Gang-rape, Sodomy, Female Genitalia Cutting, Social Injustice, Kidnapped on a Foreign Soil…. These are a Few of the Horrific Atrocities Exposed When These Wounded Yet Thriving Visionaries Blow the Lid Off Their Stories of Resiliency, Relentless Determination, and Unyielding Strength.

FEARLESS VISIONARIES™ Vol 1.1

Tear the Veil!
GLOBAL EDITION

FUMI HANCOCK
BESTSELLING AUTHOR

Psychiatric Mental Health Doctor of Nurse Practice, TEDx Int'l. Speaker, *Your Global Vision Midwife*™ & *LifeRehab*™ *Ambassador*

STORIES WRITTEN BY
Wendy Alexander, Eryka T. Johnson, Dr. Leonora Muhammad, Yolanda Dupree, Fatima Mohammed, Flerida Santana Johnas, Ramona Phillips, Zizo Mda, and Jay Kamara Frederick

FOREWORD BY
Olori Iyabowale Mariam Adebayo
Queen, Elemure of Emure Ekiti Kingdom, Nigeria

Rights Reserved. No part of this publication may be reproduced in any form or by any means, including scanning, photocopying, or otherwise without prior written permission of the copyright holder. This book is licensed for your enjoyment only. It must not be re-sold but can be purchased and given away to other people. If you would like to share this book with another person, please buy an additional copy for each person anywhere books are sold. If you are reading this book and did not purchase it, or it was not purchased for your use only, then please go to the online bookstore and purchase your copy.

Authentic leadership begins with exercising a genuine character. Thank you for respecting the hard work of this author.

Disclaimer and Terms of Use: The Author and Publisher have tried to be as accurate and complete as possible in the creation of this book, even though she does not warrant or represent at any time that the contents within are accurate due to the rapidly changing nature of the internet. While all attempts have been made to verify information provided in this publication the Author and Publisher assume no responsibility for errors, omissions, or contrary interpretation of the subject matter therein. Any perceived slights of specific persons, peoples, or organizations are unintentional. In practical advice books, like anything else in life, there are no guarantees. This book is not intended for use as a source for legal, business, accounting or financial advice. All readers are advised to seek the services of competent professionals in the legal, business, accounting and finance field.

DR. HANCOCK IS GIVING A FREE CHAPTER OF HER INSPIRATIONAL LIFE NUGGETS VIDEO SERIES - EXCLUSIVE TO HER VIP READERS GROUP:
http://bit.ly/millionaireinfluencersecrets

Copyright © 2019 Dr. Fumi Stephanie Hancock, DNP.
The Princess of Suburbia® Publishing
All rights reserved.

ISBN-13: 978-1-7328898-9-7

TEAR THE VEIL
FEARLESS VISIONARIES!

Gang-rape, Sodomy, Female Genitalia Cutting, Social Injustice, Kidnapped on a Foreign Soil. These are a Few of the Horrific Atrocities Exposed When These Wounded Yet Thriving Visionaries Blow the Lid Off Their Stories of Resiliency, Relentless Determination, and Unyielding Strength.

GLOBAL EDITION

FUMI HANCOCK
BESTSELLING AUTHOR

Psychiatric Mental Health Doctor of Nurse Practice,
TEDx Int'l. Speaker, *Your Global Vision Midwife*™ *& LifeRehab*™ *Ambassador*

&

Wendy Alexander, Eryka T. Johnson, Dr. Leonora Muhammad, Yolanda Dupree, Fatima Mohammed, Flerida Santana Johnas, Ramona Phillips, Zizo Mda, and Jay Kamara Frederick

Tear the Veil,
FEARLESS VISIONARIES!

Gang-rape, Sodomy, Female Genitalia Cutting, Social Injustice, Kidnapped on a Foreign Soil. These are a Few of the Horrific Atrocities Exposed When These Wounded Yet Thriving Visionaries Blow the Lid Off Their Stories of Resiliency, Relentless Determination, and Unyielding Strength.

GLOBAL EDITION

More Books in *Your Vision Torch*™ Series
365 Daily Vision Nuggets
Wise Quotes for Life, Home, & Business
Wake Up Girl: YOU ARE WORTHY!
AVAILABLE ON AMAZON

Fumi Stephanie Hancock, DNP.
The Princess of Suburbia ® Brand
Psychiatric Mental Health Doctor of Nurse Practice
TEDx Int'l. Speaker, *Your Global Vision*™ & *LifeRehab*™ *Ambassador*

EMAIL(s):
askdrfumi@webpsychnp.com
successlaunchbp@theprincessofsuburbia.com

WEBSITE(S):
https://bit.ly/millionaireinfluencersecrets
www.drfumihancock.com / www.theprncessofsuburbia.com

MASTERCLASSES:
www.storytellerbistro.com

BLOG(S):
www.yourinneryou.com

FACEBOOK(S):
https://www.facebook.com/fearlessvisionaries/
http://bit.ly/fearlessvisionariescommunity

WATCH & SUBSCRIBE TO MY POPULAR TV SHOW
https://www.facebook.com/IAmPrincessofSuburbiaTV/
https://www.youtube.com/c/princessofsuburbia

DR. HANCOCK IS GIVING FREE INSPIRATIONAL VIDEO SERIES, LIFEREHAB™ NUGGETS. THIS IS EXCLUSIVE TO HER VIP READERS GROUP:
http://bit.ly/millionaireinfluencersecrets

DO YOU WANT FREE INSPIRATIONAL LifeRehab™ VIDEO NUGGETS?

"I am **ready to position** myself as an expert in my industry. I thought of writing a book or perhaps co-authoring with a bestselling author but I don't know how to start! **Can You Help Me?**

SUCESS BEGINS WITH INSPIRATION
Get your FREE 6-part inspirational video series!

"I Am An Advanced Nurse Practitioner. Books & Documentaries Are My Legs to the World."
-Dr. Fumi Hancock

CREATE YOUR OWN OPPORTUNITIES. FIND OUT!
Receive my video series, empowering podcasts, practical tips & tools, inspiring "vision rehab"" delivered directly to your inbox!

First Name

E-mail

+1 United States ▼   Phone Number

SEND ME MY 6 VIDEOS!

http://bit.ly/millionaireinfluencersecrets

No matter what people say or do, remember that the power to change the trajectory of your life is solely in your hands!
DAILY VISION NUGGET™
DR. PRINCESS FUMI HANCOCK, DNP.
amazon.com

DEDICATION

To all the women across the globe suffering and itching to #TeartheVeil but are unable to; I salute you and declare that your day has come to push past fear... your time has come to release yourself from old-age secrets. The time has genuinely here when victims transition into ex-victims and begin to tell their truth.

To all who have gone silently in pain before us; taking these groans with them yet leaving unsurmountable pain for generation s behind them to display... we say, we stand and push beyond your secrets and we dare to stand.

I dedicate this to all the women and children globally who because we dare to tear the veil will be inspired, motivated, and empowered to walk their truth journey without the guilt, shame, and fear of repercussion or persecution.

I dedicate this to our men who stand by us... protecting us and ensuring that we are heard. Those who have decided to g against the grain of society to say, "No More!". No more will you weep in silence. No more will you, and my sisters carry shame like a torch of life. No more will you lie helpless, desperately looking for a savior who will come out to deliver from atrocities committed against you.

This journey is dedicated to you, our men who are standing solidly for us and with us - bearing our pain and tearing down the walls of disappointment.

Lastly, a big thank you to all my storytellers in this book You came, and you conquered. The beginning of this journey was quite rocky. We had no idea where this journey would lead us. We just knew we had to share our stories with whoever would dare to listen. Little did we know that as we genuinely tore the veil, the gloves were coming off, the masks are falling off our faces, we were peeling shame off as we were solidly behind one another, cheering each other when one person's story triggers the other.

"These women are writing from a place of strength as they decide to tell their truth and set themselves free once and for all."
~ Dr. Princess Fumi Hancock, DNP.

CONTENTS

DEDICATION 9
FOREWORD 15
INTRODUCTION 17
    THE ROLE AND IMPORTANCE OF AFRICAN QUEEN
A *LOVE LETTER* TO THE WORLD FROM YOUR GLOBAL VISION MIDWIFE™ & LIFEREHAB™ AMBASSADOR 21
    by Dr. Fumi Stephanie Hancock, DNP.
CHAPTER 1 27
    ONE EVENT CAN CHANGE YOUR LIFE FOREVER! by Dr. Fumi Stephanie Hancock, DNP.
CHAPTER 2 35
    THE KNOCK-ON EFFECT by Jay Kamara Frederick
CHAPTER 3 57
    ARISING by Eryka T. Johnson
CHAPTER 4 77
    MY DESERT STORM by Wendy Alexander
CHAPTER 5 109
    HIGHER HEELS, BIGGER DREAMS by Fatima Mohammed
CHAPTER 6 139
    ENJOYING THE JOURNEY by Yolanda Dupree
CHAPTER 7 161
    FOOD COLORING IN A GLASS FULL OF WATER by Flerida Santana Johnas
CHAPTER 8 185
    DESTINATION UNKNOWN by Dr. Leonora Muhammad, DNP BSN APRN AGPCNP-BC CCHP
CHAPTER 9 223

TRAUMADEFEATED! by Ramona Phillips
CHAPTER 10 .... **243**
   GIRL OF PRAYER by Zizo Mda
ABOUT FUMI HANCOCK **255**
MORE RESOURCES **258**

FOREWORD

When someone is inspired to gather a group of women to write about their lives, child kidnapping/abuse, female genitalia cutting, sexual violation, domestic violence, unjust sexual accusation, failed relationships… all leading to mental illness or mostly on how to overcome life's obstacles; it is not meant to be an attempt for scholars' glorification but, a platform to contribute to solving social problems as being experienced throughout the world today.

This was with a view of providing a genuine opportunity for future generations to learn from how such women overcome their challenges in life.

My choice of being nominated for writing the foreword to this well-researched work may certainly surprise many people particularly being from Nigeria, Africa.

I was fortunate to know the Author- **PRINCESS FUMI OGUNLEYE HANCOCK,** shortly after my husband ascended the throne of his forefathers as the King and Paramount Ruler of Emure Kingdom … some years back as my sister-in-law and President of **ADASSA ADUMORI PROJECT** (The Princess of Suburbia® Foundation, Inc.) based in the United States of America – a non-profit Organization, bringing quality education to the less privileged in Nigeria. Since then, she has accepted me as her sister-in-law, friend, Confidant, Close Associate and a Queen in her Royal family **(ADUMORI ROYAL FAMILY OF EMURE – EKITI)**

I have also seen her as a Philanthropist, (Adassa Adumori Scholarship/yearly Bursary Award), a Mother, Mentor, Competent, Reliable and Trustworthy Princess and an Achiever of our time.

Logically, she is humble, respectful and entirely committed to hard work.

The whole essence of the book provides quality reading materials about today's life challenges, loaded experience, useful and helpful Companion for those in distress who desire to learn a lesson in delivering life solutions for people committed to making a living for themselves, despite all odds.

Having gone through the book, I am impressed by the simplicity in the presentation and language. I believe that it will make a good consolation and companion to many who are significantly in distress and ready to drink from the experience of the author (& co-authors) with an idea to be strong even at the peak of human distress and challenges but, with an ultimatum to become a total person in life.

Without necessarily taking the chapters of the book one after another, **PRINCESS FUMI OGUNLEYE-HANCOCK,** our African Princess living in Diaspora has presented this Book of Missions™ to outline the challenges facing many homes and families regardless of culture, tradition, creed.

This is a must-read for families and certainly one I hope the media will rally around for massive impact, therefore, recommend it as a companion in homes and for families.

Queen Iyabowale Mariam Adebayo

Olori Iyabowale Mariam Adebayo
Queen of Elemure of Emure – Ekiti
Ekiti State, Nigeria, Africa.

INTRODUCTION

THE ROLE AND IMPORTANCE OF AFRICAN QUEEN

Oxford Advanced Learner's Dictionary defines a "Queen as the female ruler of an independent state that has a royal family".

The African concept of a queen (consort) refers to this as the wife of a king who resides in the Palace with her husband (king) throughout his life/reign. At the demise of her husband, she equally retains that title till death.

Paradoxically, in the Nigerian setting particularly Yoruba race, all the wives of Male children in the royal family are equally addressed as queen but, with limited role or function in the Palace except, if the incumbent queen co-opts them into her Cabinet for the smooth running of her administration

THE ROLE AND IMPORTANCE OF AFRICAN QUEEN:- African queen (Nigerian) for example, has a very significant role to play in the day to day administration of the empire, state or community or kingdom. Thus, her importance or role complements that of the king (husband). Her role or importance can also influence the decision of her husband on certain state or kingdom issue:- Just like the Biblical King Herod judgment on the condemnation of Jesus Christ when He was brought before Herod but, his wife (Queen) advised him not to be involved in the trial. This is equally peculiar in Nigerian (African) societies today. Suffice to say that her role is unique and can be described as the pillar, budget planner, game planner, game player and game changer in the Palace. Among her other roles/importance are- Head of king's kitchen Cabinet:- The queen is the head of a king's kitchen cabinet. She prepares and serves the food of the king. She keeps and supervises the wardrobe of her husband, selects a particular attire to match the function or occasion. Such dress and above it all, accompany her husband to such ceremony as tradition/culture demands.

Since Palace is her permanent house, she receives all visitors and entertains them on behalf of her husband. She addresses issues brought before the king if such does not necessarily demand the attention/presence of the king.

Head of Female Administration: - By African Culture and Tradition the queen is in charge of all female activities in her husband's domain. She influences the selections and appointments of female Chiefs and heads of various women organizations especially, the ones that relate with Culture and Tradition.

She holds regular meetings with the various segments of the female organization including wives of the traditional Chiefs.

Issues relating to domestic abuse, child abuse, failed relationships, how to manage family affairs and societies challenges are also part of the programs she puts in place for the success of the husband's administration.

African queen is seen and viewed as a symbol of peace and unity hence, she organizes and leads prayer meetings to seek God's favor for her Community, Local government, State and the Nation at large.

Equally of her importance is the keeping of the culture/tradition and teaching the young ones especially the females.

Apart from the queen in the Palace setting, notable African queens like **Queen Amina** in the Northern Nigeria, Aba women Riot of 1929 in the East and **Moremi** in Southwest are recorded in history for championing the liberations of their respective communities during the wars.

By and large, an African queen is the wife of a king in a particular kingdom, state or empire. Her role and/or importance is enormous, and these could not be easily pushed aside hence, she is the pillar of her husband's administration as enumerated above.

Since these stories are shared by our powerful women who have survived incredible life challenges, it is only befitting that the

Queen would choose this book to be her very first endorsement.

King Emmanuel Adebayo

His Royal Majesty,
King Emmanuel Adebayo
Elemure of Emure Kingdom
Emure Ekiti Kingdom, Ekiti, Nigeria
THE ROYAL HOUSEHOLD: ADUMORI NIGERIAN ROYAL FAMILY

A *LOVE LETTER* TO THE WORLD FROM YOUR GLOBAL VISION MIDWIFE™ & LIFEREHAB™ AMBASSADOR

by
Dr. Fumi Stephanie Hancock, DNP.

We are not a feminist movement neither are we a "religious move" but strictly an empowering vehicle… a book of missions™ under one umbrella. With one focus in mind… to inspire, motivate, and empower other women and children… We share our difficult and triumphant moments to save our future generation, both male and female regardless of creed, culture, traditions, religion."
~ Dr. Fumi Hancock

Allow me to clear the air as I usually would in my books, to those who are wondering why now? Why would these ladies choose to release their burdens? Why are they choosing this moment to tear the veil? Why of all times have they decided to bare it all, risking societal shame and uproar? Why are they wanting to risk their family ostracizing them and guilting them into another wave of silence? You ask again, why have these women chosen to unlock their silence to finally share their stories? Let me help you out! This journey is not about you.

This is a journey that every woman in this book of Missions™ has taken years to think about. It is a journey which is releasing and freeing them from time-bombs they have on for years... secrets which have affected every area(s) of their lives: Home, Business, Careers, and relationships. These incredibly brave women have finally understood the dangers of keeping silent. They are ready to break the curses off their boys and girls. They know it is time to empower our mothers who are still in hiding to use the tool they have, their voices, to share their stories. They understand that they no longer must suffer in silence and alone but that they can reach out to their sisterhood to help them through moments of PTSD, anxiety, depression, suicide ideation, and whatever imprint or residue their past experiences may have left behind. In fact, as we write many are still in therapy dealing with their thoughts /emotions and the effects of atrocities committed against them.

Sharing their stories have empowered them enough that they too are ready to enable others. These stories are not just another set of stories told ahead of us. These stories are triggers to success. While you our readers may not identify with all the stories, e guarantee that at least one will cause you to get up and be counted! If you are one of those that's never stood for anything, these stories will first prompt you to shutter, then encourage you to help be part of a global solution.

We are not just a group of women ranting and raving about sexual abuse... our stories are diverse. We bring solutions alongside our stories, inspiration for our men to reconsider specific thought patterns; equipping our mothers and daughters with tools to release themselves from toxic secrets... #PowerofUS using our viable tools to save our families.

I invite you to come along with us if you so, please. We move in unity... knowing that this is our moment to #releasethetoxins. Just as these stories have given us the wings to soar like eagles, we challenge you to push past fear... it is time to blossom where we are planted, and we will not be carrying life baggage on our backs.

This is the #PowerofUS, putting that the heavy back bags we have been carrying on behalf of ourselves, generations who died with their secrets and generations to come who have no idea why they may be feeling tortured by events they know nothing about.

WHAT THEN IS FEARLESS VISIONARIES TEAR THE VEIL™

Fearless Visionaries: Tear the Veil is an evidence-based work highlighting real-life role models and leaders that have overcome sexual abuse, mental illness, human trafficking, and gender inequality to live normal lives as mothers, doctors, lawyers, engineers, filmmakers, international business owners, and educators.

The path to rescue, recovery, and hope starts with Fearless Visionaries: Tear the Veil as the voice for gender equality and empowerment of women and girls is heard loudly throughout all 19 stories. The journey continues once these women enter the Fearless Visionaries Community and an ongoing support is delivered through the Fearless Visionaries Global Taskforce.

As each woman reads this book of Missions™ and joins the Fearless Visionaries mission, they will:

Understand the necessity of breaking the silence of secrecy around sexual abuse, mental illness, human trafficking, and gender inequality and instead challenge the culture to create real solutions and interventions based on that community's needs

Experience healing from the trauma of their past and move into areas of more confidence and courage to stand up for their human rights and fair treatment.

Help to remove the stigma of female genital cutting and sexual assault to encourage communities to increase safety for women and girls.

Turn their recovery from emotional, physical, and mental trauma into a roadmap that helps other women and girls find hope and help and come out of their challenges.

These are the 4 pillars which trend in our stories and what is currently causing people who encounter our stories to be steered into action, no matter how stoic they may have been in the past. These pillars and the vehicles we have chosen to help others…evidence-based practice storytelling is what set us apart from others. Our goal is not just to unleash our horrific stories on you but to give you tools and point you in the direction of available resources to help with whatever is being triggered. WE DARE TO SAY TO YOU… YOU ARE NOT ALONE.

How do we seek to empower YOU … our reader?

WHEN A MOTHER IS TRAINED, A DAUGHTER HAS A GREATER CHANCE OF ACHIEVING SUCCESS.

Our stories will bring healing and recovery. It will empower the faint at heart to push beyond the pain. When mothers are steered, children are positively affected. When children are positively affected, our nations become healthy and when nations are healthy, the global communities rip the benefits. This is a ripple effect of what our stories are about…. Being steered to find sustainable results to all that is ailing our society at large. Either a young girl is raped in Nigeria or America, rape is the same! Whether a young baby was stolen in America or India, the ripple effect on that child when he or she grows up is the same; whether a mother dies from cancer in Kenya or in Camden New Jersey, the effect the death will have on a young family is same… loss and grief look the same way. A woman is beaten to the point of almost dying in East Africa or here in North Carolina… domestic violence has its face … the pain, the feeling of betrayal is the same across board. A woman who is contemplating suicide several times because of hopelessness in Ghana or in Wyoming USA… suicide is an evil force which is running rampage through our global communities. Many are taking that route because they feel they have no other recourse.

Fearless Visionaries Tear the Veil ™ is not just a conversation starter, it is also a foundational or rudimentary pathway to finding solutions acceptable to the global communities.

Why? We represent the fabric of our global communities: From Saudi Arabia, Dubai, UAE, Algeria, South Africa, Nigeria, London United Kingdom, and USA.

Fearless Visionaries™ is a social cab™ bringing resiliency, healing and recovery to our global audience in the areas of education, health and wealth. We unanimously concur that a healthy mind is a wealthy being.

"We are fearless visionaries on a mission of hope for humanity to every girl and boy, woman and man. Nineteen women have embraced their pain to tell their story and together we are healing. It has been an amazing journey as a student under the leadership of the Dr of Nursing Practice with a specialization in Psychiatric Mental Health, Master Storyteller, Indie Film & Hollywood African Oscar Award Winner, Princess Fumi Hancock. Today, our stories became Amazon bestseller. Thank you to all who have joined our mission to speak POWER to our truth around the globe."
- Dr. Eveangel H. Savage

Let healing begin ….

CHAPTER 1

ONE EVENT CAN CHANGE YOUR LIFE FOREVER!
by
Dr. Fumi Stephanie Hancock, DNP.

I sit in my white Ford car on Verrazano Bridge, New York, everything I have to my name... all gone! My money is gone, the house my father paid off and gave me collateral for business...gone and husband I thought loved me...gone! Here I am, a very young twenty-something-year-old mother in a strange country with boys who are 3 ½ and 2 years old. The shame and disgrace I just encountered in the "loving arms" of the one who promises to love me for the rest of our lives are beyond what my little mind can fathom.

People are famous for a lot, but here I am on this quaint island, famous for being thrown out of her own business in broad daylight! Here I am standing as the greatest fool because I chose to trust despite what every part in me was telling me.

I hear echoes of the judge deep tone as I rev the car pushing harder, closer to the edge of the bridge. Mrs. T, judges are not the devil. There is a thin line between Christianity and Stupidity. I am afraid you crossed it! You crossed the line when you chose not to come to court early enough before you lose everything. You crossed the line when you were thinking only about yourself and not about the children you have in your hands. Now, you stand before me, and everything you could have used to take care of yourself and your children is gone!"

With tears rolling down my eyes and my breathing profusely labored, I look ahead at shimmering waters below the bridge. I know if I hit the accelerator hard enough, my car will push against the railings and plunge feet's down the bridge. Echoes of me questioning myself merges with that of other voices in my head. A family friend who is also a business partner visits and tells me do not expect him back home. He is never coming back! My bottom drops! With all, he had done… the emotional abuse and the physical one day where I roll down the stairs, why would I still yearn for him? Why do I still desire someone who has not been kind to me? Why am I craving the one who brings a secretary or assistant into our marital bed? Why am I rooting to have someone who has taken a lot from my family and I yet denying nothing like that ever happened? His disapproving voice, "You are nothing! You will never amount to anything! You are a wealth depleter! Don't mind her mummy, all of them want to reap where they did not sow!" Here I am holding down two jobs while he is back in college! Why is my soul yearning for more pain by wanting him? Here I am, dragging y family name down the mud because I choose a man with motives beyond loving me. Why am I willing to take him back after sleeping with someone else and didn't apologize for it? What was in me that decides to accept all the abuse?

How can I go back home to my royal family in Africa to tell them I was a failure? How can I face them with the emptiness I feel on the inside? What will I tell them? How will I reconcile the fact that few of them had predicted that the marriage would not last and they are right? His friend who had visited and had wondered why I was taking the abuse, how could I say they are right? I rev up the accelerator again as the noises in my head increases. As soon as I removed my feet from the clutch, suddenly appear in front of me is a film reel! I see my two boys crying in the arms of another woman! I see them hungry and not taking proper care of. Another voice yet again interrupted my experience… is this the legacy you want for our children? The legacy of suicide! Do you want your children always to think they were not enough for you to live for? Do you want them to blame themselves for the rest of their lives, that they were responsible for your death? Would you believe that this pain you are feeling, you can turn into victory lap? While I was to convince of the latter statements, I knew right there I had to live for my two boys. These boys had not asked to be born into chaos. Why will I choose suicide over them?

I reverse off the edge and drive right back home. Funny, all the while on the bridge, not one car surfaced. It is now 12 midnight, and I decided that I didn't have to lie for myself but for my children.

My name is Dr. Princess Fumi Stephanie Hancock. I am an African princess living in Diaspora. I am also a Psychiatric Mental Health Doctor of Nurse Practice, a 21 years bestselling writing veteran, celebrated international speaker and award-winning filmmaker and this is my story.

While I do understand that certain persons may feel slighted about sharing my story, this is my truth. This is but a teaspoon of what I encountered in the "loving arms" of my beloved. I return home that night determined to live to tell the story.

I remember walking into the cold 3-bedroom house so afraid of what the future holds. I was afraid of what tricks I would be dealt with.

Determining to live did not preclude me from all that happened after that! It was indeed a raise that if truthfully did not allow GOD to guide me, I wouldn't have survived it.

With all the noises in town about my then husband and I, I knew I needed a fresh start, but I had no money and no one to discuss this with. After much deliberation and having been warned by my banker that he had called them and insisted they foreclosed on me… after another banker calls yet again, thinking I was Mrs. T who came with her husband and delivered a $9,000 down payment on a house in another part of the state. The same money I had seen move from my business account, and we had argued over! It was time to put a distance between the shame and figure out how to live my life without him. For three years, my children and I slept on the cold floor of an apartment in New Jersey while he paraded himself in a sports car whenever he picked them up for visitation. I will never forget one day when he sets up a meeting at a McDonald's shop. Even with all I had been through, I still wanted the marriage to work. Somehow, I concluded that if I prayed hard enough, he will change his mind and come home. What I left out of the equation was his will power and him continually telling me that I can pay all I want he is no longer interested. While I was busy praying for the marriage to be restored, he was busy doing his own thing… dating and trying to figure out ways to take the children from me! When he tells me to walk down the road to the restaurant to meet him and didn't care to pick me up was a clue I missed! When he decides to meet me at the neighborhood franchise restaurant instead of one worthy of someone will love was yet another clue I missed. I remember sitting in front of him, tired from going out to find a job and when he opens his mouth, it was more than a threat! He brings his contract out and insisted I signed it so he can have full custody of the children since I was now "jobless."

    I excuse myself, quickly find my way to the bathroom and wept! I wept at the marriage I thought would last a lifetime! I left at seeing what length my beloved would go to prove to his family that he was right, and I was wrong! I came out of the bathroom and garnered the courage to say a resounding "NO!" My children were my lifeline! Without them, I would not be a life to face another day! Why will I the hand them over just like that! I walk into the cold, watching him drive his sports car right past me. There and then, I knew what I had gone through was just a tip of the iceberg. I knew I was in store for the most significant fight for my life... to hold on to my boys!

    In all of my experiences, what was most painful is my mother-in-law serving me with the final divorce papers! I remember going to pick up my boys, I was invited in as if everything was okay. I was at ease because I thought since she was there, she would make things right. You see, I knew what my parents tried to do! I knew how much sacrifice they made for my marriage. After all, against all the odds my father was the same one who took most of what he had at a tie placed it in a brown bag, handed it over to me and asked me to give my then fiancé so he could travel! Just imagine you being invited into the house, you going downstairs where your children are playing, you praying with them, you hearing someone call you wicked, screaming at you and accusing you of coming down to pray over your children, imagine her then turning around smiling and saying "your husband told me to give you this envelope." Now, imagine you opening an envelope which you were made to believe was a letter for something else and you find out that you were just served divorce papers by someone you thought if anyone could influence your beloved to fight for his marriage, was the same one who helps you! Now, imagine you in the courthouse and looking right back at you is the affidavit she signs stating she served me, and I knew I was being served.... Just imagine!

    While I have chosen to share this piece of my life, it's been over 25 years! My truth is in no way written to shame anyone but to release myself of toxic thoughts and experiences. The fact is we were young and had no clue what marriage is Those who were supposed to help us be responsible about it chose to turn deaf ears. Many decided to pick sides instead of picking our marriage. I was made out to be evil and a money squanderer. Those I thought was even called to see if I was alright, chose to be silent. I was raised to understand that once I was married, we were all ONE. My family showed me in man ways when I would see my mother purchase things and deliver to my mother-in-law in my name. During this war, because it was a war. I finally understood that e had two families and not one. It was painful because those I loved deeply, let me down.

As I write this chapter, I do the final release of the residual of pain in my life. So, I ask that if by some reason, they read this book... don't allow hatred to rule but let truth prevail. This is my truth, and it is all about my final push to healing. God has restored and allowed me to recover by giving me the greatest love of all... LOVE! Hat special kind of love which will lay his life down for me if need be... the one which is not anchored on money because he ha given it all...Now I know what real love looks like and can share with generations coming behind me what it looks like, feels like, smells like, acts like. I can genuinely say, I may not be a billionaire yet, I will never trade the love I have now for anything in the world. First, God's endless love that He chose to save me on that fateful night on the Verrazano bridge; the love of my wonderful husband, Dr. David A. Hancock who has spent over 15 years teaching me how to trust and love again; and my boys....whew... who have grown into incredibly young men, there unfailing love toward me, continually reminding e of how proud they are of me; my family... the Ogunleye's' (siblings and their spouses, my parents, and the Adumori Royal House and Alale families) who cheer me on with everything I do.

As I introduce these wonderful women who have triumphed over extraordinary circumstances, I ask that you be open. Rather than be angry, be in gratitude as these women are living... letting go of their past regardless of the pain it caused them.

Together, we are fearless women inviting other fearless women and men who are ready to encourage and support us. We are powerful, resilient, determined, committed and we raise a resounding #TeartheVeil! We are encouraging and empowering other women (and men alike) to tear their veil! We can no longer continue to perpetuate the culture of secrecy; where generational curses are being passed down the bloodline because we chose to be silent. Truth is that this is not about anyone who may feel insulted or exposed. These are our stories and others may have been characters in our plays of life. It is not our intention to belittle anyone. We are merely choosing to love and free US…..

CHAPTER 2

THE KNOCK-ON EFFECT
by
Jay Kamara Frederick

I'm laying down on my back on the uneven ground. They tell me not to move, not to be scared, but, when I'm blindfolded, and naked from the waist down, it's hard not to be scared of the unknown.

What I did know was that I was outside, in nature, surrounded by tall trees and bushes. The ground underneath me is uneven, and it feels like it's on a slight slope. The sound of hens is crowing - I don't think it's even 7am in the morning. The leaves of the trees or maybe it was a manmade roof covered me, as I couldn't feel the morning sun anymore.

We had walked from Granma's house, 2-bedroom home in Kenema a village in Sierra Leone, that was about 5 hour's drive from Freetown - the land rich in diamonds and holds the bones of my ancestor's -queens and princesses. Covered in white baby powder from face to toe, with hair roughly wrapped in a scarf with a tight knot at the back. I remember, the scarf feels uncomfortable on my head, and the powder irritated my very sensitive eczema prone skin, and with the heat from the morning sun, my skin starts to feel itchy.

Led through the courtyard of my Granma's house, under the mango trees and through the gate, we were greeted by what seemed like hundreds of women from the village and other villages who came to see us. Singing loud and proudly in Mende and dancing around us as we were led to the secret place where we would become women. Shy, nervous and apprehensive about the unknown, everyone around me was happy, greeting each and singing while I just shuffled along and beside them. Being the center of attention, I'm self-conscious as we walked down the road, the red dust rising off the road covering my toes as the women sang, danced and laughed around us. I don't see any specific faces as we're told to keep our eyes down, looking up occasionally I see a hue of brown and black faces smiling faces with shining teeth, everyone is happily celebrating. My cousin and I are walking side by side, the first time we've met, and this would be our first, worst and forever memory together. It's a memory that bonds us like twins, we felt so much on that day and even now when we speak about it, there is a bitter sadness, and silent anger towards a tradition that hurt and almost killed us.

There was an infusing of singing and talking. The jubilant harmonious singing is almost mesmerizing. The talking seems instructional, one person giving orders and others responding to them.

I try to raise myself up, off the floor, I am uncomfortable, where is my mum? I don't know what to do. Am I alright? What is happening? Why am I laying on the floor like this? What's going go? I say to myself.

"Mum" Where is my mum? If she heard me calling her, I know she would come. If I can hear her voice or see her face, I know that I'm alright. My heart is beating so fast now, it literally feels like it is going to jump out of my chest. I'm scared.

Simultaneously someone puts their hand over my mouth, holds down my arms, and my right and left legs are pulled apart roughly. My muffled scream is lost in the hand that covered my mouth. I feel hands and hear the voices of strangers reassuring me. A voice said. "If you fight it will hurt."

"What will hurt?" I mumble into the hand. At this point, my eyes are wide open like saucepans behind the blindfold. My body becomes stiff, it knew it was in danger. It is a familiar feeling, my body is about to be touched, attacked, violated and there was nothing I could do about it. What I know is that I don't want to be touched down there.

I gasp, my back arches and my head falls back, in reaction to the first attack on my vagina. The pain is so intense that even though my mouth is open in a scream, nothing is coming out. I can't breathe. Gasping for air, I use everything I have to kick whoever is doing what they are doing. I bite down hard on the hand that's covering my mouth, a sound unfamiliar to me comes out of my mouth, I'm screaming. I'm crying and screaming for help. The pain. The pain is searing through my body, starting from my vaginal area to the head what are they doing to me? Kicking, screaming and wriggling to escape, whoever is holding me, and whoever is attacking my vagina is taken off guard. For a moment there is no sound, no one restrains me, I'm free. But I'm confused. The sharp pain persists. Then in the next moment, it seems like double the hands are working to hold my body down and still, my mumbled screaming is drowned out by the singing. Someone tells me to be still. Someone sits on my chest, knocking the wind out of me. My head is held down. My right and left legs are pulled apart for the second time, this time with more forced power. Worse than then the first time, this indescribable pain engulfs my body. It's like fire I feel as slicing motions cut through the flesh of my vagina. The sounds are fading and with it the pain. As the world becomes darker, it feels like I'm rising out of my body! I want my mum, and I think, *'how did I get here? Am I going to die and what is being done to me?'* Then everything went black and silent.

If I'd known the knock-on effect this part of my life's journey would have on my life, I wonder what I would have done differently. In hindsight, I always wonder about the events leading up to 'that day' Had I'd said nothing, maybe what happened wouldn't have. Or maybe, irrespective, it would have happened anyway as part of my life's plan.

It was early spring, April I think, six months after my dad had died of pancreatic cancer - just six weeks after he was diagnosed. The family was settling down to the changes, it was a tough and confusing time. My mind was stuck in a place of denial of my dad's death. I felt his presence still so strong in the house. When I got home from school, I smell his strong and spicy cologne in the passage, and when I look at his chair, there is a dent where my dad is sitting. No one sees him. I do, he is still very much alive to me.

The last few months have been hard, leaving everyone distracted. Even when I "say" to him, he doesn't get mad, rough or force, or threaten me. What I know for sure is that I don't want him to touch or look at me anymore, I just want it to stop.

Trying to find the right time to tell my mum about it has been hard. There is never a good time. She is busy working or, we have relatives around. Dad's sudden death has thrown everything off. The plan I'd made to tell mum and dad when we came back from our summer holiday in America vanished the second we arrived back home. First there where whispers between my mum and my stepmother as soon as my mum, brother and I got in. A few days later, dad is rushed to the hospital. It's my third day back at school ... a Wednesday. The school bell rings! I grab my bag and race out of school. My dad is coming home from the hospital today I tell myself. My heart is super happy about this, and as I race home, I think about his feet, peeking out from under the sheets of the hospital bed yesterday. Today he's coming home, I know it. He'll get better, and then I can tell.

The doorbell rings and I run to open it, expecting to see my dad. It's my mum! She's crying. Dad's not coming home, he's dead. I'm frozen, I don't understand. Dad was going to make it stop, and now it will never stop. I think who will protect me and, prevent this from happening to me now. Reflecting on this thought, I realize that no one protected me while dad was alive, so it was unlikely to change. I had to stop it myself, and with all that is going on to sort out dad's affairs, this is the last thing mum needs right now. I am on my own, so I will have to find a way to protect and look after myself.

Dad left such a mess behind. A wife with her young child, my baby brother. An ex-wife (my mum) with two children and his other son which my mum raised as her own and we all lived under the same roof. Before my dad's death, we all get on relatively well, co-existing harmoniously to the best of everyone's ability.

However, I have this secret that is busting to come out of me. But, I 'm afraid of the ramifications. Will I or wouldn't I be believed? What would happen to my family – my mum and my brother? I don't want to be taken away from them, also what would people say?

I had done a bit of reading in the library of what can happen to children if they are being abused at home – they are taken away, people arrested, families torn apart. I don't want to be separated from my mum or brother.

I live a pretty normal life in Shepherd's Bush, London, just off the Askew road. My parents first home together, which they bought in the late '70s. They arrive in the UK from Sierra Leone in early '70s my mum was in her early twenties my dad early 30's. A black family owning their own home back then in the UK was a great achievement.

When I close my eyes I remember, every part of that house. The house, of laughter, strict rules, delicious west African food, takeaway Fridays and chicken dinner Sundays, hurt and tears. The house …the cream door with the arch glass effect windows. My dad's favorite colors are blue and red, which is reflected throughout our home. The entrance hall is light blue. The living room is painted a deep burgundy red with brown/red leather chairs and the sash windows covered with vertical cream blinds. My dad loved music, so there are two enormous speakers on either side of the living room and one near the entrance. The sitting room is cozy. We laugh, watch TV, play games here. It's also the place where he touches me when no one is looking.

Behind the living room was my dad and his wife's bedroom. The kitchen and bathroom are at the back of the house. He used to touch me here too.

I shared a bedroom with my younger brother who was upstairs at the front of the house above the living room, and my mum's room was in the middle, though she rarely slept in it as we always seemed to have guests so, she slept in the living room most of the time. He never touches me in any of these rooms. My dad's eldest son's room was at the top of the stairs. He always touches me and gets me to touch him in here.

It's a spring Saturday the month of May maybe, the sun is out. The radio is on as usual in the kitchen, Mum has just finished doing my hair in a bun in the kitchen. She, my younger brother and I are going to a wedding, so she was in preparation and dress up mode.

As I jump out of the chair she says, "go and get your big brother, tell him I want him." I know which one she means. I run up the stairs calling his name. "Mohammed mum wants you, Mohammed mum wants you" There's no response, so I swing open his bedroom door without a thought. Typically, I wouldn't have just opened his door like that. In fact, it usually takes me to beat and deep breath even to knock, then enter his room. But, on that day to be honest – I don't think about it. I just swing open the door.

That's when I see his girlfriend, on her knees on the floor face down between his legs as he sits on the bed. Her hair is covering the side of her face closest to me. But I know what she's doing. There is no mistaking what my young eyes are seeing. I'm confused. Isn't that what he makes me do to him too?

His room is long in length, and wide, the walls painted blue. A desk to the left of the door, a sink, window and wardrobe to the right. His bed is on the left facing the window and at the foot of the bed is a bookshelf filled with books on Bruce Lee and comics. Bruce Lee is his idol. There are a few posters of him on the wall.

Standing in the door frame – he looks up and at me and shouts at me to get out. My 13/14-year-old self can't move for a few seconds as it tried to compute what is happening. I'm confused. Why does this girl look like she's enjoying this? He forced me to do it to him most days, and I hated it, it was disgusting. I knew, and he knew it was wrong.

I stand feet clued to the entrance of his door. A few seconds seem like a lifetime. Then pulling the door closed, turned and went back down the stairs as if in a daze walk down the stairs back to the kitchen. My mum must have seen something on my face "what's wrong?" she asks me.

"nothing" I respond she asks again looking at me dead in my eye "what's wrong? You went upstairs bouncing, and now you look like you've seen a ghost. Tell me what's wrong."

"She is doing to him what he makes me do" was my response as I looked down at my feet in shame. I hadn't planned to say this, it just came out. Apart from the radio playing in the background, there was complete silence, for the second time, time stood still.

Mum's face doesn't show any expression, it's like she hadn't heard what I said. Her eyes showed that she understood. Her body became erect. Then she said in a super calm and clear voice,

"My God. Do you know what you're saying? Are you telling the truth? This is serious if this is in fact true." It wasn't an inquiry. Not disbelief, I think she just wants to be sure.

"Yes mum, I'm telling the truth, I'm not lying. I wouldn't lie about something like this. I'm telling the truth." My heart was shaking, my body was vibrating, the room was spinning really slowly. Did I just tell mum? With no planned outcome, I'm really not sure what to expect, or what will happen. Maybe a hug, screaming and shouting, tears maybe, any sign that I'm believed.

What happens next is hazy at best. Mum called him downstairs. "Mohammed! Come downstairs now!" The shuffle of feet moving can be heard above us. He bounded down the stairs with a look of innocence on his face "yes, mother" he said. That's what he calls her.

"close the door," Mum said. He shut the kitchen door.

"Your sister has just told me something alarming. I'm going to ask you a question, and I need you to tell me the truth is that understood?" "Yes mum" he responds

"I asked your sister to call you on her way to her room. She came back to the kitchen as if she'd seen a ghost. So, I asked her what was wrong. After some pushing, she finally said that Michelle is doing to him what he makes me do. What does that mean?"

"Mum we weren't doing anything wrong." is his response.

"You had to have been doing something. What does your sister mean?" Mum's voice was still wholly calm, non-confrontational. I'm shaking from head to toe.

"I don't know what she means mum. Michelle and I were just in my room talking" he said. Then I blurted out "No! No, you weren't she was on her knees in front of you, she was doing what you make me do to you.". "Mum, she had her mouth on his private parts, that's what he makes me do" At that time, and I didn't know that putting your mouth on someone's penis was called a blow job.

"Mum she's lying," he said, "I would never do that she's my sister."

"Mum he's lying" I screamed, the golden son was going is going to be believed over me, and now I'm going to be punished.

My mum then said, "A few weeks ago your sister wrote a story for school, her teacher called me in for me to read it, as it was so good.". I didn't even know she knew about that piece of homework. "it was very touching, it was about a young girl who was being abused at home. I know she reads a lot, so I thought she made it up, because, there is no way, this little girl could know what someone goes through if they are abused no way. So, let me ask you again. Have you been touching your sister in ways that you shouldn't?"

"No, mum, she's lying." He said with a slight shake to his voice

"Mum I'm telling the truth I promise" I shouted as tears started to roll down my face.

Mum then turned to me and said, "go to your room and get ready." What does that mean 'get ready' I'm in shock. I thought this would be serious. We can't go anywhere after this. We go to the wedding and have a good time. I'm still very much confused on how we got from the kitchen to the wedding. However, here we are. Today, I realize I'm on my own.

'He,' by all accounts he is a good looking young man. Tall, black and remarkably fit, his passion, karate and everything Bruce Lee, who he strived to be like, physically and mentally. There wasn't one film of his he hadn't seen, book or article he hadn't read. To the outside world including those in our family, mum, dad, cousins, aunties, and uncles, he was the 'golden boy.' From what I have been told he was in his early teens when he came to live with us from Sierra Leone. My dad's oldest son, from an old girlfriend – I think. So, I would have been 3 or 4 years old toddler when he arrived. As the years went by he grew into this tall, handsome young man who was charming, polite and kept pretty much to himself, and from what I remember his only failing was his poor academic ability, which frustrated my dad a lot. He had this way about him that was charming and captivating, it hooked and held me close. He became both my hero and the 'bad person' the person my mum had warned me about, to stay away from. Every time I got into trouble, he was there to make sure I was alright, making sure that it was him I went to find solace. He looked after me from a very young age when my parents were at work or out. My mum warned me from a young age that if anybody even if it was my dad, touched me in between my legs or any part of my body that I should tell her because it was wrong. Till today, the only reason I can give for not telling my mum sooner was that she didn't include 'brother' as being the evil person who would hurt me.

It shames me to admit that he groomed me well. I became both obsessed and scared of him. I loved him as a sister would a brother. I looked up to him. It has taken me many years to acknowledge that the feeling I had for him was born out of manipulation and grooming.

I was scared to say no to his requests and demands to touch me, for me to touch him, to have me stand before him naked as he inspected my body giving full commentary of his thoughts of my young body. He called it 'inspection.'

Growing up with him caused such a conflict. My mum would give instructions to wear PJ's rather than a night dress. He would demand that I wore a nightdress with no underwear 'or else.' Mum wanted me to have bathed by the time she got home from work which was usually about 6pm. If I soaked before he got back from his activities, I would be in trouble as he liked to watch me and even wash me. As I grew older as in 10, 11 and 12ish, I started to rebel. When I didn't do what he wanted. He would punch me, or threaten to hurt my young brother, or do what he did to me to my girl cousins.

He told me that one day many men would want me and want to do what he was doing to me. The thought made me sick to my stomach because this was not fun.

He was the one that came to my rescue when I got into trouble.

Strangely he was my hero to external eyes we are close almost inseparable, which only happened because of the hold he had on me.

A few days or is it a week, I forget, mum says that I should only have a bath when she is in the house. I tell her "it happened while you, dad, and everyone has been home, what can you do to stop it now?" I go up the stairs to my room. Am I wrong in saying that? It's the truth. A few days after, I'm sitting in a car around the corner from our house with my mum and a family friend Uncle Tony. He knows. Mum told him. Mum says "what do you want to do? We can go to the police. If we do, they will take you away. Or we can keep it between us here and don't talk about it again it's up to you. What do you want to do?" No words from me. Does this mean she believes me? All I want is to stay with my mum and brother. I don't want to live without them. What should I say? So, I say, "I don't want to be separated from you," and I wasn't. And it wasn't mentioned again, well not directly anyway.

A few months later, mum starts talking about joining the 'secret society' in Sierra Leone. "what happens when you join? I ask. "You become a woman. You know how to handle yourself as a lady, you can become anything you want, so if you wanted to become a member of parliament in Sierra Leone, you can. Your Grandma has been through it, so has your aunts and even me..." "So, what happens?" "Oh, nothing much. You get dressed up, relatives and friends from all over will come to see you, they will give you gifts and wish you well". I'm not sold "I don't like getting dressed up, and I have everything I need, I don't think I want to" was my response. Mum leaves it for a few days then my aunty her sister wades in. She says the same thing mum says and adds the importance of 'joining and being part of a community of strong women.' That got me. I want to be part of a community of strong women. In my mind, I visualise us – other girls and me sitting around a fire being told stories of our ancestors, the warrior women. I imagine, being taught how to cook and braid hair, I imagine being taught how to be a great woman because I want to be great, just like them. So, I agree.

Slowly I open my eyes, things are out of focus, my head feels woozy. My eyes connected with my mum's eyes, my beautiful mum there she is. I feel safe seeing her. Something was wrong her eyes look worried, her face drawn. As our eyes lock, she asked the question in a calm and firm tone "Do you want to live? If you want to live you'd better fight..." then she points to this little girl on the opposite side of the room and says "She is younger than you, has had the same thing as you, look she is up. So, if you want to live, you'd better fight…" Those are the last words I hear as my eyes close, ... darkness feels safe, and I let it pull me back without a fight, and as I do, I pray 'Now I lay me down to sleep, I pray the Lord, my soul, to keep, If I should die before I 'wake, I pray the Lord my soul to take'. I've been saying that prayer every night since I was in primary school and every day I woke up. So, with confidence, I say that prayer knew that I choose life over death.

I don't know how many hours, or days I was out for when I finally came out of that dark space, I woke to a new body normal that I didn't understand yet and many relieved faces. My private area was on fire. As I tried to move my legs couldn't because they had been bound tightly together. Still ignorant to what had happened to me, the dots didn't start to join until several years later.

My first spear test was a problem. Laying on a hospital examination bed naked from the waist down under a sheet, I waited for the test. Nurse number 1 came in and explained the procedure and instructs me to put both feet on the bed and open my legs as wide as possible. I follow instructions then as she went to do the test, she stopped and said she would be right back. I noted that the closer the nurse got to me, my body tensed. Danger. She came back with another nurse. It felt like I was an animal in a zoo as they looked between my legs. They both left the room, then a doctor came. At least she has the common courtsey to ask me, if I'd been abused, and if I'd experienced something called genital cutting. I said yes to the first question. But didn't know how to respond to the second question – what's genital cutting? I ask? She gently guides my legs to rest flatly and adjusts the sheets around my legs. While doing that she asks if at any point in the last several years if someone had done anything to my genitals. Flippantly I said "oh I joined a woman's society, something happened down there, I don't know what though"

That's when I found out what had happened to me. I'm told that I was '*mutilated*.' What does that mean I ask the doctor? She says part of my vagina had been removed. Does that mean I'm a boy? I don't have a penis. I'm neither woman or man, so, what am I?

WHAT IS FEMALE GENITAL CUTTING?

FGC is the partial or complete removal of a girl's external genitals. There are no health benefits, and in fact, a girl's body is physically harmed and damaged as a result of the practice and the removal of healthy tissue when her genitals are cut away.

There are four different types of FGC

These are determined by the severity of each girl's case and are classified by the World Health Organization (WHO: World Health Organization) as follows:

- **Type I:** The clitoris or clitoral hood is partially or fully removed (also known as clitoridectomy).
- **Type II:** As well as the clitoris, the labia minora are partially or entirely removed. The labia majora may also be cut.
- **Type III:** The clitoris, labia minora, and labia majora are cut away, and the remaining skin is sewn or sealed together leaving a tiny hole for menstrual blood and urine. This is commonly known as infibulation.
- **Type IV:** All other harmful procedures to the female genitals including pricking, piercing, rubbing, scraping and the use of herbs or other substances.

Though the practice has been categorized into types. There is no 'type' that is alright or expectable. All types are equally unnecessary, intrusive and a complete violation of a young girl who will one day be a woman human's right to her own body.

It's important to know that the practice of FGC is global and has been for hundreds of years. It's not just a non-western practice, or a practice carried out on black or brown girls, not carried out by non-medical professionals, in filthy places and it hasn't been introduced to the west because of migration. The two most common myths. It's documented that in 1860s UK, for example, clitoridectomy (Type 1) was an acceptable treatment for a variety of illnesses including 'hysteria' and mental illness. It was also used as a treatment for behavior seen as unfeminine and as a threat to marriage. These included a 'distaste for marital intercourse,' 'a great distaste for her husband,' violent behavior, or even just answering back.

FGM/C has been a specific criminal offense in the UK since 1985 when the (UK-wide) Prohibition of Female Circumcision Act ("the 1985 Act") was passed. The Female Genital Cutting Act 2003 ("the 2003 Act") replaced the 1985 Act in England, Wales and Northern Ireland. It modernized the offense of FGM/C and the offense of assisting a girl in carrying out FGM/C on herself while also creating extra-territorial offenses to deter people from taking girls abroad for cutting. To reflect the severe harm caused, the 2003 Act increased the maximum penalty for any of the FGM offenses from five to 14 years' imprisonment. (Assets.publishing.service.gov.uk. (2015). The first case, in 2015 in the UK, resulted in an NHS doctor being acquitted in less than 30 minutes. And according to University College estimated in 2014 that 137,000 girls and women living with FGM, and 144,000 girls at risk of FGM in England and Wales: Assets: City.ac.uk. (2014).

In America in the late 19th/early 20th century physicians performed both clitoridectomies as therapy for masturbation or nymphomania also a lack of (marital) orgasm in heterosexual women. A federal law was passed in 1996 making it illegal to perform the practice in the US. However, only 25 states have laws that make FGM/C a crime. And brave women who also white are sharing their stories of being cut from as young as 3 years old in America by doctors. I share this because FGM/C is very often portrayed as not being a western practice and only done by Africans or Asians which is misinformation. FGM/C is a global issue and has been for centuries.

While my faith teaches me not to ask the question why but to understand that

Whatever I go through is a piece of the bigger picture of my life. My curiosity does want to know why and why there is a war on our vaginas? I want to understand, not to make excuses for the actions of men and women who make a conscious choice to violate but to get a better picture for myself, so I can continue to remind myself that the violations I have endured are not my fault and I am not to blame.

Because of my experiences, unwanted labels have been put upon me like a victim, mutilated, and even survivor. Understanding labeling theory make me acutely aware of the effect of labels and their impact self-identity it's been imperative that I guard myself against the influence of those terms on my life. So, I choose not to accept those terms, for as much as I have been through, do not want to continue to feed the beast of stereotyping, victimization, stigma and shame, I am much more than my experiences of sexual and genital violation.

My experiences of violation will forever be imprinted in my memory. These experiences are like the dirt that attacks the inside of an oyster shell. To protect itself it covers the dirt with layers and layers of nacre until the iridescent pearl is formed. My protection has been choosing to deal head-on with the effects of these violations on my life so that I can be a lustrous woman.

Being abused, I was told not to tell. Under-going FGC, I was told not to tell, for both I was told to keep secret. Fear of what would happen to my loved ones and my own life made me hold on tight to the secrets. In holding on so tight, it nearly cost me my life many times.

The battle for my own sanity and being able to articulate my experiences has been intense since my mid 20's. Triggers have included, my first spear test, strange and horrific dreams, flashbacks of scenes and that had happened in my mind that I didn't understand. Everything was a jumble. The night terrors were the worst, several reoccurring dreams that included hands all over my body, touching and groping me, holding me down. I had blanked everything out, the abuse, the cutting. When it started to present itself, it was one of the most challenging periods of my life. It was like unraveling a ball of used Christmas lights. Though they didn't know my story, friends would suggest that I speak to someone, I assume they saw something in my behavior that just didn't add up.

I remember going out one day, and suddenly the everyday hustle and noises became a problem. I started to fear being in public, it felt like everyone knew and was whispering about and staring at me. I began to fear for my safety and being in public, close to people on public transportation induced this paranoia, and for several months I would walk or take a cab everywhere. Some smells would give me anxiety, making me nauseous to the extent of throwing up. A touch would make my body as rigid as a corpse. I understand now this is part of Post-traumatic stress disorder (PTSD), it took me years to realize and get to grips with this.

I've also battled with symptoms of anorexia nervosa, bulimia, agoraphobia – which for me was going outside. Obsessive-compulsive disorder (OCD) which for me was either bathing several times a day when I was at home or cleaning, not just wiping down surfaces, but, full on hands and knees cleaning and everything had to be done a certain way. My therapist, had to talk and walk me through the days when fear of going outside or my OCD stopped me from having a life. Insomnia, suicidal thoughts and depression have been on-going for years now and have become a part of my life, and despite this, I have created a life living with these issues. Some closest to me knew about the depression, the other issues I hid, they were my shame and secret which I kept hidden from others. I didn't want anybody to find out how pathetic, weak and sad I was. What I realize now with the eating disorders, OCD and agoraphobia are that this was my way of gaining control over the things I could control. Me. It was a knock-on effect of the power taken from me. From the times my body was groped, from my no's being heard, to how unclean I felt inside and out. The road to healing is on-going, it's an unpredictable windy road that provides many milestones to more understanding, forgiveness, and love for myself and others. It challenges my stubbornness and forces me always to look within first rather than out. Sometimes it concerns me that I'm becoming too introverted, "am I being selfish?" my answer to self is "yes," and that's alright. Being self-aware is the most powerful gift to have. It has given me the gift of honesty and truth to myself. It forces me to consider the needs of my heart and mind, the pain in my mind and body. It forces me to think and image how I will and can live my life once I genuinely surrender to the healing process rather than avoiding or removing myself from my ultimate healing. I have been in pain for over 30 years, so I know that I will be in the recovery of healing for the rest of my life. But it in no way means that I can't or am limited to thrive. The road may have down days, I may occasionally get stuck under my duvet for a day too long.

Nevertheless, I will keep it moving, and strive not to give up, because I have the right to be here and the responsibility to empower others and in turn give them permission to heal. Not to recover is to accept second best for my life, you do that when you live from the sidelines and or do the things that work ultimately to keep you down and not your best life, because it affects your health, finances, your character your mental state and even how you interact with others. You have to decide to take ownership and responsibility for you.

It had been such a long time since I'd made the decision not to report my sexual abuse when I was 14. I chose not to report because I didn't want to be taken away from my mum and brother. I was fearful of the outcome. As the years passed, I became increasing ashamed of my experiences, what, I'd done and hadn't done. I blamed myself entirely and didn't want to be discriminated or stigmatized. Then unexpectedly in 2015, without thought, plan or support, I picked up the phone, called NSPCC (a leading children's charity in the UK)

To make an inquiry on how best to report actual child abuse. This call turned into me reporting the crime of child abuse from my father's son. I had a case which came to trail in July 2017. Leading up to that call, I had started to feel an immense sense of guilt and shame. "I am such a hypocrite." I would say to myself. Talking to young people about protecting themselves and reporting any instances of a sexual crime to the authorities when I hadn't done it myself. What about others? Has he hurt others? What if he works with children or has children. The thought and the guilt came suddenly and affected me deeply. So, I had to tell to protect others. He was found not guilty. When the words "not guilty" came through the phone, connected with my ears then registered with my mind. I found myself transported to the place I used to hide from him, the safest place in my house my bedroom – under my bed. The left side of my body tight against the wall, my eyes squeezed tightly to concentrate on controlling my breathing so as not to be heard, and not to inhale the smell of the carpet. With thoughts of what would happen to me if he found me. I had told. They said he wasn't guilty. Now what?

Disappointed in the outcome, I literally shut down mentally for over a year. Immersed myself in work. Functioned as if nothing had happened and kept life moving.

His life was disrupted for just 2 years, mine has been interrupted for much more. I'm disturbed by my outcome the injustice and the fact that a jury of 12 of my peers both men and women choose to invalidate the crimes of abuse and incest I had received from the age of 3 to 14 years old by him, my father's son. Who actually qualifies the jurors to judge a case such as mine and dictate my fate.

Coming to terms with 'not guilty' is a challenge. Another part of me died just hearing those words 'not guilty' has been soul destroying. The verdict threw me into another dimension. Space where I felt self-doubt dance on my soul, taunt and laugh at me. I had waited for so long for justice that didn't come. I spoke the only truth I know, it was the truth, but it seems that that wasn't enough. I'm also reminded that the defense used several images of when I was maybe four or five smiling with him. They used my smile against me as if every abused child looks like an advert - broken and tearful in the corner of a room. A part of me has been numb ever since it's hard to smile without feeling a sense of guilt that my smile lost me the case. My heart is sore, it hurt to breathe without pain for a while and for several months it was hard to speak and at night as I slept 'his' hands would touch my body, and I would wake up in a sweat fighting him off. The last year has been the loneliest and mentally draining for me as I've struggled with the numbness self-doubt, increased flashbacks and really not knowing what to do with or how to express myself. I escape by closing my eyes and force myself to howl, to be free and to become a wise woman. Each time I see three animals. A wolf, head back howling at the midnight moon, an eagle flying high and free in the sky, gliding along with the clouds above the chaos of the world and an owl, perching on a branch of a tree, eyes wide open, silently observing and contemplating taking the actions of the world, with no reaction. At the time when I would see those animals in my mind's eye, I didn't realize what they symbolized. An eagle symbolizes power and strength, a wolf, a strong connection with intuition and an owl, feminine, fertility, and wisdom. I'm humbled by the symbolic meaning that these spiritual gifts from God are reassuring me of who I am, while I was in my most doubtful phase.

The 'not guilty' outcome not what I had envisioned or prayed for, broke me down. However, I refuse to be discouraged from the injustice for me. My truth and closure didn't come from the legal system, that is a hard pill to swallow. The shame I felt and still feel is because I think I have let others down. I am deeply sorry about that. If you have experienced any type of violation, DO NOT BE QUIET about it. Please tell someone. Do not be discouraged by my outcome.

The only way I see to recover from this is not to give up the fight against sexual violations, to share my story to keep it moving despite the outcome, so while disappointed I refuse to be discouraged. In her poem the "Caged Bird," Maya Angelou describes a bird with clipped wings in a cage prevented from flying away. Despite its fear, the caged bird sings of the unknown and freedom. Equally, she describes the liberty of a free bird, its thoughts of choice. A caged bird that's how I express myself and to others who have experienced the same as me. We may be clipped and caged, but we still have a voice to sing.

In the FGM/C space much debate happens about disclosing/reporting, prosecution, and women not going to health clinics, speaking to experts because of mandatory reporting, they fear their situation being recorded, especially if they have children. It is a requirement, for improved health and social care professionals and teachers in England and Wales to report known cases of FGM/C in under 18-year-olds to the police. We as woman need to become brave in our responsibility to themselves first and our family especially other girls and the young women that could be at risk of FGM/C, and abuse. Your bravery will make a difference in reducing FGM/C, early forced marriage and abuse it could save a young girl and empower others to be the same.

There are so many reasons why sexual violations go unreported.

We all have to become bolder and braver and stop making excuses for the inexcusable. To those who have had a forced, non-consensual sexual experience abuse/harassment/assault, rape, FGM/FGC, early forced marriage, exploitation, trafficking. Again, I say, do not be discouraged by my outcome. Believe your truth. Believe every flashback and emotion about the event(s). Find the strength to report it to the police. Don't let fear or even my case discourage you.

The more of us that stand up and take action against those who violate us and shame sexual predators rather than live in shame, the wall that has been built will start to be chipped away until finally, it crumbles. We must take our power back because it's our power and we are much stronger than those who hurt us. We must believe that. You have a voice, and it's a strong voice, it may not be as loud as you'd like it to be, but you have a voice. When we keep quiet, we indirectly give strength to perpetrators to continue the war on our bodies.

We need to let our rage lead the charge if not for us then for others. For too long we have been docile under the shame which is not ours or felt the need to protect our loved ones — that's not our responsibility. It must end, it is not our responsibility to protect others from the 'ugly' truth. It is our responsibility to liberate the fact to protect future generations. We can only do that when we challenge the patriarchal legal system and matriarchal constructs that have the power to render us powerless in times of trauma.

This part of my journey has changed me — it's forced me to grow up and add a raging woman as part of my character traits. I've been nervous about how to express that change. However, today, at this moment I think to myself enough is enough. This has to end, the fact that in 2018 stories of sexual violations are trending online and survivors are either not being believed or mocked is just twisted and incredibly sad to me. Equally, it makes me so mad that the power seems to remain with the violator.

It's disturbing that in the 21st century every day, every sec somewhere in the world a girl, woman, boy, and man is being sexually abused, raped, assaulted, groomed, forced into sexual slavery or experiencing domestic violence. Every 11 seconds a girl is having her genitals cut. All for what? To be controlled mentally, physically emotionally and to be disempowered to make money for others and satisfy the lusts of sick individuals It seems that the Governments of the world are not seeing this as an epidemic. This epidemic is real, and as much as social constructs may suggest that this only happens to a particular type of person, a specific ethnic group, culture or religion, bull shit. You just have to read a paper, go on social media to see a hashtag or statement that reflects this. And unless you live on Mars, not one person on this planet doesn't know at least one person who hasn't experienced one of these violations. Yet, the epidemic persists, prosecutions are lost, and many suffer in silence, fear and shame, never reporting or disclosing their experience(s).

We all have a responsibility to do better. To speak to our family and friends about this issue and demand more from our government to protect us from harm through early education in school to services. You can no longer be complicit and think it doesn't involve you. IT DOES. Each time we observe a friend acting out of character we have to ask them why. We have to create spaces and make it alright to talk about these issues. The more we do that. We will win over the demon of shame and division and empower those who have been disempowered to speak their truth. I'm an advocate of therapy and also reporting to the police. I haven't always been strong enough, I just took a blind step.

In 2005 I was recovering from tuberculosis, that's actually when the flashbacks started to really kick in and my depression first diagnosed. I was struggling to get up and dressed. Since being diagnosed with severe depression and refusing to take medication, I had to go and see my doctor every day for about 3 weeks. It was her way of getting me back in the flow of life, supported and also a way for her to keep an eye on me without admitting me to hospital. So, there I was thinking of a hundred ways I could kill myself on the way to the surgery. Which was being counteracted by 100 things I should keep living for. It was a battle of the mind. That when I heard the words "sister just keep it moving one step at a time." It was like I was given a superpower the heaviness left my body, and I was desperate to see the light of the sun. I unwrapped myself from my duvet, put my right and left the foot on the floor got dressed and went to the doctor. It was a 30-minute walk and each step I took I said "sister keep it moving" I must have said it a thousand times throughout that day and a billion's times since. Especially on the days and in those moments that I'm struggling to function the term 'Sister keep it moving' gives me hope, determination and focus that helps me to power through.

Pain and hurt change us, that can't be helped. I have cried a lot, walking down the street, while driving, on the floor, under my duvet. I have been sad a lot, empty a lot and angry a lot, but despite that, I have been challenged in that I refuse to let my experiences get the best of me because I know I have a destiny. I'm not in a race, so it will take as long as it needs to take, for me to catch up with my destiny and, everything I feel in-between is something for me to get through and over. And each time I do break through, I know that someone else can do the same too.

If we are to change the cause of the epidemic that we all need to do our part.

My scars are invisible to the naked eye. Unless I tell you, you would never know. And, every day I'm reminded of what has happened to me. In the past, it was hard to touch my body without feeling hate towards its. One Sunday, with the encouragement of my spiritual mum on the phone with me, I took a mirror and looked down there. Then I cried like a baby. The interesting thing is that before I knew what had happened to me, I was nonchalant about my private area and how it looked. Hearing the statement, you have been 'mutilated,' and the reactions from the nurses from my first spear test had me convinced that what was between my legs was the most disgusting thing ever. I was expecting to see a mangled 'mutilated' thing. That's not what I saw. What looked back at me in the mirror was *my beautiful* vagina, it had been through so much, irrespective I wasn't inhuman I am a woman, and, at that moment, I accepted all that is my vagina.

My vagina is my most significant war wound, my bravest hero, and she is all mine. I could have lost my life or taken my life because of my experiences. The suicide attempts and thoughts have not eluded me. And yet, here I am, still standing, breathing and living. Many who have experienced the same are in heaven. Called too soon, because of the war on women and girls vaginas. When I cry which I often do, sometimes it's for me, more times it is for those who didn't make it and for those at risk from any type of violation. For those who didn't hear the whisper 'sister keep it moving' who didn't feel the pull or just got too tired to fight back. I'm thankful to God for the grace of life and for sticking with me, even when I lose faith.

My pain is no longer my shame, it is the fire that fuels me to be the change that I want to see in the world – which is to be that woman who stands up with millions of others against the war on vaginas. To break the ancestry honour code and the cycle of hurting woman and girls. To end this practice and the epidemic of violence against women and girls. I firmly believe that change will come from us – those who have been violated. When we understand our power and stand up in front, not at the back. When we use our own voices, not the views of those who stand and fight for us. Then change will come. Like a bully, we have to stand up to shame, the manipulation and break the cycle, of silence and intimidation. If you are breathing, find your stride. It's OK to share your story, from there you can amplify your voice. Your story matters. Your voice matters.

In the prime of my life, it's not easy, to forget as some would tell me to. The unexpected dreams and triggers make that difficult, however, I am open to the magic of life, and what it will reveal to me, with that in mind, I choose to live one day and step at a time, as I navigate through, around and over the knock-on effects of my experiences. William Ernest Henley in his poem Invictus says it best 'It matters not how strait the gate, how charged with punishments the scroll, I am the master of my fate, I am the captain of my soul.'

I have grown into my strength, my character and wisdom that would not have been gained without my experiences. For that I'm thankful. I thrive more than survive. For that I am humbled. There are amazing days and some not so amazing days ahead, however, as a sister keeping it moving, I have pledged to do all that I need and can do make a difference. I am reminded by Og Mandino that "I shall pass through this world but once. Any good therefore that I can do, or any kindness that I can show to any human being, let me do it now. Let me not defer nor neglect it, for I shall not pass this way again. My name is Jay Kamara Frederick, I am SKIM – simply a sister keeping it moving.

Jay Kamara Frederick is on a mission to emancipate women from the stigma, shame and guilt of sexual violence. To empower and inspire them to take back their story, define their lives and live boldly. Jay knows all too well what's like to live with the stigma, losing her voice and after effects of multiple instances of sexual violence. However, despite her own personal experiences, has been able to carve a successful career in marketing, is a speaker, mentor and entrepreneur, doing what she loves, sharing knowledge, provoking thought and helping females to shape and share their own power story through the work they do.

CHAPTER 3

ARISING
by
Eryka T. Johnson

"No."

"Stop."

"Please, please don't do this."

"Get off of me!"

My arms tremble as I plant both hands in the center of his broad, solid chest and use my upper body strength to push him. "Push, push, push! Push just a little harder. Close your eyes. Concentrate. You can do this." When it fails, I quickly move my hands directly beneath his chin, and I push harder this time. He moves his head slightly to the right to dodge my hands. Then, I make two fists and swing tirelessly at his face. I think… maybe if I can hit him in the eye and cause him to see stars or even knock a tooth out causing him to bleed, he may give up and get off of me. But, he is not moving. My fists do nothing to startle him.

Now, I am clawing at his face with my fingernails. I open my palms wide to cover more of his face. My nails dig into his skin as I have a firm grip. I alternate left hand then right hand then left again until I pick up a rhythm for nonstop clawing of his face. I start at the top near his hairline then work my way down to his chin. On one stop down, I claw his nose, grab it, and then twist. He still is not moving.

My body bucks up and down uncontrollably like a bull at a rodeo as the rider tries to mount and ride it. I twist my hips left then right as he pins both legs to the carpet. If I wiggle just enough, I can slide from underneath all two hundred of his pounds. Instead of retreating, he covers my body completely. Both hands grip my hips as he holds on tight to steady himself, pulls me closer, then lies his head on my chest. His left ear is to my heart.

"Fight. Get up! Keep resisting him with all your might. Grab the lamp on the desk next to your head. Kick him off then run down the hall screaming for help." I feel tingling in my arms and legs like small needles sticking me from the inside out throughout my entire body. I try to move, but nothing happens. I must be numb. My body lies limp on the carpet. The whole time I believe I am physically fighting, but it is all in my mind.

I scream "Please stop" then "No." But, he ignores me... in fact, I don't believe he hears me at all. His only motivation at this moment is sexual gratification at any cost. I lie on the floor with my bottom half disrobed in the freezing cold seeing the tiny hairs on my arms at attention but not able to do anything about it.

I feel his hot breath down my neck. I see the dark, hungry desire in his eyes that boldly speaks "you better not fight." Immediately, my stomach starts to turn flips as nausea washes over me. Blatant disgust and anger run through my veins. I feel a lump in my throat. I want to vomit but cannot. I want him off me, but he refuses to listen.

Things momentarily come into view as I see silhouettes standing along the wall right in front of the window. Each one is stoking his genitals. Then, I remember I am in a dark hotel suite on the floor... drugged and helpless.

Something must be wrong with me. Something must be wrong with me. This is now the fourth time it is happening. Just then my thoughts begin to drift away. Here it comes again. The darkness is closing in around me. It is getting closer with every breath. There it is. I am unconscious for the second time.

I am Eryka T. Johnson, and this is my story.

I try to focus my vision as my eyes pop open. I glance over towards the clock as it reads 9:30. "It's morning already?" It is a Saturday morning in September 1998, and I feel it is a productive day. The apartment is quiet as I imagine my roommate is still fast asleep. I sit up and raise my arms high to stretch before climbing out of bed. My purple windbreaker shorts make a sliding noise against the sheets as I stand to peek through the blinds. It is a ghost town in my college apartment complex. There is entirely no movement outside. No one is out walking along the sidewalks, and the cars that line the parking lot still have dew on the windshields. It is so peaceful and quiet except for the birds chirping.

    I walk to my private bathroom to get presentable for the day. I stand looking at myself in the mirror. I am wearing a plain white t-shirt along with purple windbreaker shorts, and my hair is wrapped and tied with a navy-blue satin scarf. I turn on the water and reach for my pink toothbrush and apply minty Aqua fresh toothpaste. After that, I pull out the smelly Noxzema deep cleansing facial cream in the small blue jar, use it on my face, and then rinse with warm water.

    I head to the common area of my two-bedroom campus apartment to prepare breakfast for myself. I walk into the room that happens to be decorated with items my Mom sewed for me. The curtains are baby blue and tan with tiny floral designs. There are matching throw pillows on the uncomfortable sofa and chair as well. Literally, whenever sitting on either, it feels like I am sitting on a tree trunk with a thin sheet layer of cushion. In other words, the sitting area is not used often due to the brutally awful furniture.

    I quickly prepare a bowl of cereal and milk for breakfast. Nothing fancy, just my favorite Frosted Flakes with Tony the Tiger on the box. Every time I see the box, I smile because it reminds me of family and Saturday mornings in the small peaceful town of Bunkie, Louisiana, where I grew up. I always thought it was a big city, but really, we only had three stop lights and less than 5,000 people. The local legend is that this small town was named after the landowner's daughter whose nickname was Bunkie. She also had a pet monkey but could not say "monkey" so she called it "Bunkie."

    My Mom typically purchased Frosted Flakes cereal for my two siblings and I when grocery shopping. Saturday mornings meant that we could have cereal and watch our favorite cartoons on the TV. Of course, we had to take turns because there was only one TV in the living room with basic cable channels. My morning cartoons often included the Smurfs. I loved how everyone knew their unique gift and often worked together to outsmart the angry wizard Gargamel. So, Saturday mornings were the best for me.

    I sit with my blue bowl filled to the top with cereal, milk, and a sliced banana. I am now a sophomore in engineering college, living in campus apartment housing without a car. Where I attend college, it is at least thirty minutes away from Houston shopping. I map out my day as I sit at the table. The night before, I decided it is time to refresh my wardrobe and shoe collection.

My typical style, which I so love, is boot cut jeans, solid color tees, button-down blouses, and sneakers or boots with zippers on the side… if I want to get dressy. It is not the typical college attire I see on campus, which often includes mini-skirts, halter tops, daisy dukes, knee high boots, high heels, and fitted dresses. All these things are foreign to me as I did not grow up in a fast city. I prefer to dress simply and comfortably and that suits me perfectly.

While at the kitchen table, I decided to reach out to my cousin, who is close enough to pick me up from my apartment, drive me to the mall, and then back home in one day. I phone her, and she tells me about her existing plans for the day in College Station. She invites me to tag along and promises we will go shopping on Sunday instead. I am not entirely comfortable altering her plans for the day but graciously accept. I will refresh my wardrobe and, as a bonus, enjoy a live concert with backstage passes as her friend is dating an R&B performer.

We walk into a busy backstage at the concert with my cousin's friend. People are running around making sure the lighting and the sound are excellent. It's incredible what happens backstage to ensure that everyone in the audience has a pleasant experience. I am in awe as this is my first time at a concert or at any event of this magnitude, with VIP treatment. I meet the entire gang that is backstage as I introduce myself. To my surprise, it was male friends of the performer who all graduated years ago from the same college I am currently attending. I immediately feel in good company – safe and comfortable.

Although I really did not know the performer's music, I did recognize one song that I often hear on the radio, *I Really Want to Sex Your Body*. I glanced at the engaged crowd. As I stand backstage on the side looking through the curtains, I can see everyone singing along with the music and swaying from side to side. Heads are bobbing, smiles are plastered on their faces, and every woman in the building sings at the top of her lungs. They are so into the music. I too love the beat and rhythm of the song. Seeing what was happening in the auditorium is magical. A small-town girl from Bunkie, Louisiana, having a VIP experience at a concert she did not pay for…I was in heaven. I close my eyes, smile, join in with the crowd, and sing my heart out.

We are starving after the concert, and not many fast food restaurants are open this late. It was nearly midnight, and I believe tacos are on the menu. We order, sit, chat while eating and enjoy each other's company. The plan was to go back to the suite for a game night. One of the guys takes an interest in me and make me feel super comfortable. He reminds me of a homeboy protecting his homegirl, but those hazel brown eyes will later tell a different story.

The game night is fun and exciting. Laughing so much is refreshing. I am an engineering student taking a full course load who spends most of her time studying and working on projects. Since elementary school, I was a straight "A" student with the highest honors. I graduated valedictorian from high school and even received a four-year Presidential Scholarship along with an out-of-state waiver to Prairie View A&M University. So, it is good to feel normal and enjoy myself.

All twelve of us stand in a circle in the middle of the large suite and play a game called Faces. It really is a memory game. You make a face then invite the next individual of your choice to repeat the look and add a new face to the rotation. This continues if no one breaks the pattern by forgetting it. In the first round, I am the sixth person in the rotation and am overly confident that I remember the pattern. Unfortunately, I do not. Immediately I take a shot of either brown or white liquor. By the time game night is over, I had taken at least three shots.

I am exhausted and ready to sleep as it is well past 1:00 am, and my bedtime happens to be 10:00 pm. I ask for a large glass of water to drink before crashing out. "Here you are." I reach for the glass of water not knowing it is laced with a date rape drug. I drink the water and almost immediately the room goes dark, and I pass out on the bed.

I wake up for a moment, to see I am no longer on the bed, but now I lie on the floor near a wooden table with a lamp sitting on it. I see my cousin on the bed and someone over her. The hotel suite is dark, but I can still see six silhouettes lined along the wall right in front of the window. These silhouettes are of the performer's friends in addition to the one that now stares me into my eyes.

I am trembling on the inside. The hairs on my arms and neck are standing at attention. My chest begins to tighten as my breath comes in quick, short spurts. I am in danger and terror is all around me. I cannot move, resist, or physically fight. I do not understand what is happening to my body. It is like my body is here physically and cannot move, but my mind is somewhere else. I remember thinking...

"They are going to kill me."

"This is my fault."

"If I can only get away."
"If I had only waited to visit the mall another weekend."
"Why did I do shots?"
"Wasn't it my older cousin's responsibility to look out for me?"
"What if I wasn't so beautiful and curvy and intelligent?"

They stole my dignity. My ability to fight back was taken. These cowards stole my value as a woman. They stole my innocence and trust in humanity. They stole my voice. I experienced gang rape by eight men in a hotel suite and remember only bits and pieces because I was in and out of consciousness after being drugged.

I made another cameo appearance.

This time there is a new set of eyes looking at me. I am begging him to stop. What I see in his eyes is different from the last. Is this remorse and fear? He did not want to do this. He is only going along with his twin brother and other friends in the room. As he positions himself, I look him in his eyes and say, "you don't have to do this." Something clicks in this very moment. It is like what I am saying connects with a deeper part of him and he surrenders. He jumps off me so quickly and almost falls over. Then he turns to his friends in the suite and says, "stop guys, that's enough."

Now, I wear the badge of a gang rape victim. The things I believe about myself and the future ahead becomes blurry. I need serious help. I later find out that there is only one way to experience relief.

I love weekends in my small town. Growing up with girl cousins only a year or two older means we spend a lot of time together. Whether we are in the Augustine Apartments or at my house on Ash Street, we love playing Hide and Seek, Hopscotch, Tag, Red Rover, kickball, and softball. Any game you can think of that requires us to be outdoors using creativity, we do it. Instead of sidewalk chalk, we use white rocks to draw the boxes and numbers for Hopscotch. We are innovative because money is scarce, but I don't believe at that age, we really understand this.

It is interesting for me to hop on one leg within the lines without falling over. It is hilarious because I often cannot balance well enough to make it to the end. And, whenever we play Tag, I always lose. My two cousins are fast runners, not to mention the other kids in the neighborhood that join in on the fun. These kids are quick on their feet. As such, I often hear "Tag, you're it" or I chase everyone for a long time because they are faster. But we still have fun.

Whenever we played Tag at my Grandmother Madea's (Yes, I know… Madea) house, there are family and friends, mainly girls, that live on both sides of her that make the game interesting. We run around until literally passing out at the end of the day. There is no time to get into trouble unless the games turn sour and someone gets upset. This happens a few times, but we learn how to resolve conflict ourselves and prevent punishment by not involving an adult. There are lots of tears, but even more cries of "I am sorry."

We love giggling like girls. We huddle together on the sofa, laughing at each other's jokes or simply recounting our day. But Madea often says, "Baby, it's not good for girls to laugh a lot because it means something bad will happen." We would quickly stop and wait for her to leave the room before laughing again. I never realize how much that is embedded in me as a young girl. I grow up believing that everything must be serious and bad things happen as a result of fun or laughter.

My Mom and Dad separated when I was only eleven months old and later divorced. Because my Mom worked so hard to provide for us, my older sister Sabrina, who is only seven years older than me, cared for my brother Chucky and I. My life is my life. I don't remember ever starving or living without the necessities. However, the energy in our home was often so tense it was tangible. There is not much joy or laughter within the home just unspoken expectations and lots of discipline. Although young, I am intuitive enough to de-code the atmosphere and act accordingly.

I remember, however, in elementary school, around the age of nine or ten fishing in a lake not far from home. My Mom and the man she is dating brings us fishing pretty often. He is a mortician with a large family of eight kids. He is divorced but purposes to spend time with family, which is important to him. As a kid, we use fishing poles made of dried sugar cane and string with a small hook tied at the end. I place the slimy worm on the hook, throw it in the water, and wait until I get a bite.

We usually catch perch, catfish, or strange looking fish with beaks. This means a fish fry when we return home. Whenever it is perch, however, we use a metal spoon to remove all the scales. It is a dirty and fun job at the same time. My Mom seasons the fish portions well and then coats them with cornmeal. She fries the best fish and couples it with potato salad and white Wonder bread. It is a meal. We sit down to eat in the living room wherever we find space.

A couple of his kids always come to visit and sleepover. Mostly I love it… particularly when his daughter comes with her baby boy who I get to kiss and hug as he sits on the floor bouncing up and down. Or I get the opportunity to help with bath time and really feel like I am contributing as a kid. He is the cutest and sweetest baby.

I do not like it when his youngest son comes over for the weekend. This weekend he is here fishing too.

I lie in bed fast asleep in the middle bedroom right off the kitchen. I can see through the door straight into the kitchen. The room is quiet and dark, but the living room is still noisy as everyone except me is still up. I am tired from the day's activity. All I want is a warm bath and some rest. It is a long day, so I fall fast asleep.

I am asleep, but I feel his presence in the room and close to my bed. He often comes as a thief in the night. "No, not again. Why does he do this every time he comes to visit his Dad?" He stands over me at the edge of the bed. The blanket moves slowly as not to disturb me. I can imagine he tells everyone in the living room that he needs to use the restroom. And because you pass through the middle bedroom to get to the bathroom, if my Mom's bedroom door is locked, no one suspects a thing.

The bed shakes slightly as he slowly moves his hand to touch me. This is not the first time he fondles me, but it will be the last. The truth is I am too afraid to speak up and share what is happening. I am so scared to be punished because I live in a family with firm disciplinarians and expectations are always set so high. I often think, "What would they think about me?", "Why does my Mom not put a stop to this?", and "How do I explain something like this?" I am not doing anything wrong, but in my mind, I will be in trouble if I tell. Confusion sits in. He violates me as a kid, but I am worried the blame will shift to me because he too is a kid and only a couple years older than me.

Whenever he visits, he only touches me inappropriately while I sleep. I am asleep on my side with my knees bent facing the edge of the bed. He places his hand on my thigh and slides down until he reaches my private area. Again, I feel his presence and wake out of my sleep, sit up, and open my eyes to find him standing there. There are hidden messages in his eyes telling me "you better not tell." I put my head down in shame and hopelessness and pull the blanket to my chest for comfort. He walks away and joins the others in the living room.

As I sit rocking in the bed and contemplating my next move, I remember my thoughts taking over. "You must tell your Mom."

"No, I can't. She will be furious at me. I will be punished and not able to play outside tomorrow."

This is my moment. I have a decision to make. I am tired of feeling uncomfortable as if I am doing something wrong. There is absolutely nothing wrong with me but he, on the other hand, is sick. I like spending family time together because I love the attention and the things we do. With Mom working so much, I just want her to notice me and take an interest. Does she not realize how tense things become whenever he visits?

I want my Mom to save me and not allow him to visit again, even when his older siblings come over. But how can I get her attention? I remember thinking that it is time to end this. A surge of courage comes over me, and I decide to stand up for myself. I must do something so out of character that I definitely get my Mom's attention. My feet hit the cold wooden floor, and I walk quickly not to lose heart.

"You can do this. Everything will be okay. Just keep walking. You are almost to the living room." I enter the living room where everyone is still chatting and laughing. My heart is beating fast, and I can feel the heat around my neck. His eyes grow worried as he sees the look on my face and feels the energy radiating from me. He is in shock for a moment. He tries to give me a look, but I am on a mission. A mission to save me from the shame, guilt, and humiliation not to mention the sexual violence. I stand in front of him, reach as far back as I can, and my fist connects with his face. The sound is so loud it echoes off the bare walls, and the attention turns to me.

The room goes silent. There is no chatter, and the noise completely stops. You can literally hear a pin drop. I feel everyone looking at me in surprise. My Mom is the first to respond as planned, "Eryka! Why did you do that?" This is my opportunity to explain and put an end to it all. I share my past experiences and last incident that took place. Of course, he denies everything, but she knows my personality. There is no way I would attack him unless for a good reason. The truth is finally out. Instead of punishment, she stands up for me.

I am surprised by the result. Let's just say he never visits again and soon her relationship ends with his dad.

One of my favorite pastimes is dancing. It comes naturally to me and many girls in my family too. Music plays, and the natural response is to move. I remember a friend of my Mom's sharing a picture of me in a white lace dress with red trim, white shoes, and a red headband dancing at a wedding reception with another friend of the family. I was only five years old. Music and dancing give me an escape and brings joy and so much light into my world.

I often compete with my sister and her friends in talent shows at Bunkie High School. Although the youngest, I can hold my own. Show me the choreography once, and I learn the entire dance routine quickly. I am their secret weapon as their originality score rises whenever I am in the front, visible to the judges, and keeping up with the older girls. One time, I wow the judges for the talent show choreographed to the song *Night Train*.

My sister and cousin are also members of the Dancing Dolls at the local high school, and I cannot wait until it's my opportunity to join the dance team. They wear red and white sequin bodysuits with stockings and white dance shoes. By middle school, I have perfected my craft by learning dances and performing for anyone willing to watch.

My older cousin choreographs a routine she wants to teach me and another cousin. It is a dance routine to a song made famous by a girl group called Salt n Pepa.

I am so excited to learn the moves. My heart is racing while my stomach is leaping. I love to dance. The dance routine is to the well-known song *Push It*. I want to be Salt. My older cousin quickly interrupts me and says, "You are too dark and too fat to be Salt. You will be Pepa." My spirit is immediately crushed. For the first time, I realize how different I look from all my other girl cousins. My response surprises her and me too. I say, "Either I'm Salt, or I'm nothing." She does not budge so I do not finish the routine.

I am quickly developing as a teenage girl in middle school. I am bigger in statue with more curves than many of the girls around me ... both in my family and in class. I enjoy food and love to eat. When I eat, it calms me and soothes the internal noises as I live in my head most of the time. I create mental pictures of how my life will look when moving away from my small town and doing something big with my life.

One Friday night when I am in eighth grade, my Mom is away from home visiting with her new boyfriend. Most Friday nights at this time are spent at the high school football games cheering on my brother Chucky or at home watching TV. I love *Family Matters* and

Hangin' With My Cooper. This Friday, I am at home lying in bed, glued to the TV while my brother goes in and out of the house visiting with his friends.

I can hear the music blaring outside as our house is not well insulated. Literally, I hear everything happening around me. My brother and his friends are laughing loud. I turn the volume up on the television, so I can hear *Family Matters* better as I am laughing at Steve Urkel when the front door opens again. My Mom's bedroom is located at the front of the house. The bedroom door opens slightly, but it is not my brother. In fact, I struggle to identify the person.

The door opens wider this time, he peeks his head around the door, and steps inside the room. I know him, but I am confused because he typically does not hang out with my brother. "Why is he here?" He has been dating my cousin for years. He attends many family functions and cookouts. He and my cousin live together in an apartment, building a life together, so he is like family. It is strange he wants to hang out with my brother due to the age difference.

He says, "Hey Eryka, what are you doing?" It is obvious I am watching my favorite television show, but I respond to his question a little annoyed. The more and more he talks the closer he gets to the bed. My senses become alert. The hairs on my arm stand up, and I begin to feel anxious. Danger is around me. When I look into his eyes, I know something is wrong. He forcefully yanks the blanket off my body. I turn and begin kicking with great force. I scream as loud as I can, but the music blaring outside drowns out my cry for help.

I refuse to allow him to take me down without a fight. I roll up both my fists and swung windmill-style. I claw his eyes, face, and neck with my fingernails all while screaming and demanding him to get off me. My entire body is working to protect my safety. He is so close I could smell the alcohol on his breath, but I am confident I can break free if I remain focused. He appears to be intoxicated and unsteady on his feet. "Stay focused Eryka. Keep kicking and swinging. He will tire out before you do." I kicked one last time. He flies back as his body collides with the chest of drawers. I hear a loud clattering noise as small figurines fall to the floor. He gives up, turns around, and leaves quickly.

The adrenaline is pumping through my body as my heart beats fast, every blood vessel is humming, and my breathing is uncontrollable. "Calm down Eryka, you are okay," I say to myself. I can only see fire as heat settles down around my head and shoulders. I rise off the bed to stand and gather myself. First, I run to my Mom's bedroom door and lock it as fast as I can. I pace the room a few times until my next move is clear. I pick up the phone to dial my Mom and let her know what has taken place. She rushes home to pick me up, so I'm with her and her boyfriend.

He is like family. Everyone loves him. He too adores my sweet cousin. But tonight, he attacked me.

I remember the first women's retreat I hosted at Camp Allen in the Houston area back in 2011 called "Renew Me" Women's Retreat. Seven women attended looking for renewal in purpose and within their spirits. To my surprise, as I prepared for the renewal session I facilitated with the group, my meeting focused on renewing our sexuality as women. This topic was not my first choice, but my spirit continued to pull me to have this discussion. I surrendered and prayed for guidance and instruction.

When I introduce the session topic, their faces visibly change. The excitement that was once in the room from the first icebreaker exercise and last night's fun no longer exists. Immediately, I feel anxious and scared because I know this discussion will drudge through deep emotions and expose wounds that some have not dealt with before. I say to myself, "Eryka, you must do this. It will not only help them heal but you too. Someone needs to hear your truth. You must take the lead and share."

I begin sharing statistics that approximately 15% to 25% of women are sexually abused as children by someone they know and 1 out of 4 college girls experience rape while obtaining a higher education. The energy in the room shifts. I take a deep breath, close my eyes, and then share my story of sexual violence during childhood and while in college. The group relaxes a bit more as each woman recognizes she is not alone and can gain insight from the session.

We are deep in conversation. Many of the women are vulnerable and share their darkest secrets. I know most have never shared before but are brave enough in this environment to tell their truth. Each story pains me as I listen. The cries in the room are long overdue. But the love in the room covers every woman as we hug and support each other through the journey and breakthrough. In fact, every woman has experienced sexual violence at some point in her life except one.

That means... six of the seven women were silenced, shamed, and devalued. That number is staggering, but it also says that six women will begin their journey to healing years of guilt connected with un-wanted sex by family, friends, and strangers. That feels good.

The topic is definitely in demand, but I must prepare the environment to allow these women to feel safe and openly share. Something happens to me while this discussion takes place. As we pray together, I experience a flashback in my mind. I remember another incident happening to me that I never shared before. In fact, I had totally forgotten all about this experience.

I am eighteen and preparing for college. It is my first well woman's appointment at the free clinic in Avoyelles Parish. I am not sure what to expect as no one prepped me for this experience. I drive my Mom's light blue Corsica twenty minutes away from home to arrive at my doctor's appointment. I pull into a parking space right next to handicap parking in front of the door fifteen minutes before the start of my appointment.

I turn the car off and sit quietly for a minute. Music softly plays in the background to calm my nervousness. My palms are sweaty, and my stomach is flipping as I think about what I must do. This is my first personal interaction with a male gynecologist. I am terrified that a strange man will look at my private female parts. What an awkward moment.

"How may I help you?" says the receptionist at the front desk. She is bubbly, and her a smile lights the room. Her blond curly hair and blue eyes are captivating. She makes me feel calm. My nervousness begins to subside. "Eryka Williams here for my 10:00 a.m. appointment," I say, as she hands me a clipboard with papers to complete. I sit down next to the receptionist desk and quickly fill out the paperwork.

"Eryka Williams?" I stand as I hear my name called by the nurse and follow her to a private examination room. The room is cold and bare. An examination table, faucet, stool, and chair fill the room. I don't remember any posters or pictures on the white walls. I am nervous again. As I enter the room, I follow the instructions of the nurse, "remove all your clothes including your bra and panties and drape on this gown with the opening to the front. The doctor will be in shortly."

I do precisely as she requests and sits on the bed awaiting the doctor's arrival. Both the doctor and the nurse enter the examination room. The doctor is scary looking. I am not sure what I expected him to look like, but he is at least sixty years old with glasses and moves around slowly. His belly bulges from his pants and his white coat is a bit dingy. He does not say much rather immediately gets down to business.

I lie back, and the gown drapes open exposing my breasts. He stands next to the bed over me and begins touching my right breast. His cold hands connect with my warm skin causing me to jump. He feels the outside edge of the right breast and works his way around to the center where the nipple is located. I lie there wishing this to be over quickly. "Think of something else maybe something funny. How about the time you made a two-pound banana split while training to work at Dairy Queen? The look on the manager's face was priceless." The touch lingers a bit too long. He goes from lightly touching my breast to groping my breast. He moves now to the left breast and does the same.

I squeeze my eyes tightly willing this examination to be over while taking deep breaths and counting in my head. "Ten, nine, eight, seven, six…" I open my eyes to see the nurse looking directly at me with worry and disgust as the doctor continues the examination. His breathing changes and I feel deep flutters in my tummy. His attentiveness is beyond looking for lumps. The nurse clears her throat and in a straightforward tone says, "Doctor, let's move through this examination quickly please." He snaps out of his fantasy and completes the examination.

The nurse helps me up when the doctor leaves the room. My head is hanging down in embarrassment. All I want is to get out of here quickly and back home to my safe place – my bedroom. I receive my contraceptives in a brown paper bag and run to the car. I turn the key in the ignition, and the car jumps to life. I sit there for nearly two minutes with my forehead against the steering wheel trying to understand what has just taken place. The medical doctor who took an oath to care for the safety and health of his patients has violated me. I am so confused. "Why does this keep happening to me?"

When I arrive back home, I remove all the trash from the car. I lift the lid from the large black trash can next to the red brick wall. Not thinking, I place the brown paper bag with my contraceptives in the trash and head directly to my bedroom. I later realize what I did in my state of mental fogginess and retrieve the bag from the garbage.

I did not realize the impact of these events until later as an adult. I told myself that if I buried them deep and did not share them, I would experience healing. My antidote was to compartmentalize and silence the experiences. However, subconsciously, the trauma and violence continued to lead my life from beyond the closet.

Humiliation. Shame. Loneliness. Isolation. Mental Torture. Unworthiness. Invisibility.

This is what I personally felt due to sexual violence. When younger, although afraid, I dared to speak up and speak out. As I got older, things began to change. I understood what shame looked like. I realized how I could be viewed as a whore, slut, or bitch if I shared my experiences. And, it was more important to be politically correct than emotionally healed.

I could also hear in the back of my mind the words from my Mom "Act like a lady." I can't say I knew what that meant, but I figured you should be respectable and low key, proper and quiet, and seen but not heard so as not to attract attention.

I was not aware of the assignment of influence on my life. My call to ascend to influence and high visibility by serving women of the world. If the enemy of my soul can keep me quiet through condemnation and shame, my life purpose and assignment can go unfulfilled. This is why I genuinely believe I was plagued with the cycle of sexual violence.

When you refuse to speak out about sexual violence, you empower the aggressors to continue to abuse you and not be accountable for their actions. In fact, you protect them while devaluing yourself. I did not speak out for years. Yes, I may have shared with a handful of individuals but never on a larger scale. This book has provided the platform and support to share my story unapologetically. The healing continues for me, but I'm so glad that I'm committed to the process as well as helping others gain the strength to reveal their ugly truth.

"The captain has now closed the cabin doors. Welcome aboard British Airways flight number BA 194 nonstop service to London England." I smile as the stewardess makes her announcement.

The seat is perfect. This is my first twenty-hour international flight, and I enjoy a level of comfort I have never experienced before, even while flying first class on a domestic flight. This is real luxury.

The individual bucket seat is cushioned perfectly. It is so comfortable to the touch and has the right amount of firmness. The headrest expands the full width of my neck providing proper support like nothing I have experienced before. I giggle as I look to the floor and notice my legs were too short to reach the foot rest. In other words, I am flying to London in a comfortable seat with ample leg room and no neighbor sitting next to me, which only means one thing… I can snore as loud as I want without the embarrassment.

I arrive at Heathrow Airport only to find myself held up for over an hour at the security checkpoint to New Delhi, India because of my natural hair products. "Madam, you will need to wait here until my manager arrives. Unfortunately, you will not be able to travel with these items," says the security attendant. "Where is your luggage and where are you traveling? You will need to purchase these items again when you arrive in New Delhi."

Somehow the hair and edger gels I placed in my carry-on bag tested positive for peroxide. The look on my face is priceless. I respond, "Sir, you mean to tell me that I can't travel with these hair products? This is so strange, considering my carry-on was checked in Houston with no issues. And, NO, these products cannot be purchased in India, so I don't know what I'll do."

"I'm very sorry Madam. This is the rule," says the security attendant.

I sigh and comply. I finally make it through the security checkpoint after a pat down by a female security attendant, my carry-on going through the scanner once more, and my fingertips and shoe soles being swabbed for hazardous materials. And now, I don't have my edger or hair gel to maintain the fly-away from my ponytail on my final 8-hour flight to New Delhi, India. It will be interesting.

I am traveling to meet my girlfriends and business partners to participate in an international gathering of over 3,000 women influencers from everywhere. Not only will I receive the Women's Economic Forum India "Exceptional Women of Excellence in 2018 Award," but I will also share my truth and story with those in the room and put my small town of Bunkie, Louisiana, on the map.

It has been my desire since 2010 to travel internationally as a role model to women, but I finally wrote it down in 2014 as part of my yearly goals. My affirmations included the following:

I am a global leader and role model to women across the globe sharing how to increase their influence and show up more powerfully for themselves. People are calling me from afar to hear my wisdom and expertise.

At that time, I had no idea how I would travel internationally to help other women. I simply recited this affirmation daily for a few years and even carried around note cards with the affirmation message in my purse as a constant reminder of what I desired for my life, family, marriage, and business. I wanted to share my purpose of teaching and training other women who felt invisible to stand up and build a brand of influence instead.

This is my first opportunity in a country I have never traveled to, except for Canada back in 2008 for my employer. I met many international women through my online community and built a global business around mentoring women through my digital products and online coaching services, but this time it is different.

I get an opportunity to experience a new culture. The climate is different. It is hot, even at 11 p.m., as I step outside the airport to locate a taxi. The airport safety regulations are different. There are armed security guards with automatic weapons and men and women in separate lines going through security checkpoints.

The food and luxury hotel rooms are different. I eat curry and rice every day, and the hotel room has two twin-size beds, opulent bathrooms with oversized tubs and high-pressure shower heads, and toilets with bidets attached to cleanse your bottom with water from a handheld faucet.

Driving practices are even different... in fact, they were incredibly scary. I think I may have gotten blisters on my hands from holding on as the taxi driver entered the highway at an alarmingly high speed while sounding his horn and shouting out the window "I am coming... get out of the way," and driving in between the visible yellow lanes on the roadway.

I am on foreign soil, living a dream I had so many times desired to achieve. I finally wake up! I am living my life without the need for permission or feelings of doubt, inadequacy, or shame, because of my long, tumultuous journey to this stage in my life.

It is never about where you come from but rather the permission you give yourself on the journey to arising. You have the same opportunity as the next woman to rewrite your life story, sing your song... even if off-key, and dance to the rhythm of your own drum. The strategy for owning your life without excuses was recorded in my first book in 2015 – *Own Your Life: A Practical Guide to Personal Leadership and Being an S.T.A.R. with No Excuses.*

S – Set Apart
T – Trusted as a Steward
A – Accepted and Accountable
R - Responsible

To make life count, you need to find clarity, confidence, and courage to stand up for YOU! My new truth is finally being shared in this book *Fearless Visionaries: Tear the Veil* and is starting a movement.

"Introducing Eryka T. Johnson, a Global Leadership Brand Strategist, Author, Speaker and Engineering Leader from the USA. You are welcome Ma'am to the podium."

It's my turn. I rise from my chair nervously as I sit on a panel with nine other women influencers, including the first Kenyan woman to own a microfinancing bank and my girlfriend from Atlanta who is a PMP expert and career coach to mid-career women in the workplace. I grab my notes and walk across the stage smiling. The lights are bright. I see the cameraman, videographer, and the faces of women, from six of the seven continents in the world, staring at me.

I look down at the table in front of the podium and see my two girlfriends with their iPhones in position and the biggest smiles in the room. I smile back, take a deep breath, and step to the microphone, while asking myself this question, "Will you truly trust yourself today to step outside the comfort zone of your fear to enter this global platform of influence to which you're called to serve and support women from across the world that need your strength, vulnerability, and message?"

I pause. Then, speak. Now, I ask you the same question.

~~~ *** ~~~

I am Eryka T. Johnson - internationally award-winning Visibility and Profit Strategist, Leadership Expert, and Engineering Leader. I am passionate about helping high achieving women elevate their visibility and profitability in the workplace and in business. I mentor over 19,000 women daily on how to go from invisibility to influence™. My signature trainings and workshops through the Influencers Leadership Institute have resulted in women getting promoted to management roles with salary increases, women becoming self-published authors, releasing their stories and expertise to the world, and women are overcoming chronic self-doubt to believe in themselves again. I am committed to helping women walk into their influential and powerful selves.

The saga continues "from invisibility to influence…"

ERYKA T. JOHNSON

Eryka T. Johnson is an internationally award-winning Leadership Brand Strategist, Speaker, Author, and Engineering Leader who is passionate about helping high achieving women increase visibility and profitability in the workplace. Eryka mentors over 19,000 professional women in her virtual community daily, shared her leadership journey for two years through her column LeadHERship in two Montana magazines, Cliffside Neighbors and Rimrock Neighbors, and hosts signature trainings through The Influencers Leadership Institute. Eryka has also been featured in Success Magazine, NBC, US News, DyNAMC International Diversity Magazine, Worldwide Business Review, The Network Journal, Yellowstone Valley Women Magazine, The Missoula Current News, IEEE The Institute, Atlanta's WDJY 99.1 FM radio, and Everyday Power Blog. Eryka is the recipient of the 2017 Business Elite Award, finalist for the Women in IT USA 2018 "Future CIO of the Year" Award, and recipient of the Women's Economic Forum "Exceptional Women of Excellence 2018" Award.

CHAPTER 4

MY DESERT STORM
by
Wendy Alexander

"Thank you for flying Delta Airlines. We are happy to have you aboard today. We're expecting a smooth flight to Dubai." As I look out the window at the sun starting to set, I'm holding one hand on my head, asking myself, "What have I done? Is this the right thing to do? But what if I don't? What will working in Dubai be like? Will they accept me? Do I have an emergency plan to leave Dubai if I need to? Is it really okay, leaving my family?" As a mom and a wife? My husband loves it here, the Middle East has become his second home, but I still have anxiety. All these questions are going through my head… I close my eyes and pray that it will all work out.

Two ladies who were traveling together sit next to me. The older lady has grey hair, and the younger lady has beautiful hair of jet-black… both dressed in black jogging suits and smell nice. I think it is a good idea to at least say hello to them. After all, I will be sitting next to them for several hours and sharing the same space. I say "Hello." "Hello," they reply in soft voices with a perceptible accent. I ask them where they are from. They respond "London." "Oh really? I would love to visit London one day, I have never been. "I have a client that I help in London, and I have never met her in person." The younger lady just smiled and shook her head, and the older lady isn't saying anything… she is just looking at me then turns her head. The look says, "leave us alone and mind your business." This is a clear sign to me that they do not want to talk to me. I need to pray anyway, and I am only talking because my nerves are on edge.

The baby behind me is crying, and this crashes into my prayers. She is only about six months old, and maybe it's her first plane ride. The baby crying brings back memories of when my kids were babies, and we took them on their first plane ride to California. They were very quiet and did well on the plane. Why may you ask? I have to laugh... we gave them what we called "night night" medicine, which was Benadryl. Don't judge me! I needed to make sure we all had a peaceful ride. We only gave them a little dose for the ride. I am praying, laughing and crying at the same time. My nerves feel bad. The younger lady next to me asked if I was okay. I replied, yes, just a little nervous... excited, mixed emotions about this new chapter in my life. I am fine, and I need to pray. Don't try to talk now, I am thinking, rolling my eyes.

I feel so cold that I put the red scarf I have in my bag over my head. I decide to watch a movie to take my mind off things and slowly drift off to sleep. Suddenly, I felt a tap on my shoulder waking me up out of my sleep. I look up, and it is a woman with grey hair and a beautiful British accent. The smell of her expensive perfume hits my nose before her voice... "Excuse me, Miss, can I get by?" I reply, yes, with a tired voice. As I'm removing my seatbelt, for her to get by, I'm confused for a minute, where am I?

I stand up, I look around, and everyone is gathering their belongings. The stewardess walks by and asks me to take a seat and put my seatbelt on. Wait, am I getting off the plane or what is going on? I am confused right now. I need to go change clothes. I read on Google that I should wear an abaya before getting off the plane. I start to walk to the bathroom to change clothes, and I notice that we are still in the air. But there is a long line to get into the bathroom men, women and kids. Oh, this is going to be a minute. What if I don't get in the bathroom to change? What am I going to do now, I must turn into this abaya! What will happen if I don't change? Oh, I don't need this right now!

Finally, after waiting thirty minutes to get into the bathroom and learning about the people waiting. Like Julie, who was from Atlanta... a single mother of a very hyper seven-year-old boy named James who will be teaching in Dubai. Linda and Bill have been married for twenty years, they have two sons, two daughters named Tom,

Jordan, Sarah' and Lisa, who will stay in the States until Linda and Bill are settled. Bill accepted a job in Dubai working for an oil company. Linda is a stay at home mom, working on her master's degree. It is nice to get to know others and see the reasons why they're going to Dubai. Or maybe it's just me being noisy. Oh, well, finally I get to the bathroom!

I'm in the bathroom looking around trying to figure out how am I going to change in this little space. Thank goodness for paper towels. I place the paper towels on top of the toilet seat so I can put my abaya and hijab down. I have a pink abaya and an off-white hijab, I choose this color because I want to look extra cute. There may be someone from the media who will like to interview me, take my photos. I mean, you never know so I need to be ready. I put on my abaya, and I notice it's a little sheer. Oh well, nothing I can do now, except to wear the black tank top under it I have on. Oh, my goodness, it's something getting into this abaya in this tight space. I am sweating, and it's hot as fish grease in here! Let me wash my face and apply my Mary Kay face moisturizer, blush, mascara, and pink lipstick. Now I must figure out how to wrap my off-white hijab over my head. I take one piece overhead and continue to cover it, making sure that none of my hair is showing. Okay, I am now ready. It's time, and I am so nervous. I take one long look in the mirror, I am really going to Dubai to facilitate training. Me, an African American woman, going to a Muslim country to provide training? I told my husband I will have a business in Dubai and Abu Dhabi! I am so close to doing just that. But honestly, who would have ever thought?

The girl who people said would never get accepted into any college. I will always remember the counselor who said my baggage outweighed my dreams.

I go back to my seat, and I sit down, place my earphones in my tote bag along with the Ebony magazine I didn't read. I notice a picture of my family, which brings a smile to my face. I notice the older lady sitting next to me with the grey hair is also packing her bags. She has two tote bags full of food, books, medicine, and a CD player. Wow, I say to myself, "how long is she staying, and I wonder if she has checked bags too? She looks at me and says, "You look rested now." I reply, "somewhat," and the entire time I am now thinking, 'why does she have on a black abaya? Why does every woman on the plane have on a black abaya? Why am I the only one in a bright pink abaya? Seriously? Now everyone will notice me a mile away and if I need an escape, they surely, they will find me. I take a deep breath and start saying a silent prayer. Lord help me get through all of this, I whisper under my breath. The stewardess walks by in her beige and red uniform, with her bright red lipstick to match. Miss, please make sure your seatbelt is secure, we are about the land. Over the intercom I hear the pilot, "Ladies and gentlemen, we have arrived safely in Dubai, it's 11:00 pm local time. For those of you who are visiting Dubai, we hope that you enjoy your stay. For those of you who live here, welcome home."

I am here, and he is speaking to me, the visitor, the one who has sweat dripping down her face. With the bright pink abaya on. Ugh, what am I doing, I thought to myself as I'm digging in my bag looking for something to wipe the sweat from my face? My heart is racing, and I feel like I'm having a panic attack. I'm rubbing my face, I start looking around the plane, and I notice that I'm the only one wearing a hot pink abaya. Everyone else around me is still wearing black! Oh No! They didn't change and it wasn't a dream. They are wearing black! Oh no, what have I done? I haven't even gotten off the plane and already breaking the rules. I don't have a black abaya, which means I will have to get off the plane looking out of place, and bright pink! I honestly can't afford to mess this up, and my family depends on me.

I walk off the plane, and a felt peace…. I walk to baggage claim, and yes, everyone is staring, I feel so out place. My heart is racing, and anxiety is coming back. I reach baggage claim and guess what? There are nine hundred and ninety-nine black bags! My grandmother told me to put those pink ribbons on my bag, but I didn't listen. I need a luggage cart, I say to myself. I see some close by, and they're free! Something is working out in my favor, and I say to myself while taking a deep breath. Finally, after checking a few hundred bags, I find mine.

As I am gathering my bags, I start looking for the taxi area. I notice everyone is still staring at me, and my hot pink abaya. I say to myself, Lord, please let me find a taxi quickly so I can change clothes. I open the door to the first taxi I see. The driver is yelling at me, "no woman, find woman taxi"! What? Am I now in the wrong cab? Do I have to find a taxi with a woman driver? Seriously? So, first the hot pink abaya, then the baggage scavenger hunt and now I am breaking the rules trying to get a taxi. I haven't been in the country 24 hours and close to being kicked out for breaking rules.

I finally find a lady driver, who is wearing a beige uniform and pink hijab, I give her the name of the hotel, still no pink abaya insight. She says, As-salamu Alaykum. I replied, wa-Alaikumussalam. Glad Google didn't let me down again. She says, "New hotel"? I reply, "I don't know." Are you kidding me, I think to myself? Now, I have a taxi, with a women driver, and she is not sure where to go. We drive around for two hours, and the roundabout and street signs are starting to look the same. We drive by The Mall of the Emirates five times. There are nice cars outside the mall, with lots of people going in and out. I'm making sure to take a mental note of the location so I could do some retail therapy which I will need after all of this.

Finally, we arrive at the hotel, which was down a dark and rocky road... very few lights, it's new construction. It is a lovely hotel from the outside, bright lights, with gold steps. I reach down to grab my purse to pay for my taxi ride, which cost more than it should. A gentleman in a dark black and red suit opens the door. "Welcome to the Oaks hotel, let me help you with your things." His warm welcome and smile help to relieve some of the stress I have endured for the past few hours. I walk into the hotel, it has white marble floors, flowers which you can smell as soon as you walk in, and everyone there has a smile!

I walk towards the check-in counter and take a few deep breaths; my anxiety is terrible right now. I scan the room to see who is around because I can't deal with any more drama right now. Oh, yes, the lady with the long brown hair, fair skin, bright smile with fuchsia lipstick. Hello, she says, how are you? Okay, just tired, excited and nervous I reply. Why? She asks. It's my first time working here, I have a lot on the line right now and just the unknown. Now, she didn't ask all of that, did she? Oh, don't worry it will be fine... if you need anything at all, please let us know. She checks me quickly, and she has my bags sent to my room. I decide to stop by the coffee shop to grab a cup of tea to take to my place. I'm mentally and physically exhausted. Not to mention confused... because of the time zone difference. Should I eat or sleep?

I walk in my hotel room, and I'm amazed by the décor and the amount of space. Wow, two bedrooms, three baths, full kitchen, washer, dryer and more. I honestly, wasn't expecting this. Wow, I feel at home, it's really weird and hard to explain.

It is a beautiful, clean room. I feel like I can rest here. I have a lot to think about and reflect on. I can't believe I am here. Me...

here... in the Middle East. What are the odds? I unpack my bags and prepare my clothes for the next day. I decide to go with a white shirt, black pants, and black heels. I can't seem to take my mind off all the issues I have at home, and tears start to roll down my face. I need to get it together, and I can't be in a mess and be a mess. I mean, I am here in Dubai to facilitate training... training... I should be excited, but I feel so unworthy of this. Maybe, a shower will help me to relax.

I walk in the bathroom, and it's beautiful! Tan and chocolate wallpaper and tan marble shower and floors, beautiful. The shower tile was dark chocolate with light tan glass-like specks in the tile. The bath is soothing... and just what I need. I get out of the shower and immediately call my family. I should have called hours ago. I am happy to hear my husband's voice on the other end of the phone. He is listening to me tell all my drama, agreeing... okay, oh, okay, I'm talking his head off. Can you believe it, I ask him? I am in Dubai... I never imagined this. Yes, I can, he says. I am proud of you. He has always supported anything I do. Well, tomorrow is a big day, so I need to get some sleep, or at least try to. Okay, bye... I love you, I love you too, good night. Ugh, I can't sleep, I guess I will read this local magazine and hopefully drift off to sleep.

I wake up the next morning, very early because I'm still not used to the time difference. I left the curtains open, which I didn't realize, so the sun is shining straight into my face. Wake up!! It is bright outside, and all I can see are the buildings everywhere. I am on the twenty-seventh floor, so the views are amazing. I'm laying here looking out the window, thinking about home, my children and my family. I'm also thinking about my financial situation and how I need to make this work. I know I can't just lay here all day... I have my first training in a few hours. I am nervous! I didn't see anyone that looked like me in the airport, hotel, etc. Umm, this is going to be interesting, to say the least!

I should have included a day of rest before having to facilitate the training. Yes, the smart one wearing the pink abaya agreed to facilitate training not even 24 hours off the plane. Not smart at all on my part. I am tired, stressed and I am finding it hard to relax. I close my eyes and thank God for another day, the lesson and the blessings. I am relaxed now. I order room service, toast, jam and a large pot of coffee. I really hope this will help me, it's going to be a long day.

I get dressed, this time in a black long skirt, white long sleeve shirt, and black flats. For some reason, I keep thinking back to the five pieces of certified mail that came before I left home. I knew what it was… bills!!! Bills, collections companies, and so on. Another reminder for why I am here, and I can't afford to be. As I continue to get dressed, tears start to roll down my face. This has become the norm for me bringing back memories of past… happy, sad, happy, sad, like a rollercoaster.

Okay, get it together, it's game time. I go downstairs to wait for my driver to arrive to take me to another hotel for training. The hotel is quiet this time of the morning… well, it's only 6:30am, people may be still sleeping. I guess I will grab a cup of coffee, it's free, which is right in my budget. Soon as I start pouring my coffee, the driver arrives. I hear someone yell, "Ms. Alexander"! I am here! Just one minute, please. The driver walks towards me. He says "hello my name is Beer "I am sorry your name is? He says, "Beer." Am I thinking to myself? What kind of name is that and is it his real name?

Now, I have never met him before, and all I have to go by is that he was sent by the training center. Okay, Beer can you grab that black training bag over next to the brown table? Sure madam. Madam? Really? Am I Madam now? Oh, this is going to be awesome! Someone is picking me up, carrying my bags, driving me and calling me Madam. We walk outside, it was a bright sunny, warm day. He opens the door to a brown van. I am thinking, I don't know him, and now he wants me to get into a van. I start praying and ask for protection and to find someone that speaks English if I need help. Soon, as I step in the van we started talking about his family and why he was in Dubai. He said to work and provide for his family. We immediately connect, and I feel like I have known him forever.

We pull up to the Hilton hotel, people are waiting to open the door and carry the bags in. Hello, Madam says the short man with a tan suit. Hello, how are you? He replied, "Fine Madam." Okay, he also calls me Madam, maybe this is the norm here. He takes my bags, and we walk to the elevator. It looks like the training is on the sixth floor from the button he pushed. I can't resist asking him for a large pot of coffee to be bought to the conference room. I am still tired, with plenty of jet lag. While I wait, I decide to look around the room, see what is here and what I need for the training. The tables are ten round tables, five on one side and five on the other. Wow, this is a large room to train only twenty people in, it's the size of a ballroom. Oh, well, I need to prepare my training handouts and projector, I am tired and nervous. Who will be in the room? Why do they have such a prominent place? Will it be all men?

I had many questions with no answers. I start to feel anxiety creeping in, so I take a few deep breathes, I take a seat and drink some water. Soon as I am beginning to relax, a man enters the room, he is dark-skinned, tall and has the biggest smile on his face. Is he American, I wonder? He introduces himself as my translator and says, "Are you Sudanese?" No, I reply. You look just like my family. I have never been asked this question. I start to reach for his hand; then I change my mind, what am I doing? I can't shake his hand; I don't think. Another Google search instead of asking someone who is familiar with the culture. He extends his hand and asks if there is anything, he can do to help me. He is nice, and I can tell he has been translating for years. He helps me to set up the room, and we go over the slides. "Is this your first time in the UAE? he asks." "Yes, for work" I reply. "Let me give you a few tips to help you during the training. Don't stare into a man's eyes or shake hands unless he extends his hand to you. Make sure you give them a break to go pray." I reply, "Okay I got it!" Oh, my word, I feel like I am going to mess up, oh my.

In walked five men wearing all white robes and what looked like scarfs on their heads, and none were smiling. I can't recall what their attire is called. Their faces are tight, and you can drop a pin in the room and hear it. Following them are ten beautiful women wearing all black abayas and hijabs on their heads. The men walk to one side of the room and sit down at the round tables and the women on the other side of the room. This is interesting, I don't remember reading about the women and men sitting separately in a training class. What am I going to do? I have a team building game planned for them.

The men are staring at me with tight faces, and the women are doing the same. Not one smile in the room but mine, I am smiling, praying and I want to cry. I am nervously scared, and all I can think about is that if I mess this up, this will affect not only me but my family as well. I have mix feelings right now, I am happy, sad, scared and excited. A hot mess! Girl, you are in Dubai, the Middle East, get it together before you mess up everything. Or, worse yet, do something stupid and get kicked out of the country.

It's time to start the training, the screensaver is a picture of my family, which is helping me to calm my nerves. I love my family and miss them, and this is all for them. I start the training with a video about team building, which is the topic I am training on. After the video, I start presenting the training material. I speak, and the translator translates afterward. The flow is good, some people are engaging, and others still have the same poker face as when they walked in. Do you have any questions? No one speaks. Okay, we will take a break and come back in fifteen minutes. Miss, I have a question, he has the most intimidating face in the room. I held my breath, and let out a "yes"? "Are you a Christian?" He asked me. My eyes open wide, my heart stops for a minute, I was told never to discuss race, religion or sex here. Before I know it, I reply "Christian," he says "really? Are you sure you're not, Arab?" "I reply, no I am not." He smiles, laughs and says, "you may want to double check." I sigh, laugh and smile. I feel so relieved that I didn't say the wrong thing. This is also a good sign that he is starting to trust me I was told when they start speaking English, they're starting to believe you. I am not sure if it's true, but let's hope so.

While they're on break, my phone rings, it's someone calling from the US. I answer because I'm thinking it might be an emergency, not because I could afford to take the international call. "Hello, is this Wendy Alexander?" "Yes, it is" "I am calling from a collection agency calling on behalf of," I hang up on her. I can't afford the call, and I can't afford whatever bill she wants me to pay. "Get in line, I say to myself." I sit down, drink some tea and refocus my thoughts back on the training. This is a great opportunity... not only financially, but from what I can see, there are not many women providing training. This training could be the start of a new chapter, something new, and I need to make sure they learn from this training so that they ask me to come back again. I have this weird feeling while being in the Middle East I feel safe, I feel welcomed and accepted. Everyone is so helpful, no one is asking questions about my past. They only want to know who the person is standing in front of them today. My anxiety is completely gone, and I feel like I am at home. I feel like I am surrounded by my brothers and sisters. I feel protected…. I feel free.

Ummm, but I wonder what other opportunities are here? I have time to explore the city, and I need to take advantage of it. I like it here, and I can start my own business here. I will do business in Dubai! I know I can do it! I can create opportunities for myself. The people here seem to really want to help and support me however they can. I feel I would be happy, and at peace here. I begin to wonder, you're probably wondering too, what makes a married woman, leave her husband and two children behind to go to another country by herself.

MY DESERT STORM

My name is Wendy Alexander, I am a Cross-Cultural Consultant, International Speaker, and International Strategist, from America and I live in Dubai, and this is my story.

It is a Tuesday morning at 6:00 am. It is still dark outside, and it's time to get up, get my children and myself ready for the day. I start my coffee, sit down to pray as I always do. But this time, something doesn't feel right, something tells me to go look outside. I have this sick feeling in my gut; my heart is racing, I fear what I may see once I pull the burgundy curtain back. I start saying to myself, "please let it be there." As I pull the curtain back, tears immediately stream down my face, I yell for my husband "it's gone," our truck is not in our driveway. The bank repossessed the truck overnight. What else could happen now? It seems like everything that can happen is happening. My husband was just laid off from his job; we are close to foreclosure, massive credit card debt that I created, two kids under three… we are young and struggling. Each day is stressful, anxiety, living paycheck to paycheck, and borrowing money from family is a norm. My mother and grandmother are always trying to help. We barely have enough to pay bills, now we need to try to get the truck back or let it go completely. I am trying to stay calm, but my anxiety is high, and I just want to give up! My husband comforts me and tells me everything will okay. I feel guilty because I know this is my fault. I should have saved more, gotten a part-time job or looked for another job paying more money. I could have done more, I am thinking to myself.

The next day I call the bank, and the amount asked to keep the truck was more than we have. We decide to let the truck go and will have to use one vehicle for the time being. My husband needs to search for work, but I work full time, I'm in school full time trying to finish my degree, and I just started a part-time job. My marriage is in jeopardy, because of the constant arguments over money and me not being able to communicate my feelings. The arguments are bringing back so many bad memories in my past, something I tried to forget whenever I could. Things in my past that I haven't fully addressed. To a time before I was married, when the only thing I knew was physical, mental abuse.

It was even at a point of me hitting my husband, lashing out in anger one time during an argument. I waited and wanted my husband to hit me back, he said," I will not hit you, I will leave you before I hit you!" His reply wasn't what I was used to because in most of my past relationships, my boyfriends, mentally and physically abused me not all, but most. I had one boyfriend in high school that was so jealous and possessive he wouldn't allow me to go anywhere without him. He went to another high school and would make sure he was there to pick me up every day when I got out of school. I guess he was tired of driving to pick me up, so he transferred to my high school. Things seem to get worse from there. He got into fights every day with other boy's because they would speak or look at me. He was kicked out of school after only being enrolled for two months. Sad, but I was glad he did because it was terrifying, stressful for me, and my grades were awful. I am not sure how I passed and graduated high school. Well, my mom had to go to the school and talk them into letting me graduate. I had one class that I had failed but, it would stop me from graduating. A lot of the things I was going through, I didn't tell anyone, not even my mom. I had my family to go to, and they would have done what they could I am sure. But I didn't...I suffered in silence. My best friends knew some of the things going on, but not all. The students at school only knew about his outburst and fights with others, not the mental, physical.......and sexual abuse that went on.

I rarely went out in high school after I started dating him. Or when I did, he would show up at parties, my school, and my home unannounced. Sometimes with a bat in his hand because he thought I was with a guy. I was always on edge when we were around other people or when I would try to go out with my friends. He had control of, all of me. My friends would tell me I needed to leave him, he was crazy, and he wasn't right for me. But I loved him, and he loved me, so, I thought. He said he loved me; he would always there for me. When he would yell at me and hit me, that was because he cared right? That's what love was and looked like for me then. Thank God for my husband, I know better now.

One day I had to stay at school late, and I walked outside to my copper colored BMW in the school parking lot. He was there waiting for me. He said, "why are you late?" I replied I had to stay after to makeup a test. Okay, he said, let's go back to my house, which was his parent's house, and watch a movie. I replied okay but found it strange he was so calm. I got in my car and followed him to his house. Soon as we got into the house, he grabbed me by my arm, I fell, and he dragged me by my arm. My blue jean skirt was halfway over my head by now. I reached for the bathroom door and held on, and finally, I was able to get up. He pushed me in the shower, and the flowered shower curtain fell on me. I went to get up, and punched him, yes, I had to fight back.

He dragged me into his room, pulled up my navy-blue jean skirt and forced himself on me. He was saying, I love you and I will never let you go. Asking me if I loved him, making me say it and promise to stay with him always as tears rolled down my eyes. I can still see the look in his eyes today and smell his cologne. I asked him to stop and said if you love me you would, as I cried and prayed at the same time. All he kept saying, was I love you. Suddenly, we heard the door, and it was his mom or dad. He jumped up and said I better not say anything and to go to the bathroom to straighten myself up. I went into the bathroom, I was trying to gather myself, I couldn't stop crying, but I knew I had to or suffer the consequences. I walked out of the bathroom, and his mother was in the kitchen putting up groceries. She said, hello Wendy, and I replied hello in a low voice, I picked up my keys and said goodbye. I got out of the door before she could turn around. He came out and said, "why are you leaving?' I said I have to go and what you did…. I stopped because I didn't want him to get upset, yell or hit me. He said, call me as soon as you get home. He meant that, or he would be at my house if not. I drove home and cried the entire way. Once I reached home, no one was there, and my mom was at work. I never told her or anyone.

    A few weeks later, I was in class, and I wasn't feeling good. I went to the bathroom and threw up everywhere. What was wrong with me? Maybe it was something I ate. No way I could be pregnant I was on the pill. After a few episodes of him forcing himself on me when he was upset, I thought it was best. Even though once he found out I was on the pill, he would throw them out the window while driving. I cleaned myself up and went on about my day and went to basketball practice that same day. If you're wondering if he watched me at practice, yes, every day. A few weeks later I notice I was still getting sick, mostly in the morning. I had also missed my period as well. So, I went to Planned Parenthood to take a test which is where I also got my pills. I had insurance, but I didn't want my mother to know. The test came back positive, what am I going to do now? Weeks went on, and I never told anyone not even him. One day, he got upset because I wouldn't stay at his house longer, it was a school night. He started yelling and screaming at me. I was afraid he would hit me. I shouted I am pregnant! Hoping it would stop him from yelling and not hit me. He looked at me, and he said? Are we going to have a baby? I said, no, I can't keep it, I just can't. He yelled you would not kill my baby, that is my baby!! I said I don't believe in abortion, but I can't. The way it happened, our age, the child will suffer and so would we. But for me, the truth is, I knew if I kept that baby, he would never leave me alone. I would be attached to him forever unless he killed me first. He started crying and said, promise me you won't do it. I replied okay, I promise. Knowing I had an appointment already to get an abortion. But I missed the first three appointments because I couldn't get rid of him. He was always around and threatening to harm me if I had an abortion. My mother eventually found out, her, and my uncle took me to get the abortion. My boyfriend didn't find out till after it was done. I lied and told I had something to do with the family that day. My mother thought I was mad at him and I just didn't want him there. This was the worse day of my life! I prayed and asked God for forgiveness, I asked him not to punish me later by not allowing me to have kids. I prayed and asked God to forgive me of my sin. It wasn't easy to deliver a stillborn. Till this day, I ask and pray to God for forgiveness.

The next day, I told him over the phone and that I also needed my space. He cried, told me he was going to kill himself then it turned to me. Was I scared, yes, I think, honestly, I really can't tell you what emotions I had? I was confused and controlled by him during this time just a mess. The school year was about to end, and he goes out state for work during the summer, which was a break for me. It seemed nothing I would do or say would make him leave. I would remain in fear that he would do something to himself or me if I left him. We went on dating my Senior year high school. Nothing changed, just another year and he was banned from attending my school again, so he went back to his old school. I am sure you are asking, "why didn't she leave?" "Why didn't she tell someone?" It's easier said than done.

I remember one day towards the end of my senior year; he asked me where did I decide to go to college. We were watching a television show at his parent's house. I replied, not sure, I should know by tomorrow. I lied, I am attending a Norfolk State University four hours away which would take me away from him. Later that evening he found an envelope in my purse with the acceptance letter to the school. I was leaving, the next day, and this was why the letter was in my bag. I will never forget the dark blue shirt, jeans and brown boots he was wearing that day. I will also never forget the anger and rage in his eyes when he found out I was leaving the state. He yelled, he screamed at me, and all I could do was cry. I was praying that he wouldn't hit me. But he did, he hit me in my chest and slapped me across my face. "Why are you leaving me he said? I replied I couldn't get into another school, but again I was lying. I was going to this school to get away from him, and I felt it was the only way. I had never seen the school, had no idea what it looked like or anything! Only what his mom had shared with me because she attended the University. Yes, she knew, she helped me to get into the school to get away from him. She knew of some of the incidents but not all. By now, he had grabbed me by my arm and said: "we're leaving." I grabbed my favorite black leather book bag, matching purse and blue Polo jacket and told his mother goodbye. I remember his mother asking me, "What's wrong," "I replied nothing." He started yelling at me to leave. We got in his brown Mercedes, and he yelled and yelled. "Why are you leaving me?" I sat quietly and praying to make it home safe. See, one month prior we were in a car accident. He fell asleep at the wheel and ran into a dump truck. I had the hood of the car on my back. I didn't have my seatbelt on which saved me. I was able to look up in time before impact and leaned over in his lap. The police said they had no idea how I made it out without one scratch on me.

We continued to drive, and he started pulling over into a park near my house. It was dark, only one street light on in the next parking lot over from us. I asked him, "What are we doing here?" He said, "I need to talk to you." He said, "Are you going to leave me?" I said, "I am going off to school." He was starting to get angry, I could see it in his eyes. He, reached in his blue bookbag, pulled out a gun and said, "If I can't have you no one can." My eyes and mouth were wide open. The white t-shirt I had on was soaked, from sweat and fear. I said, "please don't do this and I won't leave." "Just let me go home, and you do the same, we can talk tomorrow." His breathing started to get heavier, and I was now looking down the barrel of his gun again. Yes, again.

Three weeks prior, I was at a party with some friends. After it was over, we went to the parking lot and listened to music. It was around fifty or more people outside at the time. One of my male friends had a Toyota Camry and said, my four girlfriends and I could sit in the car and wait. He had just started recording music and wanted us to listen to it. We were all in the car, listening, singing, dancing and having a good time. I was in the front seat in the middle beside him, my other friend on the other side, and three other girlfriends in the back. All of a sudden, we heard screaming, and then someone jumped on the hood of the car, it was him, my boyfriend. Holding a gun and pointing it at the crowd and inside of the car at me. "Get out of the car"! I was shaking my head no. My friends were telling me to get out and run, but I couldn't. It was almost like I felt like if I moved, I couldn't save my friends. I needed to calm him down, while others got away. Someone had called the police so when he heard the sirens, he jumped off the car and ran. I jumped out of the car and ran to meet my friends. Once we reached my best friends mother's car, no one said a word. I am not sure if they ever told their mom or not. I know I once again didn't mention it to anyone.

No one was in the park, but us and it was pitch dark. I couldn't believe I was there again, with him, with a gun in my face. I closed my eyes and prayed, and I opened my eyes and started telling him how much I loved him and how much I couldn't live without him. I said, "I know you're upset, I will walk home, and you can go home and get some rest." I reached for the latch of the door and opened it. He said, "No, you're not leaving." Yes, I am, please I am tired, and I don't feel good." I put one foot out of the car, slowly the next. I was so glad I had on my sneakers, just in case I needed to run. I didn't turn my back, I kept watching him and the gun. I stepped out of the car and started walking. It was dark, and it was only one street light in the park and one more down the street leading to my house. All I saw was darkness and trees. I was scared to walk home, but I knew this was the only thing that would save my life. As I started to walk, he said he would take me home, he was sorry. I said, "No, I will walk." "No, he replied, pointing the gun at me. Get in the car, and I promise to take you home. I didn't know what to do. I was confused and scared. I got back in the car, he grabbed my face and was trying to kiss me. He said, "I love you, and I am sorry." He started to drive and dropped me off in front of my house. I turned and said, "thank you and goodbye." My goodbye was for good, not for that night because I knew I was leaving for college the next day. I went to my house, took a shower, cried, prayed, never spoke a word about it to my mother, grandmother who is my heart, my rock or anyone.

The next day, my mother, stepfather and I, packed the motorhome with all belongs and we headed to Virginia. I slept the entire way because I was mentally exhausted and depressed. I also didn't want my mother asking me any questions about anything. We arrived at Norfolk State University, I unpack my belongings and meet my two roommates we had a large suite with a bathroom inside of the room. They were both from Virginia, and we were all studying Political

Science. My mother and stepfather decide to leave and head back home. My roommates and I went to eat lunch in the cafeteria. They had fascinating stories to share as to why they selected Norfolk State University. I couldn't relate at all. I can't remember what exactly I made up, but I didn't tell them to escape my boyfriend. They were brilliant, friendly and praying ladies. Just want I needed right now.

The next day, I was leaving class, I was walking looking down at the syllabus my professor gave me. I heard someone say, hey baby you miss me?" It was him; he was there, I thought I saw a ghost. He drove from North Carolina to Virginia, not just that day, but every day for the next four months. He would get off work in North Carolina, drive to Virginia, slept in his car until I got out of class. I never told him we weren't together because the last time I tried to leave, I had a gun in my face. He would come, each day, see where I was, who I was with and leave maximum stay one hour. One day, he came, and I had gone home with one of my friends who lived in New York. My other roommate who was at the dorm called me to tell me he was there. He had been there all night, outside of the dorm in the rain, waiting for me. Once I arrived at the school and was walking towards the door, he jumped out of the bushes. He was wet, cold, shivering, and yelling, "where were you"? I replied with my roommate, why are you here? I pulled my umbrella closer to me, shaking and fearing for my life. Also, embarrassed because people were walking by. I started to walk towards the dorm thinking; I only need to make it to the door and run in. The door will lock behind. So, took off running, and it seemed that it took forever to reach that big green door, I ran in and closed it behind me. The door locked behind me and I kept running once inside. I can still see him banging on the green door, standing in the pouring rain, no coat or umbrella yelling for me to come out. Shouting, that if he catches me with another guy, he will kill us both.

By now a guy approached him, asked him to leave, and they got in a fight. The police came and took him to jail. His one phone call, he called to tell me he was going to kill me. By now, my roommates found out, and they prayed for me and with me. The next day I had to go to court because I was the reason he was on campus. As we sat in the courtroom, he made his fingers like a gun, and I read his lips, and he said, I am going to kill you. I was at a place where I could ask for help, for a restraining order. I was scared and feared for my life, but I knew if I was going to do anything to stop this, it was now. The judge was going to give him thirty days in jail until he said he was going in the

Navy. So, they granted the restraining order and waived the thirty days of jail time. But no one asked him where he would be stationed. It was in Norfolk, right there with me. Soon as I left the courthouse, I submitted my application to attend North Carolina Central University. I had four weeks left before the semester ended.

I went to the Chancellor office and told my story, and they allowed me to take my exams and leave early. I called my mom and told her I didn't like it, I wanted to come home, and there was a lot of violence happening. Which was true about the violence, but that wasn't the real reason. She came to get me later that week, I moved back to North Carolina and started school at North Carolina Central University. I also started seeing a therapist as well. I never saw him again until years later. It's amazing how life works. My husband also attended Norfolk State University, but I didn't meet him there. I met him years later after him, and his family moved to North Carolina.

The arguments continued between my husband, and I was hoping the part-time would help us stay afloat until my husband was able to secure employment. It doesn't, and we argue every day and were growing farther apart. I can't eat, sleep or smile about anything. How is this happening to us? Why are we in this situation and how can we get out of it? As days go on, things only become worse; the bills are piling up, the bank and bill collectors are calling, we have one vehicle between us, and we're in survival mode. We have tried everything we can to keep the things we had left, like our home. Something needs to change; we must do something drastic, which also means more sacrifices.

My husband is applying for jobs in the Middle East, which will take him away from home. Which can also strain our marriage even more because of the distance. He will also be away from our children. All of this is scary for us, but I know we have no other choice. My husband is getting interviews for jobs overseas faster than he is in the US. He has a few offers on the table. Most of these jobs will take him away from home for over three months or more at a time. The money is right; we can get out of the debt and start living again. It looks like things are about to change for us and we are heading in the right direction. I was nervous because I knew nothing about the Middle East or anyone working there. But I knew I had to support him, he was willing to risk his life, and sacrifice for his family.

I receive a call from the bank, and they said we have 30 days to move out of our home. We are now in foreclosure, and there is no way we can come up with that amount of money in 30 days. I had asked my mother for money, but that wasn't enough. We will have to let our first home go and move in with my grandmother. This is so embarrassing, what will people think? We are homeless and jobless. Some may say, "You are not homeless because you have a family you can live with." But it isn't our home, it's gone. I start thinking of what lie am I going to tell people. At this point, I am depressed, frustrated and just ready to give up. Thoughts of suicide cross my mind. I stopped seeing my therapist because I couldn't find the time. I can't take it anymore I scream! The only thing that is saving me from suicide this time is my children... I need to live for them. This situation is triggering me, I whisper to myself while shaking my head. I need to make an appointment to see my therapist today.

Flashbacks, of when I was seventeen laying in the hospital bed, with the bright lights and nurses poking me with needles and asking me questions. "How many pills did you take?" "What kind of pills." Then the nurse is coming in to insert the long tube down my throat to pump my stomach. I can still smell the room, it smells like amoxicillin. I can still hear the nurse with blonde hair yelling, "swallow," swallow" the tube. I can still see the dark charcoal in the tube as my stomach is being pumped. I remember staring at the ceiling hoping it was all going to end soon. No, not the stomach pumping, my life. I was in a bad place during this time, including being depressed. This was my closest attempt to succeeding at suicide, out of the five times before. Pills were my choice. I was able to hide the pain and hide all but one of the suicide attempts from my family. My mom had great insurance, and I was able to keep hospital bills, co-pays away from her. She never knew my pain, none of my family, I never shared it with them.

My life has so many moving parts. It seems like nothing in my life is going right. I am walking around smiling as if nothing is wrong. I am the strong one, the one that everyone calls for advice... there's no way I can be going through anything. Wrong! Life sucks right now, and it always has!!

Reality is setting in, we must move, and it's not to a place of our own... it's with my grandmother. Thank goodness my grandmother has a home that could fit all my family, but it's nothing like having your own. There are four bedrooms in my grandmother house, one for her, one for my husband and I and the kids. I am grateful for my grandmother allowing us to stay with her. She had never told me no and has always been there for me when I allowed her to. A few days after moving in, my husband got a part-time job. I am still in school, working full time and no longer working part-time. He is still waiting to hear back from the companies overseas; the process is long and daunting. We need to have a plan B to look at other options so that we can move out of my grandmother's home. But just like everything else during that time, nothing seems to be working out. I mean, yes, he has a part-time job, and every day he is looking for a full-time job, but we need to move. My depression is getting worse. I keep it to myself and can't even think of sharing my story with someone.

I have a fear of being judged or of losing people close to me because they don't want to deal with my drama. I am in this dark place alone and feel trapped. I am not eating, or when I do it is emotional eating, and adding pounds… just great, right? Sigh.

On top of that, I don't know what sleep is. I am up all night worrying and trying to plan how we can move out of my grandmother's home. This is even though she said we could stay there as long as we want to visit. It doesn't feel right for us to do that… my husband wants us to have a home, and he is doing everything he can to make it happen.

My grandmother and husband tell me every day that things will get better, not to worry. Honestly, I can't see the light at the other end… all I see is darkness. I am a mess, my marriage, and my frustration are coming out and affecting my kids, which is not good. I am yelling at them, snapping at my husband and not returning phone calls to family and friends. I know I need to get it together. I am losing everything, including myself, again.

The next day I am laying down taking a nap and the phone rings. I miss the call, so I used *69 to call them back, afraid it could be about a job for my husband. "Hello?" "May I speak with Wendy Alexander?" "Yes, this is she." "I am calling to collect a debt," and I cut her off. "Miss, get in line with everyone else. Or contact my other bill collectors and ask them if you can jump to the front of the line." She said, "what?" I said, "you heard me, bye." Five minutes later the phone rings again. I know she isn't calling back… I'll fix her, and I let it go to voicemail. No! I'd better answer it. On the last ring I try to catch it, but they hung up. I decide to use *69 again to return the call.

"Hello, this is Amanda from the recruiting agency call to speak with Mr. Alexander." OMG!!! I said. "I am sorry, let me see if my husband is available." "Boo! It's a recruiter who wants to speak with you." I yell for my husband again, to come to the phone and he whispers to me "who is it? I am watching the game." I say, "it's a job" gritting my teeth, with raised eyebrows, I shove the phone at him. "Hello, this is Mr. Alexander." "I would like to see if you're still available for work Mr. Alexander." "Yes, I am!" The recruiter offers him a full-time job at a company not far from my grandmother's home. He told the recruiter, "let me think about it." "Think about it?" I said, "No you don't need to think about it." I have no clue what the offer is or anything. I just know it's a full-time job. He hung up the phone and explained why he told the recruiter he would think about it. He said he has received another offer as well, about thirty minutes before this one. I threw the pillow at him and said, "Why didn't you tell me? I thought you had lost your mind". We discuss the pros and cons of both jobs and decide to take the first offer.

    The next day, during breakfast, my husband calls the manager with the first offer back and accepts. Then he calls the other proposal to thank the recruiter and to let him know he has decided not to take the position. I have not seen my husband so excited in a while. I'm glad too as we are heading back in the right direction. I am so happy but not as comfortable as my husband. It's hard to smile when you are so used to being sad and depressed. My husband turns to me and says, "Let's go to dinner to celebrate." "No," I reply, we can't afford it. You have a job, but you haven't received your first paycheck, so no, let's wait.

    The next morning, I arrive to work early and am asked to come into a meeting with my boss and the Area Manager. I'm nervous and afraid… and I'm trying to figure out what the management team wants with me. What is it now? Fire me? Lay me off? We don't need any more financial problems. I walk into the bright office, with natural lighting, a beautiful cherry wood desk, and dark chocolate chairs. The Area Manager says, "Have a seat. We need to talk". Please… I think I'm going to be sick… right here and all over his clean tan suit. He is going to fire me!

    I start sweating, it's fifty degrees outside, which means I look crazy. As the area manager begins speaking, he asks if I am okay and if we can meet another day. I said no… I am fine… we can talk now. I want to say, "Are you crazy?", No way I could leave now without knowing what he wants. He said, "Great, I want to offer you a promotion." Promotion? Yes, why do you seem so shocked? I guess I wasn't expecting it. These days, I wasn't expecting anything good, I think to myself. I am shocked and excited, thinking this is a great opportunity and will help my family financially. Then he says, "The job requires you to travel fifty percent of the time." My face goes from a smile to a look of puzzlement. I think, "How will I travel with two young kids and a marriage that is already struggling?"

I went home and told my grandmother the news. I am excited because this promotion means that we can move into a home of our own again. Maybe an apartment… something small and affordable. I open the door, and she is sitting in her blue recliner, rolling up her beautiful silver-grey hair, and watching Westerns. Oh, grandma, "How can you watch Westerns? They're boring?" She replies, "No, they are perfect, you just don't sit your bottom down long enough to watch them," she says. I laugh, "Grandma, I have some exciting news to tell you! I was offered a promotion today!!!" "Congratulations, she replies, and she hugs me and kisses me on my forehead." I had heard about this position a year ago, and I wanted it… it has been one of my goals. "I am so happy for you Wendy, but how will you travel with the kids?" She asked, "I don't know, I need to speak with Mr. Alexander first." "Well, I can keep them and help you out in any way I can" she replies. "Thank you, but you have done so much for us, and I don't want to ask you to do that." "That's what families are for Wendy." My grandmother is super sweet, or she is ready for us to get out of her house, I say to myself. My husband walks in, and he looks like he is tired, frustrated and had a bad day at work. I am not sure if I should tell him about the promotion or wait. "Hey boo, how was your day, I asked." "It was stressful, and honestly the responsibility and amount of work do not equal the pay." "I am sorry to hear that," I reply. "It's okay, it is what it is right now." "Well, I have some exciting news to tell you, well, I think it is. I was offered a promotion at work!!" "That's great," he replies, "I am so proud of you." "Thanks, but my concern is that I have to travel and who will keep the kids?" "We will be just fine, and we can work it out, you just take the position, we need it." "But what happens when you have to work late or get overtime?" "Wendy, it's not like we have a choice. We need the money." "Fine!" I yell and walk out.

The next day I walked into work and had a follow-up meeting with my manager. The office feels so cold, damp and dark. It was a cloudy day, and I knock on managers door. "Come in" he replies. I walk in, nervous and excited. "How are you today I ask him?" "Fine, did you decide to take the job?" Dang, I am saying to myself, give me a minute to reply." Yes, I have decided to take the position. Thank you for the opportunity." The room stills feel cold, I ask when I would start traveling?" "He said next week to New York." I said, "Next week?" "As in Monday next week?" He replies "Yes." Oh okay. "How in the world will I plan this in just three days?" I say to myself. What seems to be a great opportunity is turning into a hot mess! "Okay, thank you. What should I do next?" "Go to Human Resources and Jackie will have the paperwork for you to sign."

I walk out of his office and take a detour to my office. I am thinking, maybe this isn't such a good idea until my office phone rings and it's another bill collector. Quickly, my mind changes and I come to my senses. The phone rings again, and this time it is my husband, he says, "Guess what?" "What?" "I finally got an offer." My eyes are big and my mouth open, "offer for what"? He says, "a job in Iraq." "Iraq where?" Like there's more than one Iraq! He says, "The Middle East, what's wrong with you"? I said, "Nothing, that's great"! I have a fake smile so he couldn't hear the fear in my voice. I am holding my head with one hand thinking, "How will I travel, and now he will be out of the country? I mean, can anything just work out in my favor? Anything? "Okay, that's great congrats, we can discuss more when I get home, I have a meeting." Lying so I can get off the phone because I am speechless. How will all this work?

I go back to my desk and sit there staring at the computer until it's time to go home. I can't think. I don't feel like talking or being bothered. I went to grab my black sweater, without looking at what I was doing, the left-over coffee ends up on my shirt and the floor. "Are you serious?" I yell. My co-worker comes in to help me clean it up, and I head home. I am over today.

I stay quiet and get into bed at 7:00pm. I didn't eat, and I even asked my grandmother to give the kids a bath… my kids. I am a mess, more of a mess than I was before. I am so tired of the roller coaster, tired of being happy one minute and sad the next. Whenever I think things are going right, something else goes wrong. This should be a time to be excited, but I am depressed. I am going to have to ask my husband not to take the job, or I can't receive the promotion I worked so hard to get. What comes first? My dreams or our family financial stability?

It's Saturday, and on Monday I must fly to New York. No way can I cancel now and not show up; I would risk losing my job altogether. I honestly can't think and with only three hours of sleep. I must tell my husband that I am concerned about him being gone and me traveling. My husband said, I am excited about your opportunity but what will we do about the kids? I really hate to ask my grandmother to anything else. We have no choice, let's go sit down and talk to her. We know that for this to work it will take the help of our family. I called my mom and told her the good news and the bad news. I ask her if she could also help us with the kids, picking them up from school and maybe watching them overnight sometimes. She and my grandmother both said, yes, they will do whatever it takes to help us. I am so grateful and thankful for my family. We hate to ask anyone to take care of our kids, but we have no choice right now.

The phone rings, "Hello, can I speak to Wendy Alexander?" "This is she" "I am calling from a collection agency to a collect a debt. You have a balance of $426.00 that needs to be paid today." "I don't have it or anything to give you today, but I will call back when I can." I hang up the phone on her. I am frustrated and embarrassed. I have the money, but it is to pay gas and daycare. Daycare needs to be paid so that my husband and I can work. I can't ask my grandmother to keep them… that would be too much to ask, to keep them during the day and at night when I travel. I am not sharing this with my husband either, he has enough on his plate. If it comes down to asking her, I will, but it will be the last result. I also don't want to keep changing their environment, they need some stability. We have already moved from our house to my grandmother's house.

We continue to discuss our plans over dinner. My grandmother's food tastes so good. She loves to cook chicken, cabbage, macaroni & cheese, and cornbread. For some reason, I have an appetite to eat today. Taking care of myself isn't and hasn't been a priority. I will either emotionally eat or not eat. I decide I will take the promotion and my family will help with the kids. My husband is happy, and he is excited about my new position. I still hate asking my mother and grandmother to help us. I mean, we have gone from borrowing money to living with grandma to her picking up the kids, and now our family is taking care of them overnight. It's family, but it's still hard to ask. We just need more time to save and get on our feet we are heading in the right direction, I think.

The next morning, I arrive at the airport with one brown carryon and my laptop bag. I am wearing a brown suit, light blue shirt, and brown shoes. I have a meeting as soon as I get off the plane. All I can think about is being away from my family for a week. I am not excited at all about that. I have to leave early, and my husband has to be at work before the daycare opens. My grandmother has to take the kids to daycare. All I can think about is her getting two small children up, dressed, and brought to daycare. Way too much! I start to cry, and people are looking at me, I don't care. I am asking myself, how did we get here? Is it buying clothes and shoes... trying to live like the Jones's? Or is it mismanagement of money, living outside of our means? We are young, with kids, and maybe it's all the above? I have so many questions yet no answers. We must get out of this... do whatever it takes, which can mean many sacrifices. One is boarding this plane heading to New York. It is the start of many sacrifices to come.

I arrive in New York, tired, not motivated and honestly not prepared for this presentation. I am a Business Development Representative, and I am presenting on behalf of the company to secure a new client. I walk into the building, it is in the middle of Manhattan surrounded by tall buildings. I take the elevator to the tenth floor. I know I must get it together, and quick. I say to myself, "Look, girl, get yourself together... now!" I stop by the restroom to wash my face and brush my teeth. I feel like I have a hot breath and I can't take the chance that they will not do business with us because I have funky breath. That will be all I need. I look in the mirror and say to myself, "You got this!" as my husband always tells me. He is, and always has been, my biggest supporter, in whatever I decide to do. I regroup and focus on my why... the reason I am here. Some will say focus and be thankful for the blessing. At the point where I am in my life, I can't see the benefit or happiness... my depression has taken over again. I could hide depression as no one would.

I walk into the office, and it is filled with flowers that you can smell a mile away. The receptionist is looking in the mirror combing her long blonde hair and putting on bright pink lipstick. "Hello, may I help you?" She asks. "Who are you here to see?" "Robert," I reply, "Have a seat, and I will let him know you are here." I sit down on this plush dark gray chair and stare out the window next to me. I love the skyline of New York... the fast pace, the shopping, and everything, but I can't enjoy it. I am having flashbacks of all my problems and thinking about my family and being away from them. I hear my name, and it's time to go in, Get it together Wendy! Do like you always do and smile through your pain. I walk in smiling, and I introduce myself, and everyone proceeds to do the same. It is go time, time to shine! The good thing is, I love to sell, it's one of my strengths and something I like to do. I stand tall, I smile, and I present like someone who owns her own million-dollar business. They are engaged and impressed with my presentation. Robert says, "you are so full of energy and passion for your work." Little did he know it is all fake, the smiles, etc.

I go back to my hotel room, which is only a few blocks away. I take my shower and then try to nap. I am exhausted from all the action. I am laying there looking at the ceiling and trying to sleep, and I can't. I call my husband to see how his day is going. He answers the phone, and the first thing he says, "Are you okay?" He knows me so well. I reply, "yes," with tears in my eyes. I don't want him to worry. But I want to tell him no, I am a mess, and I hate life right now. I wipe away my tears, and we discuss how things are going on with his new job. He says, it is okay, it is more job responsibility than they said, and the pay isn't equal to the work, but it will do. He asks me how my day went, I tell him it was great, and the presentation went well, one lie and one truth. I am tired. I think I am going to lay back down. We say our goodbyes, and I call my grandmother to check on her and the kids. She tells me the kids are beautiful and behaving. Even if things are not good, she would say to me. Little did she know her granddaughter is depressed and thinks of suicide more than living. See… I am pretty good at wearing and switching masks when I need to.

The next day, I wake up early to iron my clothes and eat breakfast before heading into the office. I am wearing black pants, a red, white and black blouse and flat black shoes. Today, I am walking to the office instead of taking the taxi. I'll be a real New Yorker for the day. Also, so I can do some meditation and prayer before I get to the office. I put on my sneakers and place my black shoes in my tote bag; I will change at the office. I go downstairs, grab some coffee, juice, biscuit, and bacon off the breakfast buffet. I make a quick bacon biscuit sandwich, trying to force myself to eat. I should be skinny by now, but I am gaining weight. It's like the food on the plate is still jumping inside my body and going straight to my hips!

I arrive at the office for another meeting to pitch my company's services and go for the close. Usually, this is really exciting for me because I love selling and closing deals. But it hasn't been that way lately… I must get it together. Sometimes, I ask myself, why did I leave working in Mental Health to go into Business Development? Honestly, I switch back and forth between the two. I guess I have options with finding a job. I don't know. Okay, now pull it together… the company needs the deal, and I need it to show my boss I can do it.

I walk in, mask on, and I pitch the benefits of doing business with me and ask for the deal. They immediately say yes and would like to know how soon we can start. This means that I will be back in New York sooner than I would like to be. "We can start as soon as you like," I reply. "Great, just prepare the final paperwork. Thank you, Wendy! We look forward to working with you." "You are welcome, and on behalf of my company, we thank you as well." Smile Wendy, just a few more minutes, I am saying to myself. I walk out and phone my boss to tell him we got the deal. "Great job, Wendy," he says, "we really needed this deal." "Thank you," I reply.

I head back to the hotel. Now that I have secured the deal, I can go home a few days early. I call our travel agent to see if she can get me a flight home tomorrow morning. This will give me time to prepare the paperwork for them. I need to go eat, take a nap and then I will do the paperwork. I have a headache again. I keep pain meds and may take at least twice a day. Oh yes, there is a café here in the hotel where I can grab a sandwich. They have the best chicken salad sandwiches and sweet tea. I sit down in the restaurant away from everyone. I don't feel like talking, and I don't want anyone trying to talk to me. I just want to be left alone.

Fast forward... I have been in my new position for over a month now. I have secured new clients in New York to whom I now travel more than fifty percent of the time. I am hardly home. My husband has been on his job for over a month now, and he is continuing to look for work in the Middle East. The kids have adjusted to the routine of me traveling and being away from home. We have started paying a few bills, but not as many as we would like to. I am tired of moving, living out of a suitcase and I want to be home with my family. My husband and I haven't spent any time together. We are stressed, frustrated and the distance at the time isn't helping.

My husband and I decided to watch a DVD and try to reconnect while I am home. We conclude that we need to plan cheap date nights. This means date nights under $10.00, so we stay focused on our goal. "Why don't we grab a movie tonight," he says. "Sure, I think they have a few good movies at the Dollar theater. Let's go!" We arrive at the theater, grab a bag of popcorn and a drink for six dollars. Yes, under budget! This is a great cheap date for us... things are going well, it seems perfect, or so I thought.

In the middle of the movie, I ask my husband if he like his job and when can we move out of my grandmother's home. Yes, during the film and I know this question will set him off... so dumb of me. He looks at me and says, "Are you serious? Right now?" I reply "yes," dumb again, and He replies, "I am trying, and I am still waiting for jobs overseas, what else to do you want me to do?" I reply "nothing" and roll my eyes. We continue watching the movie, he is mad, and I am too. I don't know why I started this argument knowing the outcome, and I am wasting a perfectly good date. After the movie, we head home in complete silence. We arrive at my grandmother's house, still not speaking, I shower, get the kids ready for bed, and I need to pack to leave the next day. My husband and I are still not speaking, and it is going to be a long, silent, restless night.

The next day, I wake up to get the kids ready for school, say good morning to my husband and he mumbles it back. Oh well, I say to myself. The smell of bacon comes from the kitchen... It is my grandmother pleasant cooking. But honestly, I don't feel like eating anything. I am frustrated, tired and just ready to get back into bed. But I can't. I need to catch this flight. I run again upstairs and tell my husband bye, I hug him and kiss. I don't like leaving mad or upset. I shouldn't go to bed upset either I guess. You know, "we need to talk and plan our next steps." He replies, " I agree, and we can talk tonight once you get settled in New York."

I arrived at the hotel in New York, and it's chilly outside today, tired, not feeling good, and just not in the mood. Leaving my family behind is starting to get to me. I know this is something I have to do to move out of my grandmother's home as well as get another vehicle. The kids, of course, seem to be adjusting, but I'm not sure. I feel like an ill mother who is all over the place... mentally and physically. I don't know. I guess I should be happy instead of sad all the time. Phone rings. "Hello. How are you?" It's my husband. I am okay, just tired and trying to understand what's going on with us.

His reply? "I don't know but it's not working, and something has to change." I agree. Maybe we need to move or at least start looking? I think we need our own place, not that, that will solve all our problems, but it could help us. When you get back, we'll start looking and planning. But that doesn't justify the arguments we are having, something must change. I reply, "I agree, but just remember it's not all me, you have a part in this too." Rolling my eyes and staring at the phone. I have to run now, I will talk to you later. This is one area I know I need to work on. I don't like facing my problems, never have. I am always looking for an easy way out or how to forget it... to avoid the situation altogether. Which is one of the reasons I am in this situation now, I feel.

A few days later, I fly back home my husband, and my kids are there to pick me up at the airport. I was standing outside of the baggage claim area, and I hear "mommy"! Any mother knows their child's voice. I am excited to see the kids, and even my husband despite the argument. He bends down to give me a kiss and a hug and says, "We have something we want you to see." I reply, "Okay where is it," I ask. We have to go there he replies. My husband grabs my bags, and we head outside to the parking lot. It is so cold I scream, it's so cold. The kids are laughing, smiling and excited about the surprise.

We get in the truck, and I immediately increase the heat. We drive about 20 minutes away from the airport and arrive in the neighborhood. "Who are we going to see," I ask? "No one," my kids reply. We pull into the driveway of a gray, two-story home, with a two-car garage. Flowers are around the walkway, and we see kids riding their bikes. It's a very nice, clean, family neighborhood. We get out the car, and I notice my husband has a house key to get in. "How did you get the key?" "Don't worry about it," he replies. "Do you like it?" "Do I like it," I ask? "I don't know, whose house we are in? We are going to go to jail, whose house is this?" "No, no calm down," he says. "This is the house we saw in the paper, and it's ours." "What?" I reply. "Yes, for us," he says. "How much is it? We can't afford this". "Just look around," he says.

I walk around the house, and it has four bedrooms, three and a half baths. It has a two-car garage, a backyard for the kids to play in and it's close to my grandmother. The rent is cheaper than moving into an apartment, and there is an option to buy. This is a great house an option for us since we have been turned down at several apartment complexes because of our credit. It's for rent by the owner, which means he will work with us, but with a larger deposit, one month's rent. We have that, so? It is the best option for us currently. We are close to our family, it is affordable and close to the daycare. One problem is that we will have to either wake the kids up early to go to my grandmothers or they stay overnight on the days my husband works late, or when I am out of town. Nothing is perfect, there is always something that has to be worked out… this is a great house.

We drive back to my grandmothers. "Are you sure we can afford this? I mean, how did you come up with your calculations?" I ask. "Yes, why do you always doubt me?" he asks. Let me handle this for once… you don't have to be in control of everything. Okay, rolling my eyes, as I mumble you better be right. The kids will be disappointed now if this doesn't work out. I will also do my own budget, I say to myself.

We arrive at my grandmother's, and I walk in and see her sitting in her recliner and watching westerns. I run and give her a big hug and kiss. "How are you, grandma?", I ask. "Fine," she replied. "Did your husband tell you about his little plan?", I ask her. "About the house?" "Yes, they did," she replied. "How do you feel about it?", I ask. "Fine, because you will always have a home here," she said. "Thank you, but I am praying we will not have to come back again. We are thankful for your support", I replied. "But I am scared grandma, I can't lie. One missed work, loss of job or hours and we are back at square one. One wrong move and it's over just like that. But okay, I am going to trust you know what you are doing", as I turn to look at and up at him.

It's moving day. Time to pack up and move into our new home. I am sick to my stomach instead of being excited. The day before I was under the covers in bed all day. The thoughts of moving and losing the house are all I can think about… the what ifs. Everyone is asking me what is wrong, and I tell them I have a headache… as I always do. The movers are finally finished packing, and I ask my grandmother if can I leave a few things there. Why? I don't know. It's time to go, and the Uhaul is packed. Outside, the kids are jumping up and down with excitement. My husband is at work, and he will meet us at our new house. The kids and I pile into the truck and head to the house. Tears are flowing down my face, tears of joy, sadness, and fear. Lord, please let this be the right decision.

The next day my husband and I are in the kitchen unpacking boxes and talking. The phone rings, and I just stare at the phone. Oh, my goodness, it's a bill collector. Who else would be calling I say to myself? I answer the phone, "Hello." "Yes, my name is John, Can I speak to Mr. Alexander? Hello, this is Mr. Alexander. John is a recruiter for overseas jobs." My husband puts him on speaker for me to hear, I can hear. "Mr. Alexander, would you consider working in Iraq?" My heart drops, "Iraq" I whisper. The recruiter explains the risk, housing, and pay.

The pay for one month is almost more than our monthly paychecks put together, but the risks are more significant. "Ask when you will have to leave," I say. "When will I need to leave John," my husband asked. "You will need to be ready to leave in one to two weeks." "What???", I say out loud. "Shhh," my husband says. I know this is the perfect opportunity for us to get out of our financial situation, but it is dangerous, and he is going to be away from home for several months at a time. We will see him every ninety days. All money isn't good money, but we also need the money.

I think I am going to order some Chinese food for dinner. "Is that okay?" "Yes, and we need to talk about me leaving and how will this work with us and the kids" "I will call my grandmother to explain to her what is going on after we eat." "Are you worried?", I ask him. "Not worried but I will miss being home with you all, and we will have to work on communication between the two of us.", he replies. "I agree. I have mixed feelings about it. I know it will help us, but we are not in a good place, well I'm not, and I am praying the distance will not pull us further apart." "Well, I have a few more days here, so let's make the best of it and come up with a plan." "I agree."

"Boo," I yell. "My mom will pick up the kids for us and bring them to the house. Have you talked to the kids?" "No, I am getting ready to do it now," he replies. "Kids, I will be leaving tomorrow to go to work in another country, which means that I will not see you every day, but you will be able to talk to me. I want you both to be good and listen to your mother and grandmother. Okay?" "Yes, daddy," they both reply. "Babygirl, I will miss your Birthday, I am sorry, but when I get home, we will make it up." This is the start of many Birthdays and holidays not together. But those are the sacrifices my husband is willing to make for our family.

It's been three months since my husband left for Iraq and he is coming home for his first R and R trip. I am so excited to see him, and the kids are also. The past few months have been challenging with balancing the kids, work, school, and a new house. I spoke with him before he boarded the plane. I told him things are okay, and I can't wait to see him. Why don't you meet me in Dubai? Not, on this R and R, but the next one? I think you would really like it. Dubai? The Middle East? Ummm no, I reply. I have never heard about anyone going to the Middle East, and I have never heard of Dubai. "Wendy, relax, it's fine, you need just to consider it. Sometimes you will need to meet me out of USA. So, do your research and think about it." "Okay, will do," I reply... while saying to myself, I don't know any parts of the Middle East or Dubai, I have no idea where that is, nor have I heard of it.

We talk a few more minutes, but one thing I left out, I lost my job a week ago. I haven't bathed in two days, hair isn't combed, and I'm barely eating. I am back in that dark place... the place that feels like there is no return. My husband keeps asking me what's wrong and I'm telling him I am sick. I fear that we could head back down the same road we were on not too long ago. We are still playing catch up and paying current bills. The only way out would be another sacrifice. "I can't take this anymore!", I scream. I am in the feeling of no return, confused and hopeless. I know I need to see my therapist today. What will losing my job due to my family now? What will happen to my marriage? I just want to go away, some place where I never have to be reminded about problems or my past. Maybe I should……

My story of resiliency in the face of fire, my commitment and dedication to ensuring my family's needs are met continues…. If you or someone you know is suffering from depression, domestic violence or feeling suicidal, seek help. There are hotlines and facilities to help you.

Wendy Alexander is the founder of Inspiring-Decisions, LLC and the Global Success Society. She provides business solutions and guidance to help entrepreneurs and organizations improve their business results by teaching them advanced marketing strategies Wendy, is a Cross-Cultural Consultant and International Business Strategist and a member of Forbes Coaches Council. Businesses and leaders from different diverse areas of Ghana, Thailand, China and to The Middle East; along with many other countries and cities, from entrepreneurs and organizations of all sizes rely on her extensive background and more than 20 years of experience to transform their business.

CHAPTER 5

HIGHER HEELS, BIGGER DREAMS
by
Fatima Mohammed

Sorry I was born a girl!

It is one of those December days, merciless cold makes its way into a small bedroom where I, a little girl of no more than 3 years, dressed in one of my many colourful feathered outfits, sitting arms tightly wrapped around my weak knees. Bleak walls hang around in eagerness staring as I whimper in cold feverish tears. There is something in my hands, a picture of my mother, with someone else's figure torn. My eyes freeze on the realisation that a part of my mom's arm is missing, and a downpour of tears flows along "Why did they cut you, mommy?" I raise the photograph closer to my beating heart and hold it tight, then take a look at the beautiful features of my mom, her hair dangling like a dark night around her neck, her blue dress contrasts her creamy skin, but then there's that missing arm, and it makes me squeeze with agony. I trace my mamma's face in a sigh: "Oh! Where did they take you, my beautiful mommy?" I am too young to understand, but I remember seeing my mother in pain before she disappeared. "Did daddy do this to you," I wonder, I have seen him make my mother cry before, I still do not know why; maybe he did it again. I keep asking questions, but there is no one around to answer me. Perhaps they forgot about me, they forgot that their 3 year old granddaughter is still upstairs on her own, on a cold December day. How can they not? Today is the glorious day when they finally get what they have waited for, a baby boy. That is my sin, to be born a girl, in a society where everyone hoped to see a little wee-wee come out of each woman's womb when giving birth.

In a world that boasts of open-mindedness and evolution, there remain some corners here and there where women have to endure various forms of oppression. I am from Algeria, a glorious land in North Africa, a heavenly stretch of Mediterranean beaches and majestic Sahara, homeland to brave women and men, marked for its history and countless riches, and yet so burdened by rustic societal codes that date back to antiquity, so shackled with outrageously biased double standards. I have come to this world as an Arab Algerian with a heavy load that only became heavier as I grew older, and I had to carry all my life. To be born a girl in a country and a society like mine is a mistake in the first place; why? People want boys! How do I know? I was born on the 7th of September, and up to this day, my birth certificate says 11th. While my father played a hand in it, it was rather his mother, a woman, who was dismayed at his first-born being a girl. She was all blizzard and storms upon hearing the not so happy news. My dad, ecstatic at the idea of beholding this tiny creature that he

helped bring into this world, was not left at peace to enjoy it. His mother and sisters, all women, haunted him every time he went near me with comments that made it feel unmanly and unbecoming to hold one's baby girl; and so he disappeared and only later did he go to register me. My mother made very well sure that I knew about this from a young age.

What no one knew is that for a child of no more than 3 years old to feel that your birth has not been quite the joyous news, and to watch as everyone celebrates that of your newly born brother, is not such a great thing. I grew up with the feeling of being less loved than my brother, and that did not encourage brotherly affection at all. If anything, I made it my mission to get him in trouble. I would break his expensive toys and watch him be blamed and grounded. For long summer afternoons, I would corner my brother in our yard and tell him all sorts of horror stories, and he would be so terrified even to move until one of our parents comes to his rescue. Things got better as we both grew older... no therapy needed for either of us. We now laugh at it all.

That bitter feeling of rejection did torment me during my childhood, and I had to get some closure, so I asked my dad once before he died, why is it that my birth date is not the day I was actually born. I could tell by the reluctance in my father's voice that he felt a hint of guilt as he assembled a patched-up answer. I did not mind; by then I knew that his love for me was more significant than anything in the world. Nearing 29 now, I look at the whole thing as a blessing; at least I get to celebrate my birthday twice!

GUARD 'IT' WITH YOUR LIFE!

Birth is not the only predicament that accompanies my sex. It turned out that no matter how old you are, as a female your life is already made up for you; you are eyed a certain way, you are expected to do certain things, and you are bound to fulfill an outlined circle. If anything, females were the predicament as they have to be monitored and protected at all times. After all, they carry the family's honour between their fragile legs. Ah, yes! It was all about the 'cherry.' As young kids, we would have that important talk: Guard 'it' with your life, let no one but your mama come near 'it,' do not touch 'it,' let 'it' be... That speech was our daily sermon, and we had to memorize every word and keep 'it' safe. I remember my own mom reciting it over and over, I believe she did the same with my younger sister: "Don't let anyone come anywhere near it." We were asked to remain away from all dangers that might cause any damage to that much precious 'it', and so every time my mom sees me slipping one of her heels on, a habit that I developed from a young age, a loud scream is all I hear before I'm forced to give them up. There was fear I may fall and do something to 'it.' Likewise, I was warned against climbing trees or fences, and running out in streets for fear of falling, and of course, I did all of those and had enjoyed all sorts of trips, falls and injuries.

Whenever I go inside, looking like a battered and bleeding soldier, my poor mama rushes to me in horror and ensures both me and 'it' are safe and unharmed. "It" was more fortunate, for I had endured lots of scars.

If you are wondering why I keep referring to the female genitals as 'it,' the answer is quite simple; we were not allowed to call it for what it truly is, another body part. We could give it other code names, like some secret agents, but never reveal their true identity. It was a huge taboo, one which I made sure to challenge, as I grew older constantly. I would say the word and enjoy the bulging eyes of those around me.

Do you know what is more outrageous? Girls are not allowed, at times, to even shave down there! Let it be, those thick bushes are none of your business. I bet many had no idea how 'it' even looks like, they might have been curious, but never dared ask the question. Then, out of the blue, comes an eligible groom, and the lucky bride is given the no-talk talk that leaves more question marks than it gives answers; it's a green light for everything, you go there and give 'it' to him, it's okay, all is okay. To make matters worse, there is a squad of women, mostly, that is stationed outside the bedroom waiting for the happy news; the great invasion of the so much precious 'it.'

A LEAGUE OF MY OWN

Clock ticks 4 pm, I race through the house to the kitchen, sip my cup of coffee in a haste, then run back to my room, pry the closet open, my eyes sparkle with happiness as they land on that red that I cherish so much; it's a Bayern Munich shorts set with my favorite number, one. I put it on and rush to find my shoes, no not my favorite sneakers, instead my black knee-high boots; the look is final, and I am ready to go out. The minute I walk out the door, there are cheers and sighs: "Yay! There comes the chief!", "Oh no! She has her boots on.", "We are so winning this game.", "We are so done!" I jump right into the field and assume my position as team captain racing between the two extremes of the rocky field, giving directions, scoring goals, committing offenses, causing injuries, and having the fun of a lifetime. Then, out of nowhere, a shadow of a man that looks like my father shows up at the far corner, and I jump out of the game the same way I jumped in. I try to catch my breath before he gets home and I think of a good defense, for in a few minutes I'll be standing before his honour my father and I will be charged with committing a great offense:

playing football with boys in my outrageous shorts. "Fatimaaa!" I hear my name like a storming thunder, and I know that this patched up excuse of mine will have no effect; no one is stupid enough to believe it. I go to face my fate, upon questioning, I pull all my courage, and in a confident voice, I reply: "No, I wasn't playing football, no way, no, I was just, you know how the game is, they needed someone who knows the rules... so I was their referee". The minute I utter these words I realize how unbelievable I sound. "You are grounded, no more going out, no more wearing those shorts!" Shockingly enough, this scene reoccurred a few times over the years, minus the outrageous beloved shorts.

As girls, when outside the house we had very clear instructions, as little recruits, on what to do, who's to mingle with, where to go, and how far to go. Of course, none of that stuck in my mind, I went out and played football with boys in all neighborhoods and until very late at night. Endless were the troubles I got into over this, I was not willing to learn that lesson. People were talking about me: "That girl is always outside playing football with boys, how outrageous!" I did not know boys were extra-terrestrial creatures that we had to stay away from. Once again, my mother fell under the pressure and had to ban me for fear of being punished by my father; which I was on distinct occasions. None of it was enough to keep me away from the ball; I was so passionate about the game. One day, I told my mom that my dream was to become a football player. Her reaction is still fresh in mind, almost spat her food out, and with begging, eyes said: "You cannot be serious! Your father would not hear of that". "How about joining the army then? I fancy myself carrying some guns and going around shooting people", I replied. "Your father will kill you, will kill us all." I do not think my father would have been that extreme, he was strict, and at times I would not blame him, I'm known to push people's buttons since childhood. Nothing quite gave him a heart attack as the way I dressed, though. I have always had my way when it came to clothes, I dressed myself from a very young age at my mom's discontent. There were those cherished Bayern Munich shorts that I loved wearing, but no one loved seeing me in; they were too short and too revealing. Dad forbade me from putting them on, mom pleaded me not to, so I had to concede. Then, I'd fall sick, and my loving dad would be by my side asking me to name my wish, and I would say "I want the red Bayern Munich shorts," and they would let me have them until I get better.

There is something about playing football in knee-high boots, that everyone was scared of, which was so enjoyable to me as a kid, and still find alluring as an adult; it made me feel unbeatable and made the game a tons more fun to play. Maybe one day, I can start a league of my own where people can join in, and we can play football in heels.

MY MOTHER'S ARMY

Domestic violence has often gone unnamed and unblamed in my society. It is the norm for men to teach their wives a lesson, and for the women to bear that beating and teaching with no complaints. I bore witness to trials of violence in my own home starring none other than my own parents. I love my dad, and it pains me to bring up this side of him, but he had these moments when he turned into a man, I did not recognise nor did I love. I was three when my brother was born, my mother was in labour and was taken to the hospital. I stayed behind holding a picture of her and crying for her because I thought my father had hurt her. At that age, I had already witnessed some of their fights, and I was aware that my mom was being abused by my own dad and there was nothing I could do to help until I grew older. I wanted to protect my mother, to support her in the face of that violent man who would attack her, and the only way I could do that was to throw myself in the middle, right between her helpless body and his storming shadow. It did not please him, but it was a wakeup call; he would soon realize that his own daughter is looking at him transform into this unrecognizable hulk and stop. While he does not get physical on me, my father would ground me differently: "You are not going to school," he would say, and that's when my mom magically finds her strength to face him "Yes, she is," and I would be very reluctant to do so. It felt as if I was bailing on her, letting her down, but mother dear would hold my hands, look me in the eyes, and tell me it was okay, that she would be okay, and that I have to go to school, to one day be able to realise all the dreams she could not. I remember this one fight when I had an exam in Islamic Studies, and I had to go, reminded that my studies come first, and I ended up getting a full mark in that exam. That is how my mom taught me that nothing comes before dreams; they are the priority. I have lived on until today to know, believe and preach that tough times do not last, tough people do!

It is scary to think and know that thousands of women in my country go through all kinds of emotional and physical abuse in their own household, yet never get help. I cannot even put myself to imagine the sort of atrocities these women go through, and I could never fathom why society compels them to swallow their agonies and continue to live with a monster. They give her no options, no way out; instead, the constant advice is: Bear it with courage, be patient, it will get better, you cannot easily give up, try to change for him. What if the husband is a monster par-excellence?

I have personally always said that I could never live under the same roof with someone who would dare get physical on me; if he does it once, he will do it again. Divorce is my way out of such a marriage; it is likewise my recommendation to others. However, the word 'divorce' has such a frightening effect, I would even say a disgraceful one, that upon uttering it, I am instantly hushed, snubbed, and ignored. What do I know after all? I know that no amount of love, care, money or whatever might be the reason, is sufficient enough to deny a battered woman of her legitimate right to ask for divorce. I also know that what lies beyond is sadly sorrowful, discouraging, and bitter. No one looks forward to a stage where being labelled 'divorced' is eyed so prejudicially; society condemns you, people point fingers at you, family blames you, and friends reject you.

'Till death do us part' never meant death at the hands of the person you chose to cherish and to hold your hands for better and for worse, only to go through the worst days of your life. Everyone will stand against you if you decide to get divorced, but then no one is there for you. No one is in your shoes, no one goes through the horrors you live, no one feels the broken pieces within you, no one feels how shattered your soul is, no one bears the blows and punches, no one hears those screams and curses; so why should they make the decision for you? A man is not the only happiness that a woman can have in her life, deciding to leave him behind and save one's life is not a crime punishable by law or a disdainful society.

THAT HONOUR THING!

Fate has it that on December 31st, 2007, I make my way, this time wrapped in my cozy black coat, relishing the stingy cold as it tickles my nose and every sense, towards the house of my English teacher. She opens the door, face adorned with a smile that warms the depth my nearly frozen heart and ushers me upstairs where we can sit and talk. Something about this magnificent creature is always inviting to pour all one's deepest secrets. I am not here to confess, however, rather to seek inspiration and encouragement, which she is ever ready to provide with an abundance of love. The door opens, and a slender girl of no more than 16 walks in. One particular detail about her strikes me immediately, the colour of her cheeks, a reddish streak of pink that I mistake for excessive blusher. In vain, I try to remember her name, but I am unable to do so, yet her story is engraved in my mind ever since. She sits to our table, and we exchange cordial greetings and inquiries. All seems well until she breaks in sobs and tears.

I am still taken back by that scene as I recollect it. Our teacher pats on her shoulder and the poor teen starts accounting for her tragedy. "I am being sexually harassed by my brother-in-law." A dreadful silence befalls the room as I stare in disbelief at my teacher, not a word is uttered, and the story goes on. She tells us all, how this filthy rich scoundrel is engaged to her elder sister, how he keeps eyeing her, how he traces her every move, how he would grab her and pretends it is brotherly affection, and how he goes as far as sneaking into her bed. That is not even the horrible part, yet, she sighs heavily at how her confession to her own mother and sister, turns them against her, accusing her of seducing him, of being jealous of the lavish gifts he brings his fiancé and making her life even more miserable. It is one of those moments when I am at loss of words; what could I possibly say that would make her feel better? This girl sitting across from me, face and features faded like a dying rose from all the tears she pours, daily, has had to endure years of constant harassment without being able to get proper help or support. It is time to leave for me, and she decides to get up as well, we walk together for a few moments, there are no words to console her, I cannot even try to. I am 18 years myself and I all I can feel is this bitterness, rage, and helplessness. I make my way back home and start writing her story and name it, Dark Memories, I hope to one day share it with the world.

As I write this chapter now, I cannot help but wonder what has become of that poor little girl and think about the other females, young and old, who have undergone similar experiences and still keep it to themselves out of fear and shame. For a society that is so obsessed with honour and dignity of conduct, where women lead their life with a massive sense of responsibility carrying the burden to keep 'it' out of the hands of intruders, you would be shocked to learn of the unexplainable rates of sexual harassment within one's own household. Imagine spending your entire life protecting your girl from the beasts that lie beyond the walls of your fortress only to find out one day that she has been molested at the hands of those monsters within. The stories are quite horrendous that it is hard to even conceive their credibility. You would hear about a little girl who was raped, molested or abused by her father, grandfather, brother, uncle or cousin; sometimes two of them or more. The real ordeal here is that most of these atrocities go unaccounted for; no little girl would dare point her finger at a male figure in her own entourage and accuse them of sallying their own family's honour; who would believe her? At times, even if her story makes sense to those she would confide in, she is left with two options. The first would be to bury the truth, ignore it and act as if it never happened and speak about it to no one. The second is less compassionate, to punish the girl herself, to put the blame on her and accuse her of playing part in her own abuse. Either way, you would rarely hear of this out in public, our society is too coward to address this issue on the open, to acknowledge its existence, and to put it up for discussion and analysis. No, people would rather keep it a secret and pretend all is well. I have heard and read my fair share of accounts such as these, on newspaper, social media and in books. One day, I was browsing through the posts of an Algerian Facebook page, Femme Algerienne[1], only to stumble over more abominable stories: a girl who was abused at the hands of her maternal uncle, every time he was alone with her, he would whisper in her ear to assure her: "Do not be scared, uncle is here!" It was an awful read, especially when the replies and comments usually are against the victims. Why would you go public with this? Have you no shame? Have you sullied your HONOUR? That word again! This woman's honour has been tarnished by a man who is supposed to guard it with his life. So shame on you, people! Is it not those human animals that should be drowned to their feet with guilt, stoned with whips of shamefulness and terror; the same kind they have brought upon those women in their lives?

BEYOND HOME

In fairness, not every little girl is surrounded with beastly frustrates at home. Some are fortunate to be brought in houses full of love and compassion. They are blessed with exemplary fathers, caring brothers, doting grandfathers, loving uncles, and kind cousins. Then, they make it to the world outside, and a whole new journey begins. Can you believe that most males out in the streets have but one concern?

---

[1] French for Algerian Woman: a Facebook page dedicated to Algerian women, their daily concerns and interests

The female audience; be it young or old, pretty or unattractive, veiled or half-dressed, alone or in company; females in all shapes and forms. It becomes such an arduous task to walk down a street, go to school or work, do the groceries, have a meal or a breath of fresh air. As a female, you are stalked everywhere, your every move is under the microscope and magnified for all probable and improbable interpretations. What is even worse is that if you do not play into their game, you are likely to get more abused. There was this instance when I was walking back from high school to the bus station, it was such a long walk and being alone, it was more of a race that my legs would hurt, but I would keep going until I am safely seated. A car drove by me, the man pulled aside and was waving his hand pointing to someone to come. I remember thinking to myself: "How lucky is that person! They'll get a ride" As I walked by the car, it turned out that the guy was waving at me, and he told me to get in his car. I ignored him and kept moving only so that he follows me with his car insisting to the point I got fed up with him and said, at quite a low voice to myself: "Why doesn't he go screw himself?" The lucky punk heard it, I do not know how, and his voice turned ten notes harsher as he howled: "What did you just say? I'll come and beat the hell out of you". My eyes widened, and the voice inside of me said: "Great! On top of being tired, I will also be battered!" The random brute drove off, and I was left to finish my journey in peace.

Twelve years later now, things have only become worse. Men do still approach women on the streets, and upon being rejected or ignored, they get verbal, violent and even physical. As I write this chapter, I still come across stories that appal me to the deepest of my soul. I read about a driving woman who was hit on by a police officer, who went as far as reaching to her chest when she refused to give him her number or let him get in her car. A few others wrote anonymous messages to complain about all the constant harassment they face every single day. No matter how dressed these women are; half-naked or fully-wrapped in fabrics; no matter how unwilling they are to engage with these imbeciles; no matter how unimpressed and unmoved with the unflattering advances, they still get hounded. I have my own share of the trouble mainly because of my heels. Males would spot me wearing some high heeled shoes, and they take it as an open invitation to start a conversation or throw in a random comment "How do you walk in those?", "Sweetheart, you may hurt yourself," "That walk!". This made going out such a complex to me that I would only do it if accompanied. Most of the instances when I am approached by a complete stranger, I act deaf and blind, but at times I am so provoked I just have to say something back. I have learned that some confrontation works; those cowards are engulfed in the idea that women love to hear their cheesy lines or are too scared to face them, that they are so startled if one rebuffs them in public.

IN A MAN'S WORLD

September 7th, 2004, it is my 15th birthday, my parents, brother, and sister are gathered around a table in our cozy living room. I have never liked cake, so instead father dear got my favorite pastry, mille-feuilles. Whether there are candles, I am not entirely sure. However, once the joyous song 'Joyeux Anniversaire' is over, it is time to make a wish, and I close my eyes and breathe in deeply as my heart warmly utters a wish. I open my eyes, and it is time to attack those mille-feuilles. My father looks at me and affectionately says: "For your 16th birthday, I will marry you off to someone who sells melons." Everyone around bursts in laughter, I might have joined, but then I feel the need to reply: "I don't think so; I'll only marry the man I choose." My oh my do I still remember the dead silence that takes over, my father's face changed and coloured in confusion, but then he decides to allow me this one joke "None of my sisters chose their husbands," he chooses to assert. I am compelled to answer once more "Well, I am not like your sisters." Everyone's eyes grow twice their size, my mother sticks her head and is ushering me to keep quiet, my dad feels the need to inquire into the reason behind such a reply "What is that supposed to mean?" At this point, with the thought of preserving the lovely gathering as such, and succumbing to mom's imploring stares, I give in and laughs it out "Nothing, I guess that melon seller is quite the catch!". While my family relishes at the fact that war is adjourned, and everyone is all smiles, I sink with a deep thought inside wondering to myself: "Is that really what my future holds for me? Are my decisions that limited?" That alone sends bitter shivers through my spine.

What is it like to live in a man's world, to have your life and decisions dictated, your moves and words judged? Not fun, that is for sure. In a patriarchal society as mine, men are all over things us, women, do. Their blessing is essential for the fulfilment of any step, and their rejection means you do not get think about it anymore. I have lived a life when a woman is supposed to abide by what the men say, they decide on her behalf, they dictate her choices for her, and they expect her to nod in unquestionable obedience. It is all too unfair that they get to do all they want, and no one holds them accountable for it, while they get all storms and blizzards if a female dares to cross them. That did not sit very well with me, I made it my mission to defy all 'male' rules starting with those of my father. I got under his skin so many times, especially when it came to how I dressed, nothing outrageous really, but he was anti-jeans, anti-shorts, anti-skirts; that there was nothing left to wear!

I have also often had a male figure in my family criticise my clothes, say that my pyjamas are too tight, or that I am showing too much skin, or that my clothes are improper; "Go get changed!", I am asked, "Buy me clothes and I'll be more than happy to wear them!", This was my reply. This argument is usually sufficient to put an end to the discussion. I have never appreciated people giving orders on things that they are not even part of, how do you expect me to go on pleasing your highness when you expect it to come at my own expense?

Voicing one's opinions is not quite likable or encouraged, especially when you are a woman, after all, what do you know? This is the norm within and outside the house. One of my male teachers, once asked me as part of an exam, what I thought of polygamy, a question that was not anywhere near what we have had in class. However, I still gave an answer: "I am not in favour of the idea. It's like me and my heels, if I buy new ones, I like them better than the old ones, same will happen in case of polygamy". I could tell by the look on his face, his counter-argument that I just would not concede to and the disappointing grade I got, that he was not much impressed with what I said; though that was not the primary purpose of the assessment.

Nothing boards on the outrageous as attempting to discuss religious matters. If I so much dare to voice a personal opinion, I am eyed as a libertine, a corrupt-minded creature who is not entitled to have her own views. Politics and at times sports are seen as beyond my understanding. If I sit down and try to analyse a news headline or watch a football game; I am scorned as Miss Connoisseur-want to-be. Women should occupy their time with things that suit their sex; cooking, cleaning, knitting, and beauty tips. Countless are those times when a woman is denounced for doing something for the mere reason that it is not for the ladies to do; says who? I got no memo detailing who does what and why. The tribe of men would rather see the opposite gender confined to homes where they perform either roles. A refined lady who would be seen nodding her head in agreement, kindly smiling, and waving her hand gently; in short, an ornamental creature to behold, or an underprivileged maiden who spends her days dusting, cleaning, and cooking; in other words, an obedient maid to serve. I do not presume to have a comprehensive knowledge of everything, but I am quite sure that I use my brain efficiently and advantageously, that I am endowed with the right to have my own say in things. I am not a vase, neither am I a follower.

THE ULTIMATE CRIME

The societal scrutiny and condemnation make me always cautious about the futuristic ambitions I have that at instances it felt like it was a crime to dream, and at others, it felt like others wished to dictate my dreams for me. People around me, family, teachers and close ones, expressed their hopes for me, their expectations of me. Everyone wanted me to be a doctor, no one ever asked me what I wanted, I guess they just assumed they could name their wishes and I would magically succumb. That was never me, even though 'No' is never an easy word to say, but I love some bumps along the way. When it was time to choose streams, I filled that paper myself, consulted no one, and went with foreign languages. When it was time to move from middle to high school, my teachers were shocked at the realisation of me choosing something other than scientific major. I never liked science despite being good at it, I was more of a physics nerd, and I had my hopes on doing something related to nuclear physics, but at that time, it was not available. The more I think of it, I count my blessings for if I had majored in anything related to nukes, there is a great a chance of the world having 2 Kim Jongs at present. I had to go with the unknown, die Deutsche Sprache.

In 2007, when I graduated from high school, it was my wish to join the National School of Administration, in my pursuit of the big dream: becoming an ambassador. The school happened to be in the capital Algiers, 500 km away from where I lived. When I expressed my desire to join, my mom was very supportive, she wanted to see me pursue my dream, but my uncles disapproved of it. One of them told my mother that she cannot rely on him and she would have to count on herself if she decides to help me; if anything, 'wrong' happens, it would be on her. My other uncle was a bit more extreme, he threatened not to talk or see either of us if we move forward with such design. I remember that helpless look on my mother's face, the sour feeling down my throat as I held her hands and assured her that I no longer wanted to go, that I could always do something else, and stay by her side. My eldest uncle, who is usually reserved and uncaring, offered to help and accompany us to the 'big city.' All fell apart when I was told the school was no longer open for high school graduates, and that I had to obtain a bachelor's degree first; 4 more years. It was like someone just threw an ice bucket over my head while I was racing at full speed; I went dead cold. I could not see myself doing anything less important.

After my father's death, this has been the second greatest shock of my life. I did not know how to react, or what to do. I did not prepare myself for this scenario, for something less 'significant' or a plan B, and I was quite a loss. Nothing mattered anymore, I decided to go with the flow, for once, what I wanted was no longer my priority, and I was willing to give everyone else what they desired. I sat back as four pieces of paper were brought, with four majors written on each one. Once folded, different members of my family took turn in choosing a piece of paper, and each time a choice is revealed, there were cheers. I looked at the whole parade with a shattered heart as I saw a dear dream of mine sink into nothingness. After a few rounds of picks, the lucky choice was English; yay me! My face was expressionless, a thousand thoughts crowding in mind, and a thousand more feelings cramming in my heart, yet I said nothing. It is but a language, and I spoke four at the time, why not? English it is.

It was not the first time, nor the last that I had to bid a dream farewell or shelve it until further notice. It was not likewise the last time someone takes my aspirations for granted or looks at me suspiciously upon hearing what I want as if dreaming was a crime.

THERAPY OF A SORT

It is around 4 am, on a warm Thursday of May 2011, I am lying in bed with my laptop open and fingers all over the keyboard. The deadline for my thesis submission is nearing and with it the pressure to finalise the chapters at hand. I have not slept yet, and I have a Literature exam at 2 pm. Words and ideas are coming at me like a downpour, but I cannot take it anymore, I need a proper rest. At that thought, I hop out of bed, grab my phone, plug the headphones, browse for a good jam, then reach into the closet… there! My red high-heeled sandals, I put them on and play the song. Oh yes! The music takes over, it possesses me, and I am dancing my heart out, in my bedroom, at 4 am, in heels. All the tiredness and trouble magically fade away, and my energy is renewed, I can go on for longer. At that moment, my mom walks through the door to wake me for prayer, and she finds me in the middle of a serious choreography busting some crazy moves. She still gets taken back at the sight, but she's got used to it by now, she has seen me in all different heels, dancing all sorts of styles. She might have doubted I needed help, but she could tell that the ritual was therapeutic itself, and I did perform well in exams, so all is good.

Those high heels of mine have seen me through some ups and downs, and they have always worked wonders in uplifting my spirits, they still do. I could be having a bad week at work, and then decide to throw on a pair of stilettos one day, and I am a different woman, a happier one, a more energetic one, and more empowering to those around me. Shoes have been there at my worst moments, I have had my fair share of disappointments and heartbreak, my eyes shed outpours of tears for long days and longer nights. However, every time I fall hard, I get up even harder and put those heels on, and it feels like this massive flood of strength fills me from head to heel. It is like they mend the broken pieces within me, no matter how stressful my day or week has been, all it takes is a pair of magic heels, and all troubles fades away. I walk out to that fearsome world ever more determined and ready for the next challenge and say: "Hit with your best shot, baby!" I may stumble, I may fall, but I will land high on these heels of mine, and I would still be standing higher above all trouble, above all the ones who try to bring me down. I will march on towards my dreams and chase them to the extremes of earth.

CERTIFICATES AND ACCOMPLISHMENTS REDEFINED

It is a beautiful spring day, the chores at my grandmother's do not seem to end, but my two cousins keep going; otherwise, the scolding starts. Grandma calls in my mother, and they both have a secret conversation for a few minutes. Mother, then, comes out and announces the happy news: "We are going shopping." The two girls look at each other in disbelief, are they finally getting a break? Did someone just volunteer to take them out? Their excitement is beyond words, in a few moments they will see the outside world, they will feel sunrays on their skin, they will meet people; how beautiful! Off they throw their brooms and rush to get changed. The door opens, and there is light, there is air, there are trees and new faces; how lucky do they consider themselves, how grateful to both grandma and mother to give them this invaluable chance. Mother heads to the road, a taxi is stopped, a destination that sounds unfamiliar is described, but the girls are still ecstatic.

The car halts to a stop, the fare is paid, and the two cousins find themselves before a building that looks nothing like a shopping center, mall or store. They read the sign on the door, and it reads: Dr -- ----- a Gynaecologist. Their surprise is indescribable, sighs of disappointment sink their hopes, and their hearts start to race. "Why?" Once inside, they find out that a check-up of their 'it' has been ordered by the higher authority of her grace, grandma dear. Unable to say no, they reluctantly take turns on the magic chair and experience an intrusive and intimate examination of a body part that they are not that acquainted with. Needless to say that the shock of that day, still lives with them up to the time I am writing, 5 years after it has happened, with both of them married.

When someone says the word 'certificate,' things that come to mind range from education, careers, experience, warranty... Never would it occur that 'virginity' would come up on the same list. Nevertheless, the two words are a very common collocation where I come from, and of course, it is the women who have to take the course, or rather the check-up. For decades now, Algerian girls, and I believe many other Arabs, had to undergo a gynaecologist probing at some point during their life, before their wedding and at times on their wedding day. All of the trouble is to prove to his nobleness, her husband, that she is a virgin. A disgraceful tradition that questions the chastity of a woman, and never that of a man, who will ask to see the proof and will only ascertain of its credibility upon a bloody invasion.

On the other hand, getting married is considered as some sort of an accomplishment, something to brag about around your circle of family and friends. Even if your intellectual achievements do not go beyond basic calculus at best, scoring a husband puts you high on the social ladder. Failing to do so identifies one in the category of the 'poor and pitiful,' that are perceived as unfortunate, and are often showered with wishes and prayers for their prompt release out of the 'single zone' and into the blissful state of marriage. I remember, not long ago, that my family's greatest pride was my educational successes, my honours, my degrees, and my career. I was the first female in the family to get a Bachelors and a Masters, and they would often boast about that in front of others. However, by failing to join the bridal train, my various achievements dwindled in significance and the diplomas I have grown lackluster in comparison to that cherished, long-awaited one; the marriage certificate. What a disappointment did I turn out to be!

ROBO-WIFE

If you have lived through late eighties and early nineties, then you are likely to have been witness to the Robocop frenzy. The super machine who takes down criminals and rids the city of their evil. In a similar, though distant, fashion, a potential wife where I come from has to assume so many responsibilities and duties that only a robot can tolerate. Often the word wife is synonymous to housewife, as in she is solely made for the house and its endless chores. As a matter of fact, a thorough mastery in the arts of housekeeping, a profound knowledge of the sundry cuisines and a perpetual readiness to serve are on top of the list when looking for a marriageable maiden.

A popular Facebook page, DZ de Luxe[2], holds 'CV evenings' that are dedicated for marriage requests where men and women send their 'resumes' with details including their name, city, job, physical appearance, good and bad qualities in the hope of finding their match. Nothing quite surprising there, except that one of the descriptors is for 'dish you can make' where both sexes are supposed to give an idea about their culinary proficiency. The majority of the male 'candidates' write (nothing, I only eat, none of my business, it is 'her' job, when she falls sick) when it comes to this particular point; and I have noticed that it often goes unnoticed and uncommented. If one of the female 'contenders' confesses her lack of expertise or passion for cooking, hell breaks loose with a flood of comments that so adamantly overlooks her other qualities and zooms in on that one unfulfilled criterion. How dare she? Shockingly enough, it is mostly other females attacking her for aspiring to score a husband when she cannot make him food. The men assure the culinary-challenged lady that her way into their hearts is through their never-satisfied stomach and insatiable appetite.

Both instances provoke me, as I know there is no shame in entering one's kitchen and preparing something to eat when one's wife is still in good health! There is entirely no wrong, or harm done if a man decided to help around, cuts the veggies, or stirs the pan. I also recognise that a woman, who cannot cook, can learn, and can still feed her hungry husband and take care of his house. There are countless

---

[2] French for Algerian of Lux

ways to figure out how to make eatable dishes and not burn down the kitchen or send someone to the ER.

The expectations, and requirements, exceed the kitchen and go into the tiniest details that concern a potential bride. The Algerian man, who usually figures on these Facebook posts, that I often read with a pungent sourness, are on the lookout for a pious wife, who would resemble a movie star, who knows how to cook, take care of his house, him, and his entire family at times, without uttering an objection, without asking for anything in return. Human beings are far too fickle to handle all these responsibilities and maintain their cheerfulness, health or sanity, and so I have come to the conclusion that Algerian men are looking for Robo-wives.

MY MANY MRS. BENNETS

I really do not know how, where, when or why my mother turned into a Mrs. Bennet from *Pride and Prejudice*. I guess she just woke up one day and thought to herself: "Let us stalk all '*dem*' eligible bachelors… on a national scale!" I was but sixteen when she cornered me one day to tell me that a certain young man wishes to ask for my hand in marriage. "That's weird, what would he do with my hand? Is it some sort of a fetish?" I like to burst my mother's matrimonial bubbles with such sneering comments. As if one wedding-feverish woman is not enough, my grandmother joined the 'Let's get this girl a husband' campaign and started rallying support for this guy. I was young, too young, and from where I stood, getting married was nowhere within my foreseeable plans. That, unfortunately, never thwarted their efforts.

Each time there is a single *he* around, a well-to-do one to be sure, wishes and desires are expressed, at times, plans are made. Before I knew it, I found myself facing a whole squad of Mrs. Bennets, my mother, grandmother, and aunts, and they all have one target, me! I have had to put up with fervid exhilarations of all sorts, I still do. "This one would be perfect," "I'd not find a better son-in-law," "I'd be a most fortunate mother-in-law." How fortunate for him indeed! Many such over-zealous aspirations come along with the appearance of new single-he. Being the aspiration-killer, I am, I never let one moment pass without a little something to say, I would at times sound like the pestering Mr. Bennet. "Is that his design in coming here?" though I rejoice at provoking mama's poor nerves in re-phrasing and even mutilating her words: "You find him to be sweet? How did you tell? Have you tasted him?" My sardonic commentary often gets me some death-stares, tough-love coated threats, or a couple of flying slippers and other items.

In a similarly Mrs. Bennet way, my mother, and many Algerian moms, believe that a ball or rather a wedding is the perfect venue to fish for prospective suitors or their moms. What better idea to catch the ideal fish than a dance segment? Yes, mothers, mine included, expect their daughters to strut what they gave us in an exotic choreography with the purpose of attracting the attention of someone's mother. I have always found the idea quite repulsive and never conceded, even though my own mother never gave away her intentions behind the incessant invitations. I could still detect that eagerness in her eyes, and I would watch that shine fade every time I shake my head in refusal: "I will do no such thing, I do not know how to dance anyway." She would, then, give me a steel-coated look with an intense whisper: "Whose arse did I catch shaking in the middle of the night on that song: shawty get low, low, low?" and I turn deaf, mute and blind to all the whispers and looks that follow after I naughtily reply: "Oh mama! But that's a private show!"

I have been an expat for three years now, and every time I fly back home, I am still asked the same question: "Have you found no suitable groom?" I am startled for a few seconds, but then my sense of wittiness kicks in, and I apologetically respond: "I am sorry, they do not have grooms on sale in Ataturk Airport, nor is there a suitcase big enough to fit a full-sized human being; but I got you some chocolate!" Sighs of disappointments are uttered as hands reach high in the sky with a prayer that I am soon delivered from my singlehood.

THE FLATS ZONE

Never have I ever thought that there would come a day when I have to give up my heels and settle for comfortable shoes. Destiny had it that my teaching journey would take me to the land of myth, magic, and endless love, Saudi Arabia. For the first time in my life, I was on my feet for a minimum of 24 hours a week and the longer I worked, the more difficult it was to wear heels. Everyone around me was eyeing me weirdly: "How come she teaches in those?" I, on the other hand, was in awe of seeing people around me wearing sport shoes all the time, "How can they put up with them all day?" as I only wore my trainers for times when I played sports.

I found myself in front of a dreadful alternative, flat and sport shoes. Walking in them felt very odd and uneasy; there was no strutting, no action, and no life. It no longer felt like I am on the edge of a thin heel, on the verge of falling but still going on, I was just walking. Before I knew it, I was experiencing comfort, and it is one acutely dangerous feeling. This time, however, I did it for a good cause.

I had to put my heels, my wings, aside for a moment, but I never stopped flying. It was a chance for me to help other ladies find their wings, their inner strength and to make their ways towards their dreams. In KSA, it hit me that Saudi girls were afraid to dream, they would settle for anything within their reach. I would ask them to share their future goals, name their wishes and dearest dreams, and I would be all surprised to hear the colourless answers. Most of my students have made peace with the idea that they cannot go far in life, thus, do not look forward to the future with much eagerness. Their aspirations would not surpass a cashier, a clerk at a bank, a desk job of any sorts. Some wanted more but sighed it was beyond their grasp, but there was the confident bunch that dared to chase their wildest desires. One day, I decided to take them around the college to the wall of fame where pictures of eminent Saudi women were hung to display the great achievements, they made in domains such as aviation, science, education, sports, and business. One of my girls said: "There is no way we can do the same." At that moment, the motivational speaker within me came to being, and I had to assure all of my girls that they are marvels, that they can be anything they wanted, that they can reach beyond the stars because even the sky is no limit. I point out at prominent figures, nationally and internationally, and I tell those beauties of mine that they are unique, they are smart, and they have all it takes to dream big, and to realise those dreams.

I have introduced a segment in my classes called 'a dose of' where I give a quote followed by a short speech to inject the minds and souls with daily doses of hope, optimism, courage, love, faith, hard work, and perseverance. The new addition has been working wonders both for my students and myself as it serves as constant reminder to us all to look at the brighter side, to hope for the better, and to work for a promising future. In one of my classes, we have set a wall of dreams, in another a wall of positivity where students and I would post little notes with our futuristic ambitions and goals, or famous quotes that spark motivation and endless optimism. This idea has also proven successful as students put in the effort to look up inspirational sayings and take the time to share their dearest wishes with us.

From time to time, I would slip in a pair of magical heels and my students can feel the positive spirit that possesses me, they love how I exude confidence, hopefulness, determination and faith that they ask me to wear them more often. At times, when I feel that we all need a break from everything, I invite my girls and myself to step out of the 'flats zone' and trade our trainers for a day of heel dosage to boost our spirit and send our morale through the roof. Needless to say, the glamour and height drives adrenalin and pumps the veins with positivism and the energy needed to keep going.

MR. RIGHT OR MR. HEIGHT?

In February 2018, I go back home on visa business, and I take the opportunity to visit an orthopaedic doctor to check on my leg; it has been hurting me for quite some time, and I have not had a proper diagnosis. I have always had some sort of a phobia when it comes to everything medicine-related: hospitals, doctors, dentists, tests, medication…etc. It is never a pleasure to make my way for a check-up, no matter how ordinary it is. This time is no different, I think of ways to explain my condition; a talent that I am not quite proficient at. I once told a doctor my head felt like a pebble stuck inside a deflated football, he stared at me for quite a few seconds than diagnosed me with a severe case of exhaustion and recommended a full week of rest. My turn is up, I raise in anxiousness then make it to the doctor's cabin. Not much of that visit stands out in memory, but then the good doctor decides to give up his chair, and for the first time in my life, I like a doctor, why? He is TALL.

One of the reasons I remain unmarried, to the dismay of my family, is that I have a different perception of what my 'prince charming' would be like. Unlike their list of worldly prerequisites, I have always wanted a life partner who was far taller than I was. If you are wondering why again, just so that I can wear heels as high as I please. When I saw the height of my orthopaedics, the pain in my foot no longer mattered, I sat back in all fancies and say: "Oh! All the high heels I could wear around him, and he would not mind". I knew that a confession necessitates a proper explanation, but I failed to come up with one "You are so tall I could wear 20cm heels" was not going to be an enough reason for him, to reciprocate the feeling, I came to reason with myself.

Tall men do not come in that often, and one has to comb through a haystack of 'shorties' to finally find that one extraordinary tall man. Regrettably, that is not how the gents see me, or rather my heels, as they consider them as a threat. Wearing my peep toes meant I grew a few centimeters taller than some guys, and that was unacceptable: "I do not want nor, do I like for my wife to be taller than me," one suitor once expressed. I remembered having these negotiations with myself to debate his eligibility, and heels came in very decisive. It is not my fault someone is born lacking a few inches of confidence when around a woman in heels, I would not mind a less taller man as long as he is reconciled with his own height and my heels' might.

Some ladies, on the other hand, saw me as mastering an art that they failed to embrace. We all know that a walk would have a life of its own if you add in a pair of stilettos. I have had some girls approach me and ask for coaching tips: "Teach us how to wear heels, show us how to walk like you." An awkward laugh usually accompanies the request when they explain that the male audience is attracted to a woman in heels and they would like to learn for that purpose. My indignant, rather provocative, reply is "There is nothing to teach here, baby, I was born this way!" I do not wear my shoes for the pleasure of the other sex, but I do expect that my Mr. Right has some Height, or at least enough self-love to admire the different shapes of my heels; it would be a match made in shoe heaven.

YOU'VE GOT MAIL

If the title takes you back to the film with the same name, starring Tom Hanks and Meg Ryan, then you probably know it was about online dating, and that is where this part is headed. There are things that a respectable woman does not do, or is not supposed to do, making the first move in a relationship is one of them. That is what my society, male population mainly, and a good deal of women think. Whether in real life situations or in virtual spaces, the ladies are cautioned against being the initiator; wait for him to say and do.

Having spent 3 years in KSA, I realised it was not that easy to come across potential suitors. Solitude could be excellent at times, one would rejoice at the freedom that comes with personal space to do all that one pleases. However, there are specific experiences in life that one needs to share with an exceptional person. Segregation in the Kingdom does not play to one's advantage if we were looking for that special one. Having had enough with Algerians, my friend recommended I try a Muslims only dating app. I laughed at her suggestion, I felt it was all too ridiculous, unrealistic, and unlike me. I sat on the idea for a few months, then I stayed over at her place and told her about the tall doctor, and she brought up the dating online again, this time citing some of her other friends who tried it. How bad could it be? I told myself, it could not be worse than making a confession to someone whose height suits that of my heels. I downloaded the app and started making my way around to figure out how to use the thing. Once signed in, there were these profiles of other members that popped up, and there was an (X) and a (√), and I would choose either based on what I see. In all honesty, the first thing I checked was height; again, my heels remain a priority. To my own surprise, two days later, it turned out that I was pressing the 'like' button on people's profiles. Everything that happened was documented with notifications; people knew I was visiting their profiles and that I 'liked' them. The shock and terror at that moment was unbelievable, I went around looking for my so genius friend and told her: "Look what you made me do!"

It could be that I have solely been around women, or that I just am clueless when it comes to the other gender, but I have come to realise that I suck at this online matching thing after all. For starters, my criteria of a suitable man start with his height, anyone short of 180 cm will not do, and that is half the lot out there. If you are cute and only 170, we are not meant for each other, sorry, my heels will get in the way. Then there is the grammar Nazi within me that pines, twists and screams with anguish every time I eye a mistake. I have noticed that my interest in contacting people out of genuine care was nothing matched to a burning desire to send a message saying: "Hey, you misspelled that!", "No offense to your looks, but your messed-up grammar needs more attention." I would be impressed by someone's picture for a fraction of a second, and then I run away closing the whole thing up upon reading some atrociousness. Deep down I knew I am not meant for this, but I try to reconcile myself, to at least be ... No, I cannot; if a man is unable to get his spelling right, then we are so not meant for each other. A life of cringing over love notes or grocery lists does not appeal to me.

And so whenever a ring comes up to notify me that I have got mail or a new message, my heart contracts at the thought of it being another mistake-filled text; the horror and anticipation were far more than I could bear, and I decided to spare my grammatical sanity and quit the virtual space till further notice.

TEAR THE VEIL; KEEP THE HIJAB

By the time this chapter makes it to the public, I would have finally found the courage to share these glimpses of my life and me with the world. To some, it may look like I revealed nothing, but to a family and a society that are so concerned with propriety of conduct and conservative to-do-lists, this is quite outrageously expository, boarding scandalous at times. My intention has been, with every word I have written, to shed the light on affairs that remain in the darkness, to set a platform for the voiceless to be inspired, consoled and heard. It is not an invitation to go rogue, but rather to be brave, to have the tenacity to stand in the face of hardship, in its distinct forms, and to raise even more powerful after every fall.

Tearing the veil is not synonymous to renouncing identity: I am still Muslim, still Arab and Algerian. I merely wish to tear that faint shadow that enshrouds my life and that of many women like myself; I tear the veil of silence, of violence, of abuse, of injustice, of pressure... but I still keep my hijab. I am quite familiar with the scrutinizing, unnecessary critical, nature of my countrymen and women, that I feel the need for a justification, though by no means considered an apology, for the intentions and purposes that lie within and beyond these lines of mine. I remain very much Algerian, the boiling blood still runs through my veins, I have lived through most of the things I wrote about, I took part, I was a victim, a witness, or just a disenchanted viewer. I am not setting myself away from the pack, I am instead denouncing the atrocities that I believe should be eradicated from society, I am calling things what they are.

HEEL UP AND DREAM ON

As little girls, we are brought up to bedtime stories of damsels in distress who await helplessly for their brave prince charming to salvage them from a life of misery, and then they live happily ever after. Then, we grow up to a film industry that portrays women with superpowers that set them way apart as unattainable ideals. It takes a human being with a proportionate sense to see the ridiculous outrageousness behind these tales and superheroes. In a way, these fairy tales and movies are telling us that women are vulnerable, frail and dependent on either men or inexistent sources of power; that is so disappointing and delusional.

Let me set a scene for you. You feel the burdens of the world on your shoulders, you have work duties to tend to, a relationship that demands your attention, dreams to catch up on, and you just cannot seem to find the time or energy. That looks like a scene I have lived a couple of times throughout the years. There were days when I felt like crumbling down to a thousand pieces, I wanted to cry rivers of pain and relief, but I never found the time to do so. What are we supposed to do at instances like this? Do we sit on our front porches, hands crossed, in anticipation of our macho saviors? Or do we make a wish before bed that we would wake up the next day with some sort of superpowers?

No, a thousand no, if you are having a day of doubt, of frailty, of hardship, you need to take a deep breath, go to that closet and heel up! That is the moment where you will feel a surge of power, of confidence, of sass, of class, and you will be invincible, unbeatable, unbreakable, simply limitless. Life has taught me that I am the only hero in my story, so is everyone, and we should reclaim our stories and experiences back. I have to look up for no one but get my superpower gear on. Wonder Woman has a cape and superpowers that she uses to help others. Your heels are your super wings, they are your secret weapon, reach out for them whenever you feel in need, they are for YOU.

Dreams are our essence as humans, they shape us, they animate us, and they empower us with reasons to go on. No one should deny us that right or take it away from us. History is witness to stories of people with dreams, with visions that the world made fun of or disbelieved, but then those avid dreamers went on, never doubting themselves, to prove everyone wrong and to achieve success that is internationally acclaimed and celebrated. That tells the rest of us to hold on dear to our much-cherished dreams, however strange, unusual or distant they might seem.

Writing this chapter has taken me down the road of forgotten and adjourned wishes that I have had. While I shyed away from sharing them with those around me, I want to take this chance to lay them before readers all over the world; I have nothing to be ashamed or afraid of. As I was working on my thesis, back in 2011, my supervisor noticed that I was not writing within academic rules, as I have never been able to keep to standards of any kind, and he made the remark that I should focus on the job at hand because he knew I would write a book in the future. I was a bit flattered, but I needed to set the record right and said that I may write, but my dream is to make films. I could see the smirk building on his face, how his lips curled in a mocking smile that he contained only to make a comment: "You need money to buy a camera and the equipment to take a video of a wandering cow rolling down a hill." The sarcastic tone did not escape me, and I know that when I find my way to making my films, there will be a beautifully proportionate cow, rolling down a steep green hill. I would not deny any hater the pleasure of making their wishes come true. Until then, I keep on writing and looking forward to a day where my words turn into worlds of their own.

For longer than that, it has been my dream to become a model, to walk on a runway and enjoy the adrenaline rush as those heels lead the walk in a glamorous sway. Deep down, however, I knew it was not very possible to make that a reality; all models have to show their hair, it is after all part of the look. My modelling dream was as wild as wishing to feature in a Victoria's Secret fashion show, even once in my lifetime; why? The answer is straightforward: to wear those heels that stretch to infinite ends. Although it would be quite problematic to be a Hijabi Angel who cannot wear lingerie; a long dress with feathery wings would have done the trick for me. Then recently hijabis started invading every domain one can think of, including the show business, and I saw the likes of Haleema Adan grace the catwalk for so many prominent houses, and that long-buried dream once again awakened. I did have a taste of how it feels when I modelled for a fashion event at a female college. There was that whole backstage scene with people around doing my hair and makeup, then there was the hustle of running to the stage strutting the outfit then having to rush back to change into a different one, along with the audiences cheering and applause. A career in fashion? Maybe not, maybe it is too late, but I would give it a go anytime anywhere in the world. I would rock a pair of mountain high heels and make my way down that runway; head up in the sky, with my eyes focused on the horizon, for far beyond there reach my dreams.

I wanted to be a TV anchor, I was always told I have the presence and abilities to pull it off. But any massive exposure like that would not have been blessed by the males in my family. I would have been disowned, in best scenarios. One of my uncles once spotted me in a very showbiz outfit one day, and he was alarmed that it made me look like a famous news anchor on Al Jazeera Channel. The comment was made with the unpleasant awareness that I may have that in mind already, as I have been known for my oratory talents and presentations skills. Who knows maybe one day I will have my own show?

There is no worse feeling than living with fear of one's own dreams. There is a conflict stirring inside of me: what to do and which side to choose? I am scared of how those around me will react if I decide to write films or make, them if I ever walk a runway or just feature on a picture, if I want to have a voice and share my story and passion. In fact, I am scared of how my own family will react to this particular chapter at hand, my society is known to be merciless as well. However, I choose to do this, to go down this path; while I love them, I know that my life is all mine, no one is walking my road or wearing my shoes. Whatever comes, I have learned to take it and accept it, it is part of growing up.

Countless are the times I stand before my students to tell them that as women we have everything it takes to do anything we want; it is all within us. We are born powerful, indubitably beautiful, and infinitely resourceful. Every woman should be reminded of that. Fear is the source of all evils, make sure you strip out of it, layer after layer, challenging yourself to explore your deepest phobias, your biggest scares, your worst nightmares; and you will set yourself free from everything that holds you back or comes between you and the life you want to live. At times, you need to find the courage to push these boundaries on your own, to truly be able to recognise your own limitless strength and will. Others may wish you well, may encourage you, but it is highly paramount to find the self-awareness not be dependent on anyone who can desert you any day. Learn to be self-sufficient; love starts with self-love, care begins with self-care; strength comes from the power within. Work on yourself first, it is not selfishness, it is rather self-empowerment. Nourish your ego with qualities that will see you through the ups and downs of the road you are taking. Nurture it with boundless optimism and healthy confidence that will fuel your inner instincts when everything else gives up on you.

I know that heels are not the wonder elixir that will fix it all, nor the magic wand that will undo all our concerns away. I also know that when we have nothing and no one around to pull us back up, heels can be all we got, and we should let them work their magic. The road ahead is going to be bumpy, but the journey will be worth the ride. Saying 'no' is a course to learn, embracing one's weaknesses is a step along the way, stumbling and falling is part of nature, but it is essential to keep going. Do not lose sight of the destination, do not relinquish your ambitions; with every inch, your heels grow higher, go on a mile further towards your dreams. When people tell you that you cannot, when circumstances defy your will, when tide flows the other way, and when life tries to knock you down, put your heels on. They are the wings that will help you sore high, and not even the sky is the limit. So, go on, ladies, heel up and dream on! The higher your heels are, the bigger your dreams get.

Fatima is a small town girl whose dreams go far beyond this world. Born in 1989, Fatima was raised and educated in Mascara, west of Algeria. From primary to high school, she had a record of excellent grades. Arab by birth, Fatima went on to learn French, English and German as she majored in Foreign Languages. She did a Bachelors in English Literature and graduated in 2011 as top of her class. Later that year, she booked her spot among a 10-elite Doctoral School to do a Masters in Applied Linguistics and ESP. She started teaching simultaneously at University and took the chance to participate in conferences across the country. 2014 was the year to make the big move, from Algeria to KSA, where she joined the colleges of Excellence and has been working there since. Fatima has been a freelance writer for years, targeting topics that range from education, sports, businezess, fashion, to health and travel. She has also been compiling stories in Arabic and English with the intention, and hope, of sharing them with the world one day as books and screenplays.

CHAPTER 6

ENJOYING THE JOURNEY
by
Yolanda Dupree

PERSPECTIVE IS EVERYTHING, PART 1

She's talking, and I hear her. But I swear right now that at this very moment, I am dying a slow death. She is my daughter, Jada, and she's 15 years old. Jada started cutting herself and considered suicide primarily because of the pressures of teenage life, the pressure to have the perfect body and me. That's what she told the youth pastor and everyone else from our church during the last session of the Winterfest youth retreat.

Everything in me is torn to pieces, and I feel like those pieces are ripping into microscopic pieces. What was once my life is now all a blur because I've failed my child. Jada and I have a great relationship, so how is this happening?

We're all standing in the kitchen, the center of our home. It's the place where we gather and have so much fun together. Mike is near the sink, and I'm standing beside the island looking towards Xavier. To be clear, although we are in the kitchen, this is not a fun time for our family. Xavier begins," I told her that she would have to tell you guys, but she didn't want too. Ma, I was so mad until I had to walk out of the room. I couldn't believe what she was telling them." Jada has now come in the kitchen and is standing beside Xavier. Mike asks her to tell us what she told them at the youth retreat.

I am shaking and can't control it. I really don't want to hear my daughter's answer, but I have no choice because she starts talking. "Well, everyone was sharing about things that they had been through, and I told them that I had started cutting myself and also thought about suicide."

This is the same child that talks me to death. She tells me everything about her life and every detail of everything. Sometimes I pray for patience as I hear all about school, her friends, and all of the drama in class. We talk every single day.

Why would she lie to these people is what I thought. She just wanted to have something to say… something to contribute to the conversation, right? But she only referenced how I would talk to her about her weight and how much she was eating…

So, I asked Jada why she would say something like that. I could barely breathe by this time. I actually felt lightheaded. My breath was slipping away, my throat closing, and I'm dying. Mike is asking why too? Why Jada? Why would you tell them that?

Then she said it. She looked at me and said mommy you know how you would talk to me about my weight and how much I was eating… I really can't remember anything else because a part of me died right then. You told them that I was driving you towards killing yourself? Everyone in this house knew that wasn't true and I knew it so how is this happening? How did the devil change my words into something different that she heard?

So, are you saying that I'm the reason? Now my voice is getting softer, and I can barely see for the tears. You told them that I drove you to this point? I can't believe that something was terribly wrong with Jada and I didn't see it. But Why? Doesn't she know how much we love her and that I would die if she did something like that? As loud as I could scream through my heartbreak, "Why Jada?" Xavier is upset now too. He cuts in and says. Ma, I know how much Jada talks to you and that we're always laughing and having fun in our house. No arguing, no abuse, no cursing… nothing crazy! Jada has never ever said anything close to this at home. I was so angry!"

We are in total chaos right now. Everyone is talking over each other, this is a mess! Jada is saying that she had been trying to tell me. "Mommy, when I would tell you about *my friend*…well, sometimes it was me." Ok, now I know that I'm dying! My mind is racing in disbelief and waiting for this horrible joke to be over.

Did she really consider suicide because of me? But I'm a great mother. We have a great Christian family, and we live in a beautiful home. Again, did my child, whom I love, really start cutting herself and did she really consider suicide? This can't be happening.

Every one of those kids that attended the youth retreat will go home and tell their parents about this. The youth pastor will share this with all of the other pastors. I will never be able to go to church again. I'm a terrible mother. I can't stay here in this room with her and hear anything more. I gotta get out of here, I'm going upstairs. I'm safe in my own space... my bedroom. I'm safe from the person who told the world that I'm a monster. So many questions were roaming in my brain. Why didn't she just tell me? Why did she feel comfortable telling them? And she thought it would be ok? Why didn't she understand how this made me look? Here's the truth:

I listen to every story that Jada wants to share about school, her friends, silly movies, music, boys, food, her hair, chorus, band, everything. And we talk like this every single day. She even gives me updates on her friend at school that is depressed and cutting herself. I listen and then give her advice on what to say to her friend...how to encourage her. I even told Jada that her friend could call me, and I would try to help her. I didn't want Jada too stressed about this because she was young. One day I even told her to be careful because the enemy will try to start telling her to do the same, so I asked her to stop being the confidant for this girl. Never in my mind did I think that I was counseling my own child. This is the essence of the conversations that I have had about a child who was actually my child. I'm angry, I'm hurt. I'm scared and embarrassed. There are days when I'm tired and don't feel like talking, and I really do have to pray for the patience to listen, not just to Jada, but to all of our kids. Listening to our kids is so important, and I never want them to think that I don't care about what's happening in their lives.

I feel betrayed. Yes, I talk to Jada about how *not* to become overweight at her age. But I never, ever told her that she was overweight. Our conversations about weight happen when we're having trouble shopping for clothes, mainly pants, and skirts. The jeans that fit her waist won't go past her thighs, and the jeans that fit her thighs were like a loose paper bag around her waist. The majority of the cute clothes that she likes doesn't fit her body so we would have to purchase basic, plain jeans. The skirts would be too short, and sometimes I would tell her that I could alter them, but she never wanted me to do it. We would be so frustrated, and she would ask me why they didn't make stuff that girls like her could wear. Actually, I would smile and say, Girl, you're beautiful! You have a tiny waist and full hips and thighs. You can't help how you're shaped. God made you that way. We just have to watch how much you eat because all of your weight gain is in your hips and thighs. I even told her that we can work out together to tone our legs because I needed it too. I suggested that we should talk to my sister, Timeka, because she's a fitness coach, for help. Not because she was overweight but because she wanted to be able to fit certain clothes. Now let me say this, Jada does have a healthy appetite, and I tell her that she is entirely free to eat whatever she wanted and to get full, but I don't want her to overeat. Isn't that sound advice? I'm human, so yes, there are times when my tone is sharper because of frustration, but at the end of the day, it all comes from love.

I am a big motivator of people, especially women, but my first ministry is in my home with my family. I speak life over my kids all the time, always have. They get mini-empowerment sessions packed with scriptures to help them apply my teachings, a pat on the back for good decisions and a slap on the butt for bad ones. This happens all the time in our home with lots of hugs and kisses. They have positive affirmations to recite at bedtime, and they recite The Prayer of Jabez as they walk to the school bus stop every morning. How did the devil change my words in her head? I have no clue but now, I'm dying, and I can barely look at her. At this moment, it really doesn't matter what I said, didn't say, or how it was said because no one will never, ever believe that I'm not crazy.

I'm a mess and have left the kitchen. Mike is in our bedroom with me now trying to calm me down, but I can't calm down because I'm literally dying. He asks if I want to talk to her again, I nod "yes" and she comes to the door. She is saying that she's ok now. That she doesn't struggle anymore and that I don't have to worry. But how did I miss her wanting to commit suicide or even thinking about it and *when* did she get better? How can I be sure that she's better? I need to believe that she really is better now. She explains that the talks we had about "her friend" really helped her.

Nothing will ever be the same. Every day, I walk through this house trying to find myself. I see all my beautiful furniture and all of our family photos but is it all a lie? I can't seem to find any joy. What if she had done it? Oh my God, what if? This is too much to bear, and I fear that I am losing this battle.

We have a Christian home, and we raise our kids never to be afraid to speak up for themselves. Almost every Sunday, Mike and I are complimented on how well-mannered our kids are and asked how we accomplished having such great kids. Well, no one will ask that will question again! I have a week to try to pull myself together before going to church again. I find myself riding in my car practicing how I will walk in as if nothing has happened. I must act normal. Well, so much for that. It's Sunday, and my emotions are everywhere. I'm not going to sing today, I don't think that I can. I'm a mess. One minute I'm crying for myself and the next minute I'm crying for Jada, and then my tears are thankful tears to God. Grateful for covering her when I couldn't or didn't. I thank him for protecting her life. Everything feels the same from my front row seat. Nobody seems to be looking at me funny, maybe they don't know yet. I'm here, and now, I just want to go home.

I am Yolanda Dupree, and this is my story.

It's been a month since that day, and I still can't seem to pull myself together. The one thing that I really tried my best not to do is done. My child resented me, and I had no clue. Doesn't that equate to being a bad mother? All of the 'I love you,' hugs and words to empower her didn't matter. Even though she says that it did, her actions have left me confused. I'm fine at work because the laughter with my client takes me far, far away from my heartache. And to be honest, I don't want to be around her at all. She wants things to be as they were, but I don't know how to be anymore. I don't know what to say or not to say. When we're talking, I don't know if she's being honest with me or not. How do I continue to teach and guide her according to the word of God and give her good guidance about life? I am not my children's friend. I'm their mother, and they aren't going to like or agree with everything I say or do, but I always tell them that I love them and that they can always tell me anything and we will figure out the best solution for any problem or situation that they face.

I need counseling but where can I go? If Jada walks too close to me, I freeze up. If she asks for something, I tell her to ask her father. If she wants to laugh and talk, I wonder what part of what I say is she going to misinterpret. I know that there isn't a counselor that can fix this death that I'm carrying, only God. The *death* is the relationship that I thought that I had with Jada. That relationship is dead, and I don't know how to birth a new one. I feel like I am wandering through life, dragging my soul behind me. I want to tell my mother. Oh, how I want to tell her. I want to fall into her arms and ask her to fix it or just to take the pain away. But that means that she will know that I failed. She is a great mom, and I love her so much. She thinks that I'm strong and she depends on me a lot. She has so much going on right now and so many people that need her, and although I know that she can handle my mangled life, I sense that this is a fight for God and I. This is one of those wilderness experiences. The kind where God carries you.

I can't tell my sisters either. We don't allow anyone to hurt one of us AND GET AWAY WITH IT, NO ONE! I am hurting so bad right now, and I know that they will want to focus on me. They will definitely be concerned about Jada but upset as well. My mother and sisters understand the type of relationship that I have with all of my kids so they will be very upset because of how it was handled. We handle things "in our house"…within our immediate family not outside of it. We fix things together, but Jada has gone out of the walls of our family, and although I'm hurt, I feel like I have to protect her.

I feel so alone, but I know that God and I are on this journey together… I cry often, and I'm waiting for the pain to go away.

Every time normalcy is close, the pain resurfaces, and I pull back. I've built a wall of protection around myself. I'm not sure what to believe or what to do. I don't know what the devil is telling her, and I don't know if she's listening. Remember, I missed everything! I missed the worse struggle of Jada's life; how did I miss it? I have withdrawn from her, and she knows it.

Its been about 5 weeks and I'm not better. Mike is trying to help me. He is such a good husband. I haven't really considered how he's handling all of this drama. I'm in the kitchen cooking dinner, and Jada comes in the and says, "Mommy, I know that I hurt you and I know that you're struggling around me and it's ok. I understand" With tears falling from my eyes, I say, "Jada, it will get better, and I love you." The bible says to speak those things that be not as though they are, well I'm still hurting, but my god is faithful. I am confident that He will restore our relationship.

Jada recently celebrated her sixteenth birthday, and she wants to get a second piercing in her ear. I am in the store with her and Kayla, everything is fine until she asks about the piercing and immediately, I withdrew and got very upset. I want to scream and sit in the floor of this store and cry. It just hit me from out of nowhere. All I could do was walk away and tell her to call Mike, and if he says that it's okay, then it's fine with me. It's things like this that I'm striving to conquer. It's a process. I don't like it, but I understand it. I understand that this is a day by day restoration process and I have to fight for our relationship. The devil will not win because God already has the victory.

The death that I have experienced is now being replaced with a "new birth." It's like the butterfly, (I love butterflies!) which is born a caterpillar. It has its purpose and goes about the day, eating and crawling around. It's ultimate purpose it to transform into a more beautiful insect, the butterfly. The problem is that the caterpillar must die to live again. It has to go through a transformation that is difficult if it's going to produce its best life. Once the "new birth" has taken place, the old is still there, but it's different. And there's a new level of freedom in life that he would never have experienced without the "dying" process.

Gradually…day by day… and moment by moment my world is getting better. Jada and I are working on it, and I can see the light at the end of the tunnel.

PERSPECTIVE IS EVERYTHING, PART 2.
BY JADA DUPREE

"OMG, Jada you are so thick! I wish I had a body like you! Your butt is HUGE! You must eat a lot of cornbread." For as long as I can remember comments like this have always been made towards me. Little 6th grade Jada that moved to this new community a year prior. I didn't even know half of these people, but they already knew me. *Jada with the big booty, Big Booty Jada, BBJ, the thick Jada.* I already had the name in a place where I didn't even know these kids. At first, it wasn't an issue. I didn't care about them calling me these nicknames. I never answered them, so it didn't bother me, right? Sixth grade was the first time someone ever told me that I would be pregnant by 16 and that I would never amount to anything. I would drop out of school, be a stripper or a teen mom. **Strike 1.**

7th grade is where everyone had a crush on everyone. It was normal to hear conversations about a cute boy and who liked him or vice-versa. Looking back, it seemed so sweet and innocent, but when you're a 13-year-old that hears from a crush that if you didn't have the body that you had, they wouldn't like you, it does something to you. I can't help the way that I look. This is the way that God created me. It was at that moment that I realized that most guys were only going to like me for my body. So, I decided that I *would not* be with anyone that just wanted me for my body because I am more than that. I remember any time a boy said he liked me, I would always ask why. And either their first or second answer was because of my body. What was wrong with me? Was I not enough? I was smart, funny, and a good person. So why won't anyone like me for me? I even asked a boy that was a good friend of mine if he thought I was pretty. Not because I liked him or anything, but because he was my friend and I thought I would get an honest answer. His response was, "I mean you're not ugly, but you're not like Dang you fine. Your just cute, I guess". "Wow! I thought" - You GUESS! You guess that I'm pretty! **Strike 2.**

Eighth grade was terrific but not in a good way. Most girls did not like me because their "boyfriends" would stare at my butt. I never understood how that was my fault, but whatever and I was called a whore for the first time in 8th grade. I can remember how angry I was that day. How was I a whore? The girl who had never had a boyfriend, let alone kissed anyone. Such an amazing year, right? I made it through that year and was excited about high school because I thought that it was going to be different. I was hoping that I wasn't going to be seen as just body, but boy was I wrong. I decided to audition for the marching band, and the older girls told me that all the drumline boys would try to "mess" with me because of my body. The year had just started, and I could see that the cycle was continuing. Before I knew it, I was known as "the Jada that dances with the big butt." I would always complain to my friends like why I can't be known as Jada with the chubby cheek or Jada with the big smile or just The Jada that dances? Why does my butt have to be such an essential thing in my life?

I was slowly starting to hate how I looked. Why couldn't I just be skinny like the other girls? I would get praises at school for the way I looked, and at home, I thought I was too thick. And then buying pants or skirts for me became really difficult because they weren't making pants for girls with big thighs, big butts, and a small waist. My mom would suggest me trying to lose some weight by not eating as much. But to me, I didn't eat that much. Yes, we all have "greedy" moments, but I didn't think that I ate too much at all.

I was so confused and conflicted because I was getting both positive and negative comments about my looks and criticism from her. In my mind, I just kept thinking, I look like this because of you and dad. These are the genes that you guys gave me. I would have loved to be tall and skinny like literally everyone else in my family. I really felt like I stuck out like a sore thumb. They didn't have to stop eating as much. They didn't struggle to find clothes, so why did I have to? I would get so frustrated and annoyed with my mom when she would say something about trying to change the way I looked. I would be frustrated because as much as I wanted to do what she told me to, what 14/15-year-old wants to be watching what they eat. Like even though I knew what she was saying was out of love, I couldn't help but feel even uglier, or like I wasn't good enough. I felt like I was someone that needed to be fixed. But how could I be fixed if I didn't think that I was broken? And honestly, I was scared. For so long I had always been identified by the way that I looked, so if I changed it them who would I be? What would people say now? Do I even want to lose the weight? Why would God give me a body like this if it was going to be such a problem for me? **Strike 3**

Everything was getting to me, and I was done with all of it. It seemed like no matter how hard I tried, I would still be seen the same way by everyone. I started listening to the voices in my head, and only negative thoughts came from that. If someone complimented me or told me that I was pretty, it would make me happy at first, but once they walked away from the voices in my head would say to me that they were lying and that I was ugly. Then that happiness would turn to sadness, anger, frustration, and rage. I thought I was the ugly duckling out of all my friends and my family. I was tired of always being stared at everywhere I went because I knew why they were staring. And the media did not help at all, especially the music. So many songs had lyrics about "big booty whores" or having sex with a girl with a big butt. I was automatically put in that category like the girls in the music videos. It's crazy how you don't even know my name, but you just assume I'm out here doing things that grown women do. I just always felt angry. I believed that I would never be good enough. I was starting to wonder if I should just become what everyone had already made me out to become. I felt worthless. I felt like a waste of space or just an object that could be molded in any shape to please people. I didn't feel loved, and I hated that because I was surrounded by people who loved me. I knew that my family loved me, but I hated myself. I hated that I felt like no one saw me for me.

    I got the idea from a friend. I was trying to help her stop doing it. She would cut herself, and I hated the fact that she did it. But one day as I was wondering why she did it, I decided to try for myself. The first time I did it, I felt terrible afterward, but it was something about the pain that gave me relief. I was smart enough not to go too hard or deep, so there was no scar. This was during ninth grade. After the first time I cut myself, I would start talking to my mom about "my friend," just to see what she would say. I would change up some of the stories to be about me, but I never had enough courage to tell her the truth. I didn't *cut* too often. It was a here and there thing. To me, it was like that favorite restaurant that you go to once every year because it's so expensive, but when you go the food is amazing. Every now and then that voice in my head would say, "you know things aren't going to change so why not just end it. They are only going to remember you as Jada with the big booty anyway". I always found myself in a constant fight with my mind. I felt like I didn't know who I was. Like, I saw myself in the mirror, but it wasn't the version of myself that I wanted everyone to see. I had lost who I was. I felt like I was always forcing my happiness, and I was a darn good actress. I had to be the rock for everyone so I couldn't let them see that I didn't have it together. They needed me, and as a good friend, I had to be there for them. But the more I started to ignore the real problem, the more lost I felt. I was slowly giving up on myself. I just didn't care anymore. Why would I when no one cared for me?

It's crazy how it happened. My deliverance. It's like someone just knocked the wind out of me. I was on the phone with a boy that I liked at the time during 10th grade, and we were arguing about something stupid like we always did. This time was different though. I remember I was so upset about everything. I was upset with life. I was bothered with myself for feeling the way I did. Then all of a sudden I heard a voice say "why do you care what people say? Remember who you are". And it's hard to explain, but it was if something clicked in my head. I remember laughing, trying not to laugh too loud because I didn't want to wake my parents and my siblings. Then my laughter turned into me crying.

The people who know me know I am always preaching about self-love, standing firm in the person that you are, and not apologizing for it. And yet I did the exact opposite of what I believed in. Now I know that is not the big revelation most people look forward to, but sometimes it's the simple things that help bring you back to your senses. I knew the person I wanted to be. I didn't want to be the girl that dropped out of school; the one who got pregnant at a young age. I didn't want to be the girl that everyone assumed that I would be. I wanted to prove them wrong. Show everyone that I was much, much more than my body. I am sensitive when I want to be, but not often. I'm very overprotective of the ones I love. I am very goofy with a smart mouth, thanks to my dad. I AM BEAUTIFUL, and I dare someone to try to tell me otherwise. I stayed up half that night and just thought about the person I had become and tried to figure out how to get the real me back. I had to distance myself from a lot of people so that I could focus on myself.

I began talking to God more. Just basic conversation because I was desperate to find the real me... I could feel her, but I didn't know how to connect to her. I began to always speak positive words to myself even when I could hear that voice telling me otherwise. I started to apply the concepts that I would encourage my friends to live by. I was slowly beginning to learn how to be entirely in love with myself. I was figuring out that I was my biggest cheerleader. Even though I appreciated and loved my friends and family, I had to be the one to cheer myself on when no one else would. I was slowly building myself back up, and I was falling in love with me.

Even though, I grew up reciting this affirmation, "I was a mighty woman of God and a doer of his word," I was actually starting to believe and live by it. I could have anything that I wanted. Be anyone I wanted. Do anything I wanted. I was so proud of myself for overcoming everything by myself. I never told anyone or asked for help. This was all me and God. I felt like my relationship with God was getting stronger. I was starting to see life the way he wanted me to see it. I began to understand that everything in life is a lesson that we have to be willing to learn, and I was proud to say that I learned my lesson and now it was time to move on. Finally, it was over.

No one needed to know because I was over it, right? Later that year, my older brother and I went on our youth church trip to Winterfest. The services we went to were amazing, and it was the time away that I needed to focus on myself and ultimately heal entirely. On the last day, we stayed in the cabin and had a little service before we left. I remember our youth pastor telling us to leave what was dragging us down there. For us to go back home feeling free from whatever was holding us back, and I felt like this is my moment. I was tired of that old version of Jada and was ready to let her go. So, I told my story. I talked about how I didn't want to live anymore, and my heart broke when I saw my brother walk out of the cabin. I ran after him and apologized continuously because I didn't want to hurt anyone. He told me I needed to tell my parents what happened and that he was glad that I had moved past it. When we got home that evening, Xavier started the conversation, and I worked up the courage to tell my parents about my experience. I didn't really want to talk about it, but I knew I was dropping a massive bomb on them. I didn't think that telling them would change anything, but it did.

CONCLUSION

I have praise that no one can take from me because I have a testimony! We have a testimony! God restores, and he gives you back more than the devil stole from you. This was a horrible "valley" experience for me, one of the most difficult of my life. I still have the scars, but they are healed. Sometimes the memory of it all hurts a little, but this experience has made me a better person and a better mom.

So, you've read both of our accounts of what happened. Our perspectives are very different. We experienced it together, but we didn't see it the same. Both of us suffered some of the same emotions, but we tell different stories. Which story do you believe? Which one of us is right? We both are. My story is the truth, and Jada's story is the truth. We are both rights because our perspective of the situation is different. What she experienced is real, and it happened the way that she recalls. I can't change it. What I experienced was real, and it happened the way that I remember, and Jada can't change it.

Perspective is everything. We all should be more gracious to each other as we go through life because we don't have the same experiences as everyone else. You can watch a movie with a group of friends, and each person will have a different understanding of the film. You can attend an event with friends, listen to the speaker and eat the same foods, but once the event is over and people are asked to rate the event or give their opinion of the event, sometimes it can be hard to believe that these people actually attended the same event.

My account of this journey may have come across as selfish because I talked so much about my pain, but I don't really care because it's my truth. You see, somehow, I had helped Jada through one of the toughest times in her young life and didn't even know it. She conquered her demon and won before I ever knew it existed, but the revelation of this process stripped me of my pride and joy as her mother. I had to rely on God and his word about love, forgiveness, and restoration to pull me back to life again with Jada. One day a few months after things got back to normal, I told Jada that I had the feeling that we would write a book about this journey… when we were both ready. She said that she had the same feeling too. God is so amazing!

Recently, God answered my question and gave me total peace about how Jada shared her testimony with everyone at the youth retreat. I never understood why it happened that way. Well, God told me that I don't get to decide when or how she gets her freedom. I am her mother, but He is her God. Jada was presented with the opportunity to lay her burdens down, and she took it. She realized it as the time to be free. God told me that her freedom is not based on my feelings and how I handle it. When God offers deliverance and liberty, we should accept it immediately. What if she *had* considered me or my feelings? She would have come home with the same baggage that she left with, but my sweet Jada chose freedom. I am so proud of her. And I can shout it from the mountaintop, "My baby is Free!"

NOT YET

It's Monday, one of the slowest days of business for a fast food restaurant and he's pointing a gun in my face. Am I going to die?

There aren't many cars that are coming through the drive-thru window tonight because it's raining and it's Monday. I am working the drive-thru, which is my favorite area to work. It's a slow night, and I really don't have much to do. I just finished up with the last car and have already cleaned and wiped everything down. There's nothing else to do here so I will go see if anyone needs help on the front line of the store. As I walk over there, I see that a guy is laying across the counter trying to reach in the cash drawer to steal the money. This is crazy, and I'm not going to let him steal the money from the restaurant. He is struggling so I will just walk over and close the drawer. Very simple, right?

Now, I have a gun in my face, and I'm scared to death. It's black, and it has no loyalty to anyone. It's literally in my face, and all I can think about is my family and how I don't want to die. My nose is starting to run, and my eyes are full of tears. I couldn't speak. No words, just tears. I'm 19 years old, and my life can end now…but it's just getting started. I'd never seen a real gun, and my first introduction is a life and death encounter.

Our customers are frozen in their seats. The room is entirely still - You can smell fear. He said to get back and pointed it closer in my face. It was a shiny, black gun. How did I miss seeing the second guy? There are two of them robbing our McDonald's restaurant. One guy is reaching to get the money from the drawer and the other one pointing the gun at me. It's too close to my face to really see details but close enough to feel the coldness in the room. I immediately looked to my left just over the gun, and Mr. Johnson was sitting in his regular seat. He is motionless and staring right at me. His gaze is saying *don't move Yolanda, don't move*. I knew that he was trying to tell me something because it felt like he was staring through me, but nothing made sense.

The guys are yelling, but all I can think is to get away. He's saying to get down and stop moving, but my body won't listen. If he's going to shoot me, he will shoot me while I'm running for my life. I'm actually scooting across the floor towards the back of the room, crying and begging him not to shoot me.

So, I kept scooting backward towards the fry area. The first guy finally gets the drawer out of the holding tray but drops it. Now, the money is all on the floor. He jumps over the counter and grabs the money. In the meantime, I haven't stopped trying to get away. I'm at the fry area and turned the corner, but my eyes are on the gun. Once out of sight of the gun, I am still scared to death and want to keep trying to get away until one of the line cooks crawled behind me and put his hand on my back and told me to stop moving. That's when I stopped. He got all of the money, jumped back over the counter and both of them ran out. I jumped up immediately and ran in the office. The cook is trying to calm me down, and I can hear what he is saying, but I can't control my body... I am still running in my head, but he was holding my body.

The reality of what had happened and what could have happened was trying to catch up to the fact that I had made it. I am alive, and it is over.

The officers are finally here, and I've survived. They want me to describe the gun, but I can't. It's black, that's all I can say. It was black, and it was on my face. One officer asks me if I thought that I could identify the two guys. They had found two African American guys running not far from the restaurant. "Sir, I'm not sure if I remember what they looked like," Which was the truth. He asks me again to try, so I told him that I would. I am so scared and want to go home. The officer tells me that I will be able to see them, but they won't be able to see me. He walks me over towards where they have the police car parked, and I am in shock. One of the guys in the car is a friend of mine from elementary school. I had classes with him and his twin sister, we know each other very well. He had a funny personality and was fun to hang around. His sister didn't have many friends, so I made a point to talk with her and play with her at recess time. Maybe that's why he didn't shoot me, or maybe God said, "Not yet."

THE BEAUTY OF DEATH

My life is hectic. I'm a hairstylist with a large clientele which requires a lot of energy, stamina, and patience. And on top of all of that, I'm married and pregnant with my first child. Every day is busy, but Mondays are my saving grace. This is the day that I can run errands, clean my house and rest. Today is Monday, and it's a beautiful sunny day which is perfect for getting out of the house for a few hours. It's been a productive day, and I've crossed everything off of my to-do list: pay bills, drop clothes at the cleaners, and pick up a few products for the salon. All of this running around has me hungry, so I think that I'll go home and eat some leftovers from Sunday's dinner. I'm driving home, but my mind is on my pregnancy and the fact that I decided not to find out the gender of the baby, but I'm a little frustrated with my decision. Right now, I'm daydreaming about being a mother and everything that goes with it when the ringing of my phone snaps me away from my thoughts.

My mom is calling to check on me and to remind me that I really need to go visit our cousin who is in the hospital with complications from cancer. She repeatedly tells me not to keep waiting, but I have put it off over and over again. Well, not today. Although I'm only 10 minutes from my house and the hospital is 40 minutes away, I'm going there right now.

My cousin, Sis. Eula Ackey (it's a church thing) is married to the Presiding Bishop of the Pure Holiness Church of God. I know her to be a God-fearing, sweet spirited woman. Her husband and children have been at the hospital by her side every day, loving and praying over her. I haven't seen my cousins in a while, so I'm excited but also a little nervous, which is a weird feeling.

Once in the room, Bishop Ackey introduces me to the gentleman who's in the room with him and explains that my cousins had just stepped out of the room to get some lunch. "Why don't we step outside to talk and let you spend some time with her alone," he suggests. Now that they are gone, I realize how cold and empty the room feels. The walls are pale bluish green, the floor is the basic hospital white and white, black mosaic tiles. Besides the bed, there isn't much furniture. I can't help but smile as I walk towards the bed, Sis. Ackey is sleeping and looks so peaceful. I'm not sure if she can hear me or not, but I touched her hand and whispered, "Hey, Sis. Ackey, it's me, Yolanda." No response. Her hands aren't under the covers, so I rubbed and held them for a few minutes. She didn't respond so I decided to in the chair at the foot of her bed. Just as I'm starting to reminisce a little, something caught my eye. She is looking right at me. This is sort of scaring me, so I said, "Hey, Sister Ackey." She takes a deep breath and closes her eyes. I watched. After 3 more deep breaths, she opens her eyes again, looking right at me. It was just a few seconds, but it seems like forever. She closes them again. Then, three more deep breaths and her eyes are on me, but somehow, it feels like she's looking through me. I'm doing my best to hold her gaze. I don't know what's happening right. Ok, her eyes are closing again, and I can relax. A few seconds pass. I'm waiting…waiting for …waiting for her to open her eyes again. Instead, she takes 1 more deep breath, now they're open again but not for long. Once they were closed, she takes her final 3 breaths, and she sleeps away. Those are the lyrics of a song that people used to sing in church years ago, "Saints don't die, they just sleep away."

This can't be happening! I just got here! Not now! I'm in here by myself! Did she just die right in front of me? Thoughts are rushing in my head, and I do not believe this. She's gone. I want to go get Bishop Ackey but there is a substantial, heavy presence in the room, and I feel like I need to be still. Wow! She's gone. I just witnessed her transition, and it was peaceful and beautiful. Now, I have to go and tell Bishop. I'm not sure how I'm walking, but I'm calm, calmer than I ever thought that I would be in this situation.

Bishop and the other Pastor turns towards me as the door opens, "Bishop, you better get in here, she's gone.' Well, this is already too much for one day, but he rushes in the door past me calling her name. He's calling the nurses to hurry and get in the room quickly'. The room is being flooded with people, and I'm trying to fade away in the background. I find a place up against the wall in a corner because I want to disappear. My heart is breaking because he's emotional and asking them to do something to bring her back. I've never seen him like this. He's a strong man but now, so weak.

The nurses calmly remind him that he and their children decided a few days ago that they would not resuscitate again. They're talking to him, and he's looking at her, rubbing her hand, and I can see the moment when reality settles within him. She's gone. The love of his life is gone. He keeps saying ok, ok. I feel like I'm in a movie now or outside of my body. They ask him what happened, and he looks to me. I'm not even sure if I can remember. I feel guilty that I was in here with her and not him. Are they going to think that did something to her? Maybe I should have gotten him earlier…but I didn't know what was happening at the time. My thoughts are racing and colliding together, but somehow, I managed to tell them. The doctor comes in to confirms her death, and now he and the nurses are offering their condolences as they leave the room. Bishop walks over to the phone and calls their daughter and tells her to come back because her mother just died. To be quite honest, I don't know what to do right now so I' m just going to be quiet. I want to run out of the room, but I know that I can't do that so, for now, I'll just disappear.

I need to call my momma and I will as soon as I get back to my car. The walk out of the room was hard and navigating the halls to the exit is a blur. And now that I've made it to the car and start telling my mother what happened, I'm secretly asking God why. Why did he allow it to happen like this and why me? Why me? Mom says that Sister Ackey's spirit must have been waiting for them to leave because their love was keeping her here and she was ready to go. My being there gave comfort that she didn't die alone, but it gave her the freedom to go. Mom is talking, and I'm listening, a little. "It was meant for you to be there," is what I keep replaying in my head. That's what my mother said, "It was meant for you to be there."

Today, I witnessed a beautiful and peaceful transition. Life to death. Just me, her and the angels. They were taking her back to God, the one who created her. The one who initiated her beginning by forming her in *her* mother's belly. The same God who has now closed the book, and in my head, I can hear him saying, "Well done! My good and faithful servant.'

Death is an enormous part of life, and people have many different thoughts and views on it. Today, I will say that death was beautiful.

WHY AM I ENJOYING THE JOURNEY?

For as far back as I can remember, I lived two lives. Maybe as far back as 4 years old, I have memories of a great life with loving parents, but there was a dark side of me. I grew up playing outside with my sisters, going to church, singing in the choir, eating good food, wearing pretty clothes…everything that life should be, but I had a secret. My secret? Is the one that I prayed and asked God to help me genuinely forgive and help me love people unconditionally. I'm sure that if they could take it back, they would. I'm sure they cringe at the thought of what they did to me. I know that they have probably prayed that I would somehow forget, but I haven't forgotten. Most of the time, the boogie man isn't lurking around the corner or in the bushes. No, he's at the family gatherings, the church programs or *he* is a she. My secret life was me being touched inappropriately, fondled, being pinned against walls in corridors, behind closed doors, laid down, humiliated by being held as urine filled my mouth, and people laughed…ok, that's enough because I'm sure you get the point. I only told my mom about one incident because I was so mad.

I didn't dare share the others because it had been a part of my life forever and to be quite honest and regardless of how foolish it sounds, it was my normal. I grew to accept it and never tried to stop it although I knew it was wrong. I started having sexual desires at a young age. It was as if someone unlocked that part of me and I never really understood that my body was a precious gift, only to be shared in love and marriage. I'm embarrassed to say that I allowed some forms of this to continue into my teenage years, but one day it came to an end. *I* almost came to an end. I battled life and death on and off when I was seventeen because I almost became the "secret monster" to someone else.

I was having a horrible day mainly because I was desiring to be touched but was angry with myself for wanting it. I was scared but thought that I would try it anyway. I attempted to try it, but I couldn't do it. I didn't like how I felt, and I almost hurt myself many times after that day. I knew that I would never try it again, but I was an emotional mess. God had no choice but to help me forgive the people that hurt me and took advantage of my body. I had to forgive them to forgive myself. I didn't want to hurt anymore. I didn't want to be sad anymore. I didn't want to hate myself. I had to surrender myself to God, all of me and everyone else. One day, I realized that I couldn't find hate in my heart anymore, just love. I never wanted to hurt myself again, but it took years to remove the yucky taste in my mouth whenever I thought about it.

God is so amazing! Years later, He sent a man that loved me but most importantly, he cherished my body as a precious gift and waited till marriage to unwrap that gift. My healing was complete. Then, I had children of my own, and it came flooding back to me. It caused me to be super-crazy overprotective of my kids. I would hide and cry because I wanted to trust people, but it was so hard. I prayed like a mad woman and went overboard when telling the kids about protecting themselves. I know that I probably grossed them out a few times, but I needed them to understand the difference between good and bad touching. The older my kids got the better I dealt with them not being with me all the time.

Today, regarding my personal experiences, I'm able to interact with and be around everyone from my past because the "old" is no longer and God has made all things new. We've all grown and transformed ourselves and love has conquered all.

Our lives may not have gone the way we wanted it to go, but we have a choice for our future. We can decide to exhale and live fully or crawl in a corner allow the past to stop us and ultimately kill us. I choose life.

I am entirely convinced that God knows what's best for me. I'm totally convinced that He loves me. I am entirely convinced that He has a plan for my life. And I am totally confident that I am what the bible says that I am:

1. I am a child of the living God.
2. I'm the head and not the tail.
3. A lender, not a borrower.
4. I am the righteousness of God.
5. I am healed.
6. I am delivered and set free.
7. I am a beautiful creation.
8. I have the mind of God.
9. I walk by faith and not by sight.
10. I have the power to decree and declare a thing, and it is so!

I am enjoying my journey because God is in control of my life. I was created in His image, and I trust Him. I can sit back, relax, and follow the path that is set before me. I find peace in not having all of the answers because I gave God my "Yes" a long time ago. It's been a fantastic ride, my life has blossomed just like a beautiful flower. It has been transformed like the beautiful butterfly, and my faith is built on a firm foundation like a sturdy old house that was built many years ago. The exciting thing is that the best is yet to come!

Enjoy Your Journey!

Yolanda Dupree has humbly accepted the call of God on her life although never in her wildest dreams did she think this would be her path. Yolanda attended Arnold's International University of Cosmetology and received her Master Cosmetology license in 1990. In 2005, Yolanda started Yolanda Dupree Ministries Inc. and she and her husband hosted to first Staying Married God's Way Couples Retreat in 2006. Later, three more programs were added; Faith Walkers Empowerment Group for Women, Not You/Not Me: Teens Against Dating Violence, and Kayla's Pink Ribbon Society. Then in 2010, Yolanda became a Certified Christian Life Coach. After receiving the 501c3 nonprofit status, she changed the name to Dupree Empowerment Group Inc. Yolanda has written three books, "To God be the Glory", "Countdown to Your Last 90 Days", and "Five Key Components to Finding Your Purpose." She's a dynamic speaker, a singer/songwriter and a handbag designer. Yolanda likes to eat good food, spend time with her family and create beautiful things. She isn't afraid to cry or be outspoken and tell it like it but most importantly, Yolanda believes that all things are possible. Yolanda has enjoyed an amazing marriage to Michael for 24 years and is blessed with four children: Xavier, Jada, Kayla, and Jonathan.

CHAPTER 7

FOOD COLORING IN A GLASS FULL OF WATER
by
Flerida Santana Johnas

Disclaimer
I have tried to recreate events, locales, and conversations from my memories of them. To maintain their anonymity, in some instances, I have changed the names of individuals and places, I may have changed some identifying characteristics and details such as physical properties, occupations and places of residence.

Frame in Time
It's Jane and Brian's Story.
Linda walks into the room with a smile on her face and a swing in her steps. Her ears are covered by a headset while she nodeds to music as she turns to close the door. Linda notices that Jane, her roommate, is crying. She is not able to hear the sobbing, but the sight of the tear-stained face tells her immediately that something is amiss.

The smile leaves her face at about the same time her hands reach her head to take off the headset. She leaves it on her reading table along with her brown, leather strap bag and hurries over to her roommate's bed.

"Jane, what's wrong?"

Jane looks at her for a while, taking her time, as if she is gauging her worthiness to bear the critical secret that is weighing her down. Her big blue eyes are wider than they had ever been, serving as a resting place for fear; fear that is sitting in all the glory of its stark nakedness. She looks so vulnerable, like a little kid who is desperately in need of her big sister's protection.

"Jane" Linda speaks calmly. "You need to tell me what's wrong" she didn't know what the problem is but at that moment, looking at her frightened roommate, Linda is ready to go to any extent to deal with whatever her problem is.

"LINDA" as Jane's voice chokes with emotion. "I think I've just been sexually assaulted."

Linda feels the ground give way from underneath her as she settles down on the bed, drawing as close to her roommate as she can. The icy hands of fear grip her. The buzz she still possessed from a night of heavy drinking and partying was cut through like a knife by Jane's confession. First, she feels her limbs go cold, then she feels that chill seeps into her bones till it reached her spine.

"Oh my God."

Something is set off - It was like a fuse was blown. There was a spark.

"By whom?" she asks her roommate.

"Brian"

The voice is so low that it was almost inaudible.

"Brian?"

"The basketball guy."

For a moment Linda draws a blank, then from the depths of her memory, desperately shaking the vodka cobwebs out of her head to connect the name Jane had uttered with the person. By this time the spark had grown into a small flame.

"The one who is Josh's roommate?"

"Yes"

Jane whimpered in a fragile state. Linda wondered what she might have gone through at the hands of that beast. The beast in question was the newest guy on the school basketball team. She imagined what this black, 6-foot 2 inch, 180lbs beast must have done to poor Jane "I was awakened by him inside me."

Linda's right hand folded into a fist so tight that her long nails dug into her palms, but she did not care.

"I did not know what to do" Jane continued. "I do not even know what to do now. I'm so scared."

"Don't be. I'm here" Linda assured Jane. Then she gathered the girl in a tight hug. "I'm here okay?"

But being there was not enough. Something had to be done.

As Linda grabbed the phone, Jane yelled, what are you doing',

"Jane, we must call the police," she said.

"No" The no was followed by a shaking of the head, in sheer panic. "I don't want to get them involved."

"But he raped you."

"Yes, but I do not want to call anyone."

"We must." Linda insisted. "This guy is dangerous. If he thinks he can get away with raping you then he may want to rape someone else or worse still, rape you again."

That was what they always banked on, all rapists. They all believed that their victims will be reluctant to tell people, either because they are afraid of them, or maybe because they are ashamed. It is what encourages them, giving them the audacity to commit the act and sometimes even come back for seconds. It is not going to happen in this case! No sir, he won't. I will not let it happen!

~~~ *** ~~~

Jason's books were lying on his reading table unattended. Although they were inanimate things that were not supposed to have any effect on him, whenever he looked at them, they seemed to be looking at him with disapproval. He was supposed to be studying for his exams, but the book that everyone on campus was talking about was hard to put down. In his hands, he had something more important than any exam facing him. Some psychologist wrote this book on how to ruin someone's life. She broke it down, a playbook, step by step, this was incredible that someone would write this, Jason thought, he had to finish it by morning. After all, did someone not say that exams are not the true test of knowledge?

The sudden knocking on his door interrupted his intense concentration with his book. It was akin to the staccato bursts of a machine gun, repeatedly coming without a pause in between. Annoyed at the knock, wondering who was knocking like that at his door so early. More importantly, who was bothering him when he was in the middle of this crazy ass book, he swung down his legs from his reading table and went to open the door with the novel sill in his hand.

When he pulled the door open, he saw his neighbors who lived directly across from him, Linda and Jane, standing outside looking like people who were just coming from a crime scene. Before he could open his mouth to ask them what the matter, Linda began to talk. She sounded like the knocking. Her words were so fast that they almost fell over one another due to the haste with which they were pushed out of her mouth.

"Jason, can you please keep Jane in your room? Did you see Brian in the hall? You know... the new basketball player, the tall black guy. Can she stay here while I go find him?"

Jason stands staring at her, open-mouthed.

When she realizes how she must have sounded, Linda calmed down and explained the situation slowly and carefully this time around. When she finished, Jason opened his door wide and invited them in. Of course, only Jane walked in, hugging herself and looking downcast. The girl was just doing everything she could to avoid looking into his eyes. As she walked, she kept her eyes on the floor.

Jason felt sorry for her. He wondered who would have had the heart to hurt this girl. She seemed like a sweet girl, one of those who would always greet one with a warm smile if their path happened to cross in the hallway.

From the corner of his eye, Jason studied her as she sat waiting for her roommate. From his estimation, Jason thought that her height would be around five feet two inches. She was dressed neatly, hair combed, but her eyes were bloodshot. It was odd that he did not see any noticeable bruises. This puzzled him because he realized then that this girl's room was just across from his and yet he hadn't been aware of anything untoward going on there. Even though he had been reading, he could still have heard. He wondered if she had screamed, resisted the black guy and had lost, having to succumb in the end because the help that could have prevented this ugly incident was not forthcoming.

Linda came back into the room then. She was moving quickly like a locomotive with a full head of steam.

"Did you see the guy?" Jason asked her.

"No" she replied going straight to where Jane sat on the couch. "We must call the police immediately."

She brought out her cellphone from the hip pocket of her denim and began to dial the emergency numbers.

~~~ *** ~~~

Immediately after her report was taken by the police, Linda escorted Jane to the hospital so that she could be administered with a rape kit.

The investigator was a good-looking, middle-aged man who looked nice but sturdy as well. It was those kinds of people who can make kids fall in love with them when the kids are in the right and dread their coming when they are doing the wrong thing. He appeared to be capable. All his questions were asked in a soft, melodious voice that automatically set the rape victim at peace.

"Just before we start Jane," he said "I just want you to know that we believe you. Okay?"

She nodded.

"Now, if at any time you feel uncomfortable and want to stop answering questions just tell us okay."

She nodded again.

"We will just stop and come another time, okay?"

"Yeah"

"Okay. So, what happened?" he brought out a pad and a pen, which he held above it, ready to write.

"I fell asleep around 3:30am Friday and woke up to Brian ramming into me."

"Okay," the investigator wrote in his pad.

"I just want to make sure he didn't get me pregnant because he was not wearing a condom."

"Do you know him?" the investigator asked her.

"Yes"

"Where can we find him?"

"He lives in the dorm."

"Did he threaten you?"

"No"

"Did he gag you?"

"No"

"Did you say no at any point?"

"No"

"Did he hold you down?"

"No"

The investigator paused to collect his thoughts then he asked: "How do you know him?"

Jane licked her lips before replying "Well I met him at a frat party."

"Did you have any interaction with him before last night?"
"Yes"
"How about any sexual interaction with him?"
"Yes"
"Okay. What was the sexual interaction?"
Naturally, this made Jane uncomfortable, but she answered anyway:
"Um... when we left the party, as we walked back to our dorm, I gave him a handjob."
"That's it?"
"Yes, that's it"
"Did you interact with him any other time?"
"Yes, we often hung out, mostly because we have common friends."
As if on cue, Jane's parents came in just as the investigator was finishing with Jane.

DEER IN HEADLIGHTS

Early on Saturday morning, the court was filled with cameras and reporters. The case for that morning had drawn a lot of interest. It was the kind that the media loved to feast on, the type that drew them like flies. There was a superstar involved, or rather one could pass as a superstar at a top Division 1 university anywhere in the country. A basketball player who was a member of the St Joseph's University Division 1 team was accused of sexually assaulting an innocent young girl. Everyone wanted to know what the guy's fate would be. Well actually they did not care about the guy, he is just another black male athlete who got caught and finally the school is going to stop protecting beast like these. Excited that girls are speaking out, with the "me too" and "times up" movements, more girls on campus are feeling empowered to tell the truth, and we believe them. It is time these creeps get put away for life....

However, they weren't sure of the possibility of justice prevailing in this one. The school was known for protecting their athletes, letting them get away with almost all their misbehavior. Just last month the school had gotten into a scrap with the local law enforcement agency because they were casting doubts on the school's ability to adequately address cases of sexual assaults on campus. So who was to say that this guy was not going to get away with it?

The good thing however for those who wanted to see him get punished was that the District Attorney office was becoming increasingly tired of the misconduct of these athletes. Although DA was an alumnus of the school, he was known for his strict stance on crime and for his intolerance for the frequent misbehavior of athletes. Any guy who thought that being on the basketball team gave him the right to do whatever he wanted with whoever he wanted was in for trouble as the DA was sick and tired of this conduct and his constituents expected him to be tough on crime, and he was not going to let his constituents down. He was going to make sure guys like this one didn't get away with it. I learned through this process that public opinion is critical to all politicians especially with the pressure of Believe the Woman front and center, though it would be difficult for any politician involved in this case to not have that in the back of their mind.

The courtroom was packed with media people long before the accused was brought in. He was dressed in orange, with his hands cuffed and his face screaming out his fear. Surprisingly as his eyes darted around the court, searching the mass of face for a familiar one, he didn't look like the predator described by the stories making the rounds. He looked like what he was... a frightened kid looking for his mommy amidst the many hostile faces, faces of those who were here to see if he was going to go to jail where they would throw away the key. He saw her in the midst of the haters, just before he sat down at the defendant's table. Although he had intended to smile for her, to show her that he was holding up alright, he found that his face was frozen and his eyes wide with fright. Having spent the night in an alien environment where he had been locked up like an animal, he was disoriented, and the cuffs on his wrist did not help this feeling. So, he sat like a lost person, feeling utterly powerless and having to deal, on his own, with the bitter taste of defeat on his tongue. The Assistant DA and his attorney conferred and agreed.

The proceedings began, the room went silent, all you can hear is the camera flashes, reporters taking notes, but no one was talking. Then the Assistant DA got up to make his case;

"Your honor," he said. "We feel based upon the defendant's lack of a criminal record, and that he comes from a stable home, where his parents own their own home and a local business that he does not present a flight risk. We ask the court if he could be released without bail until we are ready to set a trial date."

Still, the room was quiet...

The judge took a while to review the arrest document. As she did, her face revealed what her judgment was going to be. It turned beet red as her eyes ran over the words on the pages.

"Absolutely not," she said, glaring at the defense attorney. "Bail set at $10,000 cash."

Brian's world came crashing down around him. As the press went into a frenzy trying to get a glimpse of his reaction, and that of his attorney who expected the lenient judge to be reasonable, Brian felt his head spinning out of control. He couldn't imagine having to spend another night in jail. His mother had promised he was going home with her today. What was happening? As he was being taken away, he turned to look at her with fear in his eyes. What he saw stilled the storm raging inside him. She sat there with the calmest look on her face, looking unruffled as if the drama that was playing out before her was just that: a drama. That alone told him all he needed to know: it was going to be alright. She would not fail him, she had never failed him. Since she said that he was going with her that day, he knew that he would not be sleeping in the jail that night.

It was as well that Brian did not have the power to read minds else he would have given up all hope. His mother's mind was churning with so many thoughts that maintaining her poise was tough. On the inside, it felt as if her world was falling apart and everything she had was being taken away from her. Sitting there watching as her son was being taken away by a beady-eyed deputy without being able to do anything was the most difficult thing she had ever done.

Totally oblivious of the true state of his mother's mind Brian thought about the girl who lied. The moment she entered his mind, confusion followed. He could not for his life think of a reason why the girl would want to get him into trouble. All through the night, he had thought about it, going through everything that had happened; from the moment he met her for the first time to the time he was arrested in the dorm. Now as he thought about it again for the millionth time, he failed to arrive at a reasonable explanation for her behavior. However, a comforting thought that was borne out of common sense quietened the turmoil in his mind.

I know this is a misunderstanding somehow, he thought. *Jane will undoubtedly come forward and tell them the truth. She can never say such a lie.*

He gave the courtroom one last glance before he was led out of it. At some point, all of these people gathered here to watch him suffer for a crime he did not commit would get to know that he was innocent, then the smirks and the condemning looks on their judgmental faces would be wiped off.

ALL YOU HAVE IS FAITH...

The Friday before the Saturday I saw my son, Brian, got arraigned in court for rape, I was as carefree and happy as any other woman. It is disconcerting how a single phone call can completely ruin a perfect day. I was in the parking lot, walking to my car when the call came in. It was from Brian, my son. Like any mother who knows her child the moment I heard his voice, I could tell that something was wrong. He sounded like he was going to fall over at any moment. My bones were chilled.

"Brian, you alright?" I asked.

"Ma, I have been arrested." My boy said.

I could hear the fear now. It was as if my son was drowning in hot bubbly lava of terror. Like most kids his age, he was tall and strong, but you would know the kindness when he spoke and how he treated people. I could not think straight immediately. The first thing that shot into my brain was that my kid was black. He was black. He was... then I made myself stop and brought the phone back to my ear. Panic was quickly spreading all over me, so I had to struggle to bring myself under control. When a mother's child is in danger, it is usually almost impossible to think straight. This is your life we are talking about; the kid you've dedicated nearly two decades to, your pride. My head was beginning to spin, but with a force that came out of nowhere, I made it stop and tried to concentrate. I couldn't be of any help to him if I allowed hysteria to take over. So I asked him in a voice that was as controlled, deliberate and neutral as I could make it "What?!!!"

"I dunno," he said shakily. "They came up to my room this morning to pick me up. I had just returned from class, and I took some Dayquil and laid down because I was not feeling well. They knocked on my door. I woke up and opened the door, and they said I was the one they were looking for. They said they wanted me to come with them to answer some questions, so I did mom. They asked me a bunch of questions, I was respectful and cooperative, and then they just cuffed me and said a girl said I raped her and they believed her."

The word hit me with the power of a freight train. Rape? Brian? I could not believe it. For the next few seconds, I could not speak. It felt like the breath had been knocked out of me. I was so shocked that I didn't hear him calling me initially. But then his weak, scared voice broke through the wall of my thoughts, and my heart followed, breaking into a million pieces. The police station was not a place to be, and if he had been there since morning, I knew he must have seen hell or what looks like hell to him. There had never been a reason for him to be there. He was a typical teenage boy, fun loving, popular because of sports, happy go lucky and innocent, I was sure of that.

Why on earth was this happening to me? What was my offense? Did I commit a crime by giving birth to a black boy? If you've lived with skin like mine, sometimes it feels like carrying it is some kind of transgression. At that moment, I found myself wishing that this was a nightmare instead. As you know, more than any crime, a rape case is never good for the male, especially when he is black.

I said, Brian I need you to not say another word, not to anyone, did you hear me, not one more person. I am calling your father, and then I will be right over there. Not a word to anyone. Scared Brian said, "I have arraignment tomorrow morning by 9am ma, please be here." I will be there tonight Brian, just sit tight, I will be there tonight.

When I started the drive upstate, I had just one thought on my mind. I did not consider the possibility of returning without him that night. I knew he was innocent but did not know how I was going to prove it. All that I focused on was bringing him back the next day. No mother who truly loves her child can rest easy when he is spending the night in a dark, dank cell where he is locked up like an animal and dressed in some jail uniform. No matter how hard I tried not to, I couldn't stop myself from imagining Brian in one, walking with shackles on his leg, with the other inmates, as they lined up for food. This thought made me sick to my stomach.

The 3 hours it took me to get there seemed like a blur. It was more like I crawled more than I drove. My foot was always on the gas pedal, and my hand on the horn as I sped down the highway. I recall being in a state of terror all through the drive, worrying that something terrible would happen to Brian before I got there and wishing that there was a way, I could teleport myself to that place and save a lot of time. Then I began to pray and sing so I could take my mind off my worries and focus on God's capabilities. I had to because worrying was not going to help me, and it also wasn't going to help my son, only God could.

When I got there, I wondered if they would let me see him. Inside was warm, so I absent-mindedly registered the fact that the air conditioning was not on or was broke. I approached one of the officers and greeted him.

"Please, I want to see my son," I said. He looked at me like he didn't hear me, and I wondered what he saw. Just another black mother who was scared about losing her son to a justice system that hates anyone accused of rape immediately without any evidence or yet another black woman who looked tired and frustrated from driving hours to see her son in a police cell for the first time? Both did not actually make me happy.

"What's his name?" He asked as he typed what I assumed to be passwords into a computer.

"Brian Jones, a student of the university here," I explained. He nodded slowly as I looked at the nameplate on the table. I watched as he typed my son's name into the computer. Then he nodded and raised his head. With a disdained look he told me to wait while he made a call.

It took a while before I was led to a room with chairs and a glass wall dividing the room. He told me to sit and wait. I could not relax since I didn't know what to expect. As I sat there resisting biting my nails, I found myself reminding myself to breathe. The molecules in my body were hyper, and I couldn't help it. Then he came out. I could not believe it. My son looked like he had been crying for so long. His eyes were now tired and had sunk deeper into his face. He sat slowly, with his eyes on me, squinting because the lights hurt his eyes. He was silent for a few seconds, and I let him. I put my hands on the glass separating us wishing that I could touch his face, hold him in my arms and not let him go.

But he looked like an injured deer, looking at me. Then he began to cry, a deep hurt kind of cry, an exhausted, disbelief kind of cry. I could not tell if it was because my son found himself in a place where he would never think he would be, or in a position that he knew caused me pain seeing him in a place he never thought he'd find himself in. But soon he was quiet, and then he said something so faint I almost didn't get it.

"I'm sorry, ma" he had said. And my heart exploded. "I do not know why I am here, ma," I told him not to speak about it. I said, let's pray. I do not remember what the prayer was other than we started with praising God. We sang a worship song, I remember that. I wanted him to learn it, I needed him to focus on it, I love you, Lord… And I lift my voice... To worship you oh my soul, rejoice... take joy my King in what you hear, let it be a sweet, sweet sound in your ear, let it be a sweet, sweet sound in your ear. I assured him that he will be going home with me the next morning, I just needed him to pray, to praise God and to know that I will be sitting in my car parked outside praying and praising God with him all through the night. All he can say is, "ok ma."

EXONERATION JOURNEY

Getting my son out of jail on bail was a hard-fought battle. It was as if everything was against me. I was required to raise $10,000 in cash, not bond. This was on a Saturday morning, upstate, two and a half hours away from where I live. To make matters worse, I do not bank with any local bank in the town, so there was just no way I could get the money needed to bail out my son. This was bad because I had assured him that he was going home with me that morning. Even when God intervened through JK helping him, to make money available for me on short notice, the officials in charge of the process became the stumbling block, telling me repeatedly that it would take a lot of time and that it would be better if I just waited till Monday. But I refused and waited it out. In the end, I got my son out and went home with him that day as promised Thank God.

But that is not the end of the matter for Brian.

The case brought him embarrassment and humiliation. His name was all over the local paper, the local tv stations, and even national stations. His hopes were crushed. All through this saga, he has always held firmly to the belief that the girl who accused him falsely of raping her would step forward and reveal the truth so that he can clear his name and put this nightmare behind him, but sadly until today that hasn't happened. Initially, after he returned home from the jail, Brian had been reluctant to unpack his things from the car due to his certainty that he would be back to school shortly. But that also did not happen, so after a month or so he unpacked. No other 4-year college would agree to take him and getting a job has been like the passing of a camel through the needle's eye... all because he was accused of rape, not because of any fault.

Naturally, he sank into depression because it looked like all the work he put in at school before this happened would go to waste. All the efforts he made to improve his grades and all the time he has put in towards becoming a better athlete had gone down the drain, just like that! Eating became difficult, and sleeping stayed far from him. No one remembered his good deeds of yesterday. Brian has many accomplishments, but the biggest joy he gives me is how many people will come to me and tell me how he did some act of kindness towards someone. And always he would keep quiet about it. Nobody remembers this anymore; all people do is just to troll him on the internet these days. There are a lot of comments from different people who do not even know who he really is describing him as a scumbag who shouldn't be part of the college community.

I had to help him find his feet again. Watching him spiral into depression was not easy for me, so I had to do something; convince him not to let his life waste away because of this. We must continue to fight. This matter is not something that will just go away. There is a lot of support for the woman or accuser on issues like this, and it doesn't help that my son is black.

There is the MeToo movement shaping the way people think in situations like this. This movement is so strong that no one wants to go against it, even if they see the possibility of a miscarriage of justice. The backlash that will come from going against the tide is too significant for some. So, whatever a woman says happened is what the mob will bully everyone to believe. Nobody wants to hear the male's side of the story. (The sign of a good attorney who unapologetically will tell you the truth and worst-case scenario even if not politically correct) ... I remember my son's attorney advising us a few days after his arraignment... he said this is not a good time for a man to face such charges, especially if he has black skin. The optics of a tall, muscular black boy and a short white girl... well, the odds are stacked against him. And then even if he emerges victorious, everything just ends there. Nothing happens to Jane Doe. There is no retribution for the false accusation. His case was typical 'he said she said,' so chances are a plea will be offered, and we should consider it. This is the conversation we were having, *pre-DNA* results. Why should we plea? Because if he loses, twenty or more years of his life will be spent behind bars. The situation is bad for the male, it is too risky. Therefore, we should endeavor to also listen to the male's side of the story. We should not sacrifice the innocent people along with the guilty just because we are trying to support women. You would think *post-DNA* results that help the male would exonerate him.... nope... the girl refuses to rescind her claim because she faces going to jail for lying to law enforcement and the force of the Public Opinion is a mighty force that gives any or at least a lot of politicians pause in standing up for justice. The push back from their constituents, with the mob ideology of the "MeToo" and "TimesUp," can be career ending. This movement ideology is that women have been abused for so long, that if a few innocent men get crucified in the process, that is fine... just collateral damage! Do they truly believe that? Then why aren't their innocent fathers, brothers, sons, and friends turning themselves in? Innocent males who are in support of this ideology would be turning themselves in and volunteering to go to jail for 20 to 35 years in support of women who have been wronged for years. That sounds ridiculous, right?

Through my experience, I can identify with women who have been abused at one time or another in their lives. My mother was abused by my father, both physically and verbally. This led to their separation when I was only three years old. Unfortunately, upon splitting with him, she ended up with a worse person; a functional alcoholic who beat and sexually abused her regularly. She also left him at some point, but not before his abusive ways had left deep scars on all of us. Now my mom runs the division for Domestic Violence victims for a nonprofit my brother founded. So, I understand the predicament of women who have suffered abuse. However, it is essential to place it in balance with the difficulty those who have been falsely accused find themselves in.

Justice should not be carried out at the expense of anybody, nor should it be made to favor anyone. The only focus should be on unraveling the truth.

I do understand and know that women get assaulted, abused and/or raped. I not only grow up in an environment where men and women both misbehaved, but I also grew up in a household where my mother was beaten and abused. I recall as a child my father being verbally and physically abusive towards my mom. I was not upset when they split, and I was only around 3 years of age. But even worse was yet to come, when the functional alcoholic man she moved in with that would beat her weekly. Many weekends, I would hear my mother asking, begging him to stop, yet still, he would beat and rape her, and she would try to console him in hopes to protect us. She finally did leave him, she just walked out with just us. We had nowhere specific to go to when my mother decided one morning to walk away, she just knew that she needed to because the beatings were getting worse and mother was afraid she may not wake up one day and who would take care of us. I remember the sigh of relief in her voice when we were standing outside near the building where we lived with this monster, and she was on a payphone calling the Picard family who offered to let us stay with them until she got on her feet. The feeling of relief, of hope… we were out of the woods by then… but depression kicked in for my mom. She struggled and coped by taking valium. She struggled so badly that at times she did not recognize us, her own children. She was physically and verbally abusive towards us. But all that came from the trauma she experienced through the abuse she endured. So, I know too well the plight of an abused woman. The impact upon her life and those she loves. Years later, my brother founded a nonprofit organization of which I am a board member, where our mom has a division for Domestic violence victims. To this day she helps women heal and get out of such situations. This has been part of my life through my mom. But I also know the other side of this. I did not raise my son to be an abuser. I was able to heal my relationship with my mom before having my son. We are great friends. Moving forward as a mother and, like many other parents, I am sure, giving Brian the care and support I did not have was important to me. Raising him up in a household where I did not abuse nor partake in drugs or alcohol was very important to me. Raising him in a home where healthy family values were modeled was important to me. Every male role model he was surrounded by showed respect, care, kindness towards women. His experience was not one where he would ever see as acceptable, for a man to raise his voice towards a woman, hit a woman nor mistreat her in any way. Also, supporting him in his music and sports pursuits, while attaining his education, was a priority for me. We would get up around 5:30am to go to the gym to work on his basketball for a long time. He started the AAU circuit as early as he could. He struggled with processing and comprehension in school so in an effort not to seem inadequate in front of his peers he would clown around. He was always known as kind and caring… and a peacemaker. Everybody knew him. Even when the opposing teams would be in town, not only would a lot of the opposing team players know him, but a lot of the parents of the opposing players know him and like him. He learned about options in life and to make decisions. Though he would not make the best decisions all the time, he was given the space to make mistakes. He grew up in a Christian home. He knew at an early age that there was no Santa Claus, that the purpose of Christmas was to celebrate the birth of Jesus. But he never blew his friend's bubble. He respected their belief system. We never celebrated Halloween, it's a pagan holiday, and we do not celebrate anti-Christian holidays. When it came to situations such as acceptable norms that are not consistent with who he is, he felt comfortable not feeling pressured. I remember one of his teachers in grade school had cancer. She was quite mean to him, at one point. He came home, complaining that it was getting a bit out of control. He learned she had cancer and ran into her. My son asked his teacher how she was feeling and prayed that she gets better. I did not know that from him. I learned that from her. She was surprised that he would care about her well being when she had been so mean to him. She saw his heart. It had no malice. Brian had many accomplishments, but the biggest joy he gave me is how much people would come to me and say that he did some act of kindness towards someone. He would never tell me... others would. It is just who he is... he did not expect any special treatment or acknowledgment from me or anyone for being kind to anyone, it is just who he is. This carried on into this incident with this young woman. It has taken him months to get angry at her. He truly believed she would come forward and tell them that it was a whole big misunderstanding between her and her roommate. He was willing to move on and go back to school. He had no ill feelings toward this girl. He is much nicer than I. I cannot say I felt the same way about her. But I did try to understand her level or lack of maturity. Hoping that she would someday own her lie, and correct it so that we can all move on. She has opted not to correct her error. But I had to forgive her. To help my son, I had to start by forgiving her. I had to look at what door he left open in the life that allowed him to get caught up in this mess. Even though he did not violate her, he could have avoided her altogether and never been caught up in her web of lies.

In paraphrasing, the District Court Judge F. Dennis Saylor noted in one of his deliberations, that whether someone is a 'victim' is a conclusion which must be reached at the end of a fair process, not an assumption which is expected to be achieved at the beginning.

I share our lives with you because though yes, there are many victims of domestic, sexual violence, there are victims of false allegations as well. Years past, it was difficult for women to speak out. So, if anything good has come from "MeToo" and "TimesUP," it is that women are speaking out. Women and men who have been violated, are feeling empowered to come out and tell their stories and, by telling their stories, others are being set free. Truth has a healing effect. But the extreme that believes the woman no matter what is a lie that has the potential to imprison not only the innocent but dilute the truth of real victims. That will set us back, and if that happens, people will have a hard time believing a woman or man who states they have been victimized because so many are falsifying that claim. I stand with any and all women and men that are actual victims. I do not consider it victim blaming to question what happened and get proof. Now that all are being empowered to speak up let's provide evidence. That is applicable in every crime, and this one should not be the exception. I know it is difficult for those cases of the past where a woman/man may have been too intimidated and or damaged to report or have proof, but having innocent people pay the price for that is unacceptable. We must begin to heal the past hurts by accepting certain truths. John 10:10 says that the thief comes to steal, kill and destroy. What is it that he is destroying? It is your peace, your state of being before you were violated... His goal is the condition you are left with after the assault/violation. The emptiness. If you do not know this, you will replace what was perpetrated with that person, with that incident, you will occupy that emptiness with the pain they caused which leads to fear, despair, insecurity, powerlessness. That is what that thief wants. Despair, uncertainty, and fear which handicaps you from becoming what you were called to be. That is why forgiveness is so important. Forgiveness is not for them, it is for you. By releasing this person, releasing the offense, you are releasing that person/incidence/the intent out of that space they violated that you continued to allow them to occupy. The best revenge, the best empowerment is that despite someone's intent to stunt you, to cut out of you, you are able to succeed. You must no longer give them more power over your life. When you were young as a child, or you may not have been young as a child, you just lacked the coping skills to deal with this intruder. Well speak up now and teach others how to see the intruder and how to stand up and fight that intruder and how to win against the intruder. We are no longer victims. We are strong enough to be vulnerable and not use anyone as a scapegoat. We do not need to perpetuate killing someone innocent to be empowered. If we do that, we are perpetuating an assault upon the innocent, we are then no different than those who did us wrong. I had to heal from what this young woman tried to do to my son so that I can help him recover. So that he can recharge his power supply again.

This incident has tested my heart, my faith, and my patience. Wanting to fight back and put this girl on blast has crossed my mind more times than I can count. But my focus must be my son's healing. We must exercise patience in God's timing. There is a reason it is taking the time that it has to resolve itself and I am confident that by the time book 2 is published, we will know. In the meantime, be encouraged for He has overcome the world. The thief meant to sift a lot of us, but God's word will prove the test of time. Let His healing power overwhelm you, take the reins and succeed, despite what they tried to take away from you.

Become a light so bright, that you empower others to avoid ever being a victim of this heinous crime of abuse whether it be sexual assault perpetrated upon you or being falsely accused. The foundation to mitigating and/or solving these types of crimes must be based on truth. A little lie, no matter how small, is like a drop of food coloring in a crystal-clear glass of fresh water. That drop can engulf the entire glass of water, infesting it with its hue. But the blood of Jesus cleanses us. His accomplishment through the cross cleanses us and makes us new again.

False Accusations: Why do accusers lie?

Researchers determined that false charges were able to serve three primary functions for accusers:

1- Providing an alibi
2- A means of gaining revenge
3- A platform for seeking attention

Accusers Who lied were also asked why they did it.
Spite or Revenge
To compensate for feelings of guilt or shame
Thought she might be pregnant
To conceal an affair
To test the husband's love
To avoid personal responsibility
Failure to pay, or extortion
Thought she might have caught a venereal disease
Wanting attention/sympathy
In my opinion, some are just bat shit crazy

THE JIG IS UP

Every experience in life provides an opportunity to serve. Here you have had a glimpse of Brian's story and, as the case is still pending, I cannot disclose the details of the case, but his situation is far from unique. It would be a disservice to just talk about my son's innocence, why some women lie, how public opinion is framed and providing cases after cases as to why our constitutional right for due process is becoming more and more critical, considering this crime without me also finding a way to serve and be the whistleblower. As parents and students graduating high school is a significant milestone to independence and going to college. We worry about the GPA, ACTs, SATs, community work, and extracurricular accomplishments... but absolutely none of that matters if you do not understand the anti-male climate our sons are going into when they go off to college. Not being armed with how this will go down, will render all this work, all these accomplishments useless for the rest of their lives. False accusations can potentially disgrace you for life, it can end your career, your livelihood, your credibility. So, this section is to address the possible doors you leave open which you MUST shut (boys and girls) to prevent ever finding yourself in the life-altering web of lies, and for parents ever having to endure this nightmare.

HOOK UP CULTURE IS A LIE!!!! Fathers and Mothers, you know that all it takes is for a soft wind to grace a boy's member and they get an erection. Equally, you know that the emotional maturity of a lot of our daughters can be a fairy tale at their young age. In my view, that is a cocktail called a disaster. For us to say that we, as women, can just sleep with a guy and have zero emotional connection to it, is a lie. Guys, if you honestly believe that you can have sex with a girl and think she does not want more than just a roll in the hay, that she is not looking for something more than you can give, you are delusional. Unless a woman/young lady, has been sexually abused, she does not have the frame of reference nor the capacity to detach her emotional need to connect from her body. For her, it is not a simple exercise of letting off some steam. I am going to say this TWICE: EVERY WOMAN THAT SLEEPS WITH A MAN WANTS SOMETHING. AGAIN, EVERY WOMAN THAT SLEEPS/HOOKS UP WITH A MAN WANTS SOMETHING. Men, your approach to sex should never be just to relieve yourself. AGAIN, MEN YOUR APPROACH TO SEX SHOULD NEVER BE TO RELIEVE YOURSELF ALONE. Let's go back to fundamentals. The man carries the seed.

Seed is supposed to be sown on fertile ground. If the woman you are looking to get involved with is not fertile ground, you have no business planting seed there. If she has thorny ground, she has the potential to hurt you. The purpose of your seed, men, is to add value to someone. Sow into their life to better their life, not to deplete from them. Ladies if your ground is arid or thorny, leave these men alone. Go deal with your issues and don't try to ruin others and invite others to your misery. We all have weeds, but for the seed to take root in our grounds, we must be able to heal our ground and provide the conditions whereby good seed can establish long-lasting roots.

In this day and age where kids meet through Instagram, easily exchanging contact information with a swipe of a finger... if a girl approaches you at a party, and without exchanging any information other than your names and the fact that you live in the same building, and in 15 minutes she is unzipping you and blowing you, she is telling you very clearly that she does not know her value. Therefore, you can easily have it without effort and without any investment from you. A girl like this is not a score, she is damaged goods. You, as guys, may lack the skill set to help her heal, so I highly recommend that you do not engage with her... flee before she touches your zipper. That 5 minutes of her engaging your member can cost you a lifetime of hurt. By the way, guys, if you did not ask this girl to help herself to your member and she did not ask if she could, she just helped herself, just because you relieved yourself does not signify you gave consent. Men are sexually assaulted by women all the time. It is proven that biologically, even when assaulted, you can experience a hard on and ejaculation. Don't let your biological response confuse you and the same goes for women.

Guys, you have seen famous athletes lose multi-million-dollar endorsements, get divorced, and miss out on raising their kids... all because of an indiscretion with a woman who did not know her worth. Her not knowing her value is not just a reflection on her but on you for not knowing to avoid partaking in her low self-esteem. Because I have a son, I do expect better... much better.

Step up your game guys. I know you do not mean any harm. But the biggest lesson you must learn about women is that they are not you. They have different needs than you. If they act like you, they have experienced some pain, and you better know what they are before you get involved, or you will pay the price of her pain with your life.

Ladies, it is not women's liberation to sleep around. Stop lying to men and most importantly stop lying to yourselves. You know every time you sleep with someone you are doing so for a myriad of possible reasons, and an itch that needs to be scratched isn't it. If you have been hurt or taken advantage of, let's support one another and heal. Carrying the hurt robs you from finding what you truly want. So, stop shortchanging yourself. Stop depriving yourself. Someone may have taken something from you, someone may have tried to hurt you, someone may have deceived you, but that is on them, their loss. Be the best you can be. Someone is out there that can and will see your value and want to share a beautiful life with you. The longer you wait to heal, the longer it will be before you meet that person.

WINDOW LEFT OPEN

So, parents, the conversations about the birds and the bees must be more profound. Must be about the truth as to who we are as men and women and our individual levels of development. How we cope, how we respond. Let's equip our kids with this earnest and honest truths so that they do not find themselves like a deer in headlights like my Brian.

As a parent, I did not have these conversations with my son in enough detail to prepare him for what was in store for him when he went away for college. I have since met a lot of parents and young men like my son, some have medicated their anxiety and depression with alcohol, with drugs and some have taken their lives. As a mother who is fighting for my son's life, I urge parents to start having in-depth conversations with your kids. Both boys and girls. It's a very tender age for them to cross each other at this level of immaturity that can have such a significant negative impact upon their lives.

The playbook as to how to ruin a man's life is not only on display every day, it is a written work of literature. Three tools, Allegations, Media and Authority. Combating this process will take the following:

Schools and Parents: Instead of spending so much time in gender identification in school-aged children, let's focus more time on the more in-depth talks about the birds and the bees. What is acceptable touching or not? Communicating in the home. Parents have the support to provide a safe environment to raise their kids and what to look at in predators. Having zero tolerance in misconduct by those in authority, teachers, etc. to establish order and being able to give kids a safe place to talk and develop. Most kids who are violated are engaged in school and with their peers and community. Balance in counseling. My pastor never counsels anyone without his wife or another person being present. That protects him and the person seeking advice. Procedures need to be established to protect all parties.

Stop the books of a damsel in distress and the prince that is going to save you. In fact, BURN those books. Women who learn how to defend themselves physically, who are strong enough to speak for themselves, never have to abuse that power, and rarely get abused. I do believe that women should bear arms.

Laws to change. Discovery laws must change, and Defamation suits must have longer statutes of limitations. In most States, a defamation charge only has a 1-year window. This should be unlimited, and the punishment should be equivalent to the purported allegation. This will discourage people from making false allegations. This will deter people from making allegations that have no evidence. Any party associated with a false allegation will be penalized for participating in perpetuating the falsehood. Allegations can never be anonymous. The days of leveraging the rumor mill (media) and the hero who needs to save the damsel in distress must end.

By having these more in-depth conversations with our sons / our daughters, we can begin to end the multi-billion dollar industry that's in place to destroy families. Do not be fooled, parents. This is not just about an isolated incident that solely hurts one family, there is a money-making mechanism driving this miseducation. Education empowers our families and is the only way to starve out those who are profiting from our pain and ignorance. Knowing the truth, helps us stop feeding this monster.

Healing can only begin with the truth. Not some form or portion of truth, BUT the whole truth. God promises healing and restoration. If we as women can heal, so can men. The fear mongering is a powerful deceitful tool based on a lie to rob you of what God has pre-purposed you to become. Let's seek the truth and restore our family back to the creator's design and participate in restoring order and healthy stable family life that will lead to success.

Flerida Santana Johnas, boasts 24+ years experience in analytical management and leadership. Flerida's career has been predominantly in the field of real estate finance, having worked with several banking companies. Her expertise lie in cultivating conducive business relationships and partnerships, the analysis and management of budgets and cost controls alongside credit, debt, and risk assessments. Aligning these factors with an understanding of business objectives, she has developed and led efficient, productive and cooperative teams during her career. In her current role she assists in the planning, funding and development of effective Public Private Partnerships and marketing models. Her extensive experience in Real Estate has positioned Flerida in spearheading major real estate development projects. Her passion still includes coaching groups as well as one on one in the field of real estate investing. In her circles she has been dubbed as "The Legacy Builder". Flerida is driven by the belief that she is part of something much greater than herself. Giving her the focus of the big picture while still being able to identify the myriad of moving pieces that help realize the bigger picture. Flerida also commits time to charitable endeavours which include, holding current position as treasurer of Community Empowerment Network Inc. an organization which provides a safe place for adolescent youth to congregate and engage in activities to prepare them for the 21st century, keep them off the streets, off of gangs and drugs; Board member of the IDA for Delaware County, NY who's goal is to enhance economic vitality throughout Delaware County. Board member of WilPau Foundation whose focus is Financial Literacy and Business development to impact communities nationally and internationally. In the past, acting as secretary of LADCE a non-profit organization that helps women starting small businesses, Board of Education Member of Stamford Central School and Board member of the Schoharie Chamber of Commerce.

CHAPTER 8

DESTINATION UNKNOWN
by
Dr. Leonora Muhammad, DNP BSN APRN AGPCNP-BC CCHP

BEFORE THE JOURNEY

Pow Pow Pow!! The sound of tires screeching, and the faint sound of cries are muffled through the window glass on a perfect sunny day. The blue skies and bouncy clouds were no indication that this day would yield any excitement as I lay on my bed unpacking items from my backpack. As I pull down on the metal window blinds to see what the fuss was, the curtains made the familiar cracking sound as it folded and dipped in the center, I could see someone laying on the green grass of the church lawn. As I hurry to put on my clear jelly bean sandals with the sparkles inside to get a closer look at the action, I hear my grandma yelled, "Chrissy, what is going on out there, get away from those windows, they out there shooting." As I quickly reach the top of the steps, I shout up to the ceiling, I think someone is hurt over the church lawn, I'm going to check it out. I quickly hop two to three steps at a time as I make my way to the bottom of the stairs. I open the screen door and try not to slam the door as I know I will not hear the end of it when I return. I run off the pouch as I start to see other people from the neighborhood head toward what they had heard as well. As I run across the intersection of St. Louis Ave and Bishop P. L. Scott, I start to listen to the cries for help from the girl that was shot and now bleeding from a single gunshot wound in her right upper thigh.

St. Louis Ave and Bishop P. L. Scott Ave are located in the center of the north side of St. Louis. This area is filled with duplex buildings not typically owned by the residents that occupy the space. My grandma has lived in this same house for thirty years so for the last eleven years of my life I have had the time to memorize every nook and cranny of the home and neighborhood. Our house is the second house from the corner across from Lively Stone Church in Christ, which automatically made you want to be on your best behavior having to live right across the street from "God." We have two big bushes that extend over the artificial green turf lined up the stairs that remind you of a baseball field's grass. In between a few of the houses, you will either see abandoned buildings that had at some point caught on fire, is vacant, or being used as a dope or crack house. Sometimes there is just an area of grass where the house used to sit, and us kids would use as shortcuts to the alley. You had to be extra careful though not to step on broken glass or needles as homeless folk, and drug users tend to use these areas as their shoot up spots. I am accustomed to the environment and know the ends and outs, dos and don'ts of the neighborhood. I know most of the people that live here, and when I see an unfamiliar face, I know that they are not from around here. They are here to buy drugs, or it's an undercover police officer waiting to kick somebody's door in.

For the most part, we did have some residents that took pride in caring for their yards and maintaining their property, but most of the yards were filled with dirt patches and babies running around with snotty noses and only a pamper on. I definitely passed the pamper stage, but my clothes were definitely in need of some styling upgrades. I am used to getting hand me downs from my sister and friends and of course the dreaded Veteran's Village or Goodwill. Mama did splurge at Grandpa Pigeons or Venture's when it was time to start school, so I can't complain. Today my outfit choice for after-school wear is my pink tank top with the matching pink and black biking shorts, coupled with my jelly beans. My hair is up in my signature ponytail. It was pressed like three weeks ago, so the beady beans were beginning to form at the base of my neck and around my edges, but I can get the gel out a little later, I need to see what the action is.

As I approach the young girl, I assume she has to be around seventeen or eighteen years old, I could tell because she had the same bamboo gold earrings my sister would wear, in which I was always told I was a little too young to have myself at the age of twelve. I move toward the girl not having thought out what I was about to do when I arrive at the scene, so I ask, "Are you okay?" She just grabs onto her leg and squeezes it tightly and reaches out toward me with her other arm. "Help me, they shot me." As I stand here in shock of what I was seeing, I could only think, I thought a bullet hole would be much bigger, as the bright red blood is dripping down her leg, settling in a pool at the top of her white ankle socks with a red pom-pom ball in the back. As I begin to yell out, everything will be okay, more people run up from behind me to see what was going on. I distinctly hear someone calling out that the ambulance is on its way, while other folks start to gossip about what they think is happening. "These old young gangsters trying to get somebody and done shot this poor girl." One lady stated. "It was probably them boys round the corner, down on Lincoln, they always out here doing stuff." It was typical for the neighbors to offer up their versions of the truth, and us kids would do the same thing when we got time alone.

My days are typically filled with coming home from school, dropping off the book bag on the bed, grabbing a snack from the refrigerator, or getting 2 dollars in food stamps to run to the corner store. After getting the snacks, next stop would be my best friend's house that lives across the street. With a family of 10 plus, including siblings and children, everyone on the block tends to gravitate toward this one house. The neighborhood people are always at their home, big family, great food, and you are guaranteed to get the real deal story of what happened while you are at school. I can't wait to get to my girl's house so I could hear, who fought who, who got beat up today, who was dating who, what such and such was wearing, and in today's case, who got shot today. It had become such a routine growing up on the north side of St. Louis, there is always something going on. But I was one of the odd kids in the neighborhood, bused to the south county through the desegregation program, a program that was meant to get inner city children integrated into the predominately white county schools in the north, south, and neighboring west counties of St. Louis. I am learning what it was like outside of the hood. I am being introduced to the world wide web, different books, single family homes, host families, and organized sports. Last week, I learned about keeping the earth clean, and I am confident that I will be teased back in the hood because I want to recycle. As I start to engage in time away from my neighborhood, I yearn the escape away from what I am used to and what I know about life and growing up. Outside of the hood, mama just put me in the Girl Scout church troop, which has been filled with camp visits, etiquette classes, fashion shows, and selling cookies. My mother, who is always working two or three jobs, fills my summers with sleepovers, day camp, and hanging out late. Even with all of that, I know what it is like to grow up poor, raised by a single parent, and the strife and struggles of the hood. It depends if the lights are on this month, or if we have to hit up the bath water on the stove, but we always improvise. We will make something out of nothing until we get a little money the next month. Sometimes we only have government cheese sandwiches, powdered milk, cinnamon butter, and sugar bread, or Roman Noodles to eat but we do what we have to do to survive. Today was no different, what was happening today, was just another example of everyday life on the north side of St. Louis.

While two grown men tend to the girl's wounds, I can hear the ambulance sirens in the distance, and the voice of my grandma standing on the porch, yelling, "Chrissy, get your butt back over here, right now." I am bummed because I cannot see any more action up close, I turn and slowly walk back across the street toward my house. As I approach the sidewalk, one of my neighborhood friends walked up. "Hey girl what happened." "Girl same old same old, drive-by shooting and girl got hurt. She shot girl, I thought her leg would be all busted open, but it's just a small hole on her leg. I bet it hurts like hell, the way she is screaming." "Okay, I'm finna go check it out," as my friend ran toward the corner. As I turn around to walk up the steps of the porch, my grandma, who we call Tine (short for Christine), was waiting with her hands on her hips.

Tine is that typical grandma, approaching seventy years young, strict to the ways of the deep south, makes sure you are respectable to all elders, engraining the "yes ma'am," "no ma'am" mantra into your brain. She doesn't tolerate much, but if you can get to her sweet side and break that exterior shell, she can actually be a kind person. "Now I don't know why you ran outta this house like that, being so noisy, you don't know what was going on out here. Now get your behind in this house." "Okay Okay, as I open the heavy black metal screen door with the gold mail slot. "And don't slam that door, and don't run up those stairs, you gonna wake Ms. Johnson." I mouth the words under my breath at the same time she said them because I had only heard that ten million times before. I run upstairs and back to my room, to finish watching from my window. I have the front room in the house after my brother moved away to live with this "baby mama," so I could see all of the action. I opened up the window and began to listen as the ambulance and police cars arrive at the scene. With all the commotion that's occurring today, I realize I do not want to be in the hood for the rest of my life. I have got to get out of here and do better.

HEADED TO THE AIRPORT

Living and being raised by a single parent, teaches me every day about independence. My father Ulysses was only really in my life up until I was five-years-old. If anyone has a twin, my father would be mine. He is short like me, average a good 5'5 feet tall with skin the same complexion like mine, ears that curl at the lobe, 3 winkles that form at the bridge of his nose, just like me and thick black eyebrows and eyelashes, that most women would pay a coin for nowadays. I remember living on Rosalee in a four-family flat and him walking me pass the Hostess Bread company to take me to school. I used to love the smell of freshly baked bread in the morning. It really smelled like donuts to me as they were my favorite when I was that age. My father has been a bus driver for years, sometimes driving the school bus. That's how my mom met him, and she states she has a thing for men in a uniform, so I guess that is how that connection started. Now I only see my father every once in a while, on a birthday or just randomly on the Bi-State bus as he is a bus driver. I actually noticed him the other day, and he promises to come to pick me up soon, but I have heard this before, maybe this time he will keep his promise.

My momma Linda is always leaving, at work, or coming back from work, so the time spent while she is away is at Tine's house, running the streets, or over my god sister's house. Most of the times, mama will drop us off meaning, sometimes she will take us, or sometimes it means getting a bus pass and catching the bus to Tine's house, so we could be "watched." Being watched in my book means running the errands, which includes going to "Maz" house, my grandma's best friend to pick something up, running to Regals Market to get hot head cheese, crackers, and Braunschweiger, running down the stairs to pay the insurance man when he comes. Most times if there was nothing to do, I will just rummage through the house looking for things to do or get into. My bedroom now used to belong to a woman, the old folk called, "Mongula." Mongula was my great grandmother's sister, so that would make her my great aunt. Mongula had dark mocha skin, a small, slender frame, the face of my ancestors who were slaves, salt and pepper hair that was always sticking from underneath the side of a fancy wig she was wearing. She was most flamboyant in style and her wild and crazy in her stories. She would tell us wild and crazy stories about her childhood and almost getting eaten by a fish while at Lake Oakachokee. When I think about it now, I realize that this behavior was just mild to moderate bipolar disorder mixed with a little dose of dementia. Nonetheless, I enjoyed sitting and listening to her speak.

My older brother Corey would come to inherit her room after she died, and he transformed it into a room full of rappers such as Ice Cube, N.W.A., DJ Quick, and sketch drawings. My brother lived in his room sometimes like a hermit just eating his bowls of rice and eggs and blasting music loud enough to have Tine hollering to shut up that noise over Ms. Johnson's head. He is the only person I know that is like me and keeps a fan in the window year-round. He is seven years older than me and likes to keep everyone out of his room with a flimsy keyhole lock on his door. Little did he know, I know how to unlock that door with a wire hanger and reconnect it all while he is sleeping. He is also fascinated with wrestling and the World Wrestling Entertainment or the WWE for short. Even though he is about 5'7 with a medium build, he often thinks he is Hulk Hogan and uses me as one his practice dummies, putting me in figure four, or doing a piledriver on me until I cry. Luckily, I haven't had to suffer from that now as he is now living with his girlfriend.

Occupying their old bedroom, I am fortunate enough to have all exclusive access to all of Mongula's wardrobe in the chifforobe which was left after she died. I play dress-up with all of the hats and clothes, except for the fur with the actual squirrel heads on both ends. I also find myself wandering down to my Aunt Sugg's old room, who was Tine's sister, to dig through her drawers as well. Today on one of my many explorations, I find some old notebooks. As I open them up to see what is inside, I see familiar eloquently scribed handwritten notes. They are written correctly between the blue lines on the white college rule paper. As I begin to read them, I realize they are my mother's old nursing school notes.

My mother Linda is a reticent, reserved and private women. She grew up the oldest of two children and raised alone by Tine after my grandfather fell down the stairs and broke his neck. She has features similar to her dad, as, during my random rummaging, I found an old photo to compare her to. She was tall to my standards, towering maybe 5'8 with dark caramel color complexion with a slender but medium sized nose, very comparable to her dads. She has a black raised mole near her upper right hairline, which I notice is a staple in our family history. Moles, all of the women in our family displayed random spots on their upper cheeks and forehead, and I have one growing on my right lower eyelid. Mama's scent smelled of Elizabeth Taylor's White Diamonds or one of the many fragrances from the Avon collection. My mom tries her best to provide for us three kids by working two jobs on time. She has worked for the Salad Bowl for a long time now, and her new job at the Science center allows me to get a big giant chocolate chip cookie when she arrives after work. We are living back with Tine for now, but we often move from house to house across town. It seems like we run about every year to year in a half or when she dumps her current low life boyfriend, and we start anew.

She never really speaks about her time as a certified nursing assistant or when she attended LPN school, but as I read the nursing notes, I began to get interested in what I am reading. The notes are filled with big words that I don't quite understand with only having a sixth-grade education, but I am doing my best to try to read through it. Up until this time, I have dreams of being a teacher and running my own classroom full of eagerly excited students. Taking care of people on a professional level never really crossed my mind before. I have definitely been used to taking care of my grandma and her friends but would I like to do this as a career. The thoughts began to swirl in my head, and I contemplate maybe this will be a second option.

About two years have passed as I grow to the tender age of fourteen, my godmother Dale who works at Jewish Hospital, tells me and my god sister Ne-Ne about the volunteer program they have at the hospital, it is called candy striping. What is a candy striper? I have no clue, but it sounds interesting. I am instantly interested in the idea of having a job, even though I will not be paid for my services. Nonetheless, I think this could be fun. Waking up on my first day and donning the bright red and white candy striping smock with the ties on both sides. We now live on the upper north side of St. Louis in the Walnut Park area of the city. It is very near to O'Fallon park on Holly Ave. O'Fallon Park is a hangout spot for the teenagers and young adults that have cars. My father and I, when I was about 5 years old, walked up on a dead body, so it's not the kind of park you want to be in late at night. The neighborhood was a little better then St. Louis Ave as these homes you can tell back in the day were homes that the upper class lived in before the migration of whites began, and they moved out of the city limits. There are less crime and gang activity over here, but you can still see a couple of wineos and pedophiles trying to holler at you as you wait on the bus stop.

    I have to catch the Lee Avenue bus to connect to the Kingshighway bus to get to the hospital. I am a master of catching the bus alone now as I have been traveling along for quite a few years at this point. Riding the bus down Kingshighway Blvd, I pass all of the typical landmarks that I had come to memorize as time passes as we approach the affluent neighborhoods. As the bus pulled up to the big hospital, I marvel at the fact that I would be working her for the summer. I enter the building and proceed to the volunteer office to receive my assignment. The lovely elderly lady who is head of the volunteer program, informs me that I will have a variety of jobs within the hospital that will range from working in the nutrition department, helping patients to understand how to make healthy food choices to working on the medical, surgical floor alongside the patient care technicians and nurses. I was a little apprehensive and nervous about working with the "professionals." I am always timid and shy as a person, and this experience is no different. Can I keep up with and understand what will be asked of me. I shall see. The first weeks start out high. I am learning all about nutrition, and I am scheduled to work with the nurses next week to help pass out food trays, empty and restock the linen closets, and empty bedpans.

    Working on the medical, surgical floor with patients is my favorite. I am fascinated being around the nursing assistants and the nurses because I really see how the care that is being provided affects the health of the patient. Sometimes when the nurses leave the room and during my rounds, I will conversate with the patients, and they always have nice things to say about how the nurses help them and teach them how to do something that they didn't know before. I see how families who were worried about their loved ones seek out the nurses for guidance. I want to be that person that patients search for, and I want to be that person that could comfort that patient when they were worried. I'm thinking now that maybe I could do this, I can be one of them.

    I did candy striping over the summer before high school, and now I'm ready to begin this exciting journey. My high school Bayless Senior High is small and has about 45-50 black students out of a total of around 200. I plan on making sure that I study hard and do well as I have always loved learning. So, I'm going to try to make this experience the best I can. I am so glad my girl bestie Taz is able to attend the same school as well. She has been my A1 one since she started at Bayless in the 6th grade. We are always hanging out after school, and we are trying out for the basketball team at the start of the season. I hope we get on the team. Taz and I always stay fly, rocking Your weave ponytails that we wet, roll and place in the microwave to dry. Don't ask how we learned to do this, but we did and can't forget about our signature swoop on the side as well. I start to notice we are getting attention from boys. The funny thing that cracks me up about boys is that they don't know whether to like you, talk about you because they want you or they are trying to fight you. But I am not about to pay them no mine, I just hope I get asked to prom, that's the one highlight on my list, but I have a couple of years to go.

We moved again recently, and now we are living on the other side of the northside on Page Blvd. This time we are right in the action of the neighborhood, as this is a bustling street. Our house stands out because it is a big red single family home, which my mother is renting. We really cannot afford to furnish such a big house, so we have no living room furniture in our living or dining room, but in our bedrooms, we have our belongings from the previous home. I tried out for the basketball team a few weeks ago and was picked to play junior varsity as a forward. I am only 5"3 inches tall, but I'm trying my best not to get bowed to much in the head as I go up for rebounds.

Sometimes after practice, I get off the bus over my bestie Taz's house and hang out with her until mama Joyce put me out. As we sit on the porch, roasting and talking about people, a light-skinned dude with gold teeth walks up trying to act cool. I look and turn around trying to ignore him as I just know he is about to come up on the porch to holler. "What's up shorties, yo Taz, who yo friend? "What up, Tony this Nony, as my bestie blasted out before I could stop her. "What up girl, you got a man? He stated. I look and roll my eyes, and say. No, I don't have a man, why? I am really not interested at this point, because I had my eye on the chocolate dude that just walked passed like 5 minutes ago and I had given my number to. He had golds too and was tall like I like 'em. "Well I'm trying to get your number, so I can call you to holler at you, is that okay, can I have your number? Reluctantly, I gave in an wrote my house number down on a piece of old homework paper that I had sitting nearby. "Nony huh, I'm gonna be calling you later, he smiled and smirked as he turned and walked off the porch. I end up dating Tony for about a few months before he gets jealous because I have another dude name Brandon whose name and phone number is written in my school planner. Tony gets mad and rips up my school planner and throws it in the street, grabbing me up by my shirt as my sister pulls up to pick me up in her brand-new Geo Metro. Now my sister Kim plays no games. She has always been tough, ferocious battles for girls in the hood, even got her head busted a few years back trying to help a neighbor from getting jumped. She is dark chocolate, 5'7 and weighs a little over 200 lbs. Folks would describe her as big boned, with the big booty that I never got. She always teases me and says I stood in the boobs line too long and she stood in the booty line to long. She is very accurate in that assessment as I dream for booty like hers. As she pulls up and jumps out of the car as she sees Tony and me arguing in the street. She proceeds to chase him down the street with a crowbar she found in the trunk of the car and yells at me to get in the car. As we ride down the road, I think to myself, this is the end of this relationship, I have school to focus on and not some boy that I didn't even like in the first place.

    Years pass as I manage to graduate on time although I contracted mononucleosis "the kissing disease" and was out of school for like 3 weeks, during my sophomore year of high school. Plus, that the fact that today I am getting suspended for 10 days for carrying a box cutter in my book bag. Everyone that lives in the hood has a box cutter, padlock, or knife in their book bag because when you get off the after-school bus, you never know who you will encounter. Teachers and principals really don't understand the danger that us young black girls and boys have to go through. Most times, we have to walk down derelict dark streets at night, wondering if a pack of stray dogs will be waiting for us at the next turn. Perhaps, a crackhead is waiting in the gangway of the house, looking to steal any valuables that you had on you at the time, or even the girl and her squad you pissed off the week before because she and her friends were jealous of the new gear you worked hard for at your part-time fast food restaurant job. Today, Principal Jose was actually looking for a butcher knife that my bestie had brought to school just in case some girl wanted to get froggy. He inadvertently discovers the box cutter during the random search of Taz's known associates. Once Principal Jose asks to look inside my bag, I don't worry because I know where the knife in question is actually hidden. As he dumps all of the contents on the table, I immediately see the box cutter that I actually had forgotten was in my bag, and he directly instructs me to head to the office. Once Principal Jose calls me into his office, he informs me of my 10-day suspension and the fact that I will need to attend summer school to graduate on time.

Having to go home and tell mama that I was now suspended for 10 days and that I needed to attend summer school is going to be the worst. But I have to do it because I am planning on being in the Co-op program where I get to go to school half a day and work the other half and to do that, I have to have a B average, and I am determined to get that. So, as I walk into the house, I creep up the stairs and head to my room. "Chrissy, come in here." I hear Tine calling from her room. As I approach the room, I realize that mama was there as well. I come into the room and sit on the couch that was adjacent from Tine's bed, which felt like you were under the spotlight similar to when police interrogate suspects for the crimes they allegedly committed. "So, what's this about you are getting suspended from school, and for ten days at that?" my mama asked. Guess Principal Jose beat me to the punch and called ahead of me making it home. "Well I had a box cutter in my bag, and he found it," I replied. As I sit there and listen to all the reasons why I am such a good student, and I'm better than this, this is not your speech, I am only thinking about the fact that I have to attend Beaumont High School, my mother's alter mater for summer school. I have never in my life had to participate in summer school, so this is entirely embarrassing as I have the 2nd highest GPA out of the black students at my school and 18th overall. Well, this is going to be an adventure as it's a public high school, which is primarily black and about 5 minutes walking from our house now. Dab smack in the hood, with fights and drama every single day.

The first day of summer school and I am huffing, puffing and pouting that I have to spend the next month going to school every day. I put on my green Tommy Hilfiger shirt with the red emblem and Guess blue jean shorts along with my white K-Swiss tennis shoes. I have to look fly today are I will definitely get talked about in this school. Even +though, here we go again with the hand me downs from 2 seasons ago, I still had to wear some type of brand-named clothes to fit in. I get my paperwork and walk down about 6 blocks to Natural Bridge. Beaumont, the home of the Bluejackets, sits right on the corner of the street across from Fairgrounds Park. The structure is massive with 1920's brick architecture. It sort of reminds you of a huge castle, and it has a track behind the building. As I walk up the massive set of stairs in the front of the building, I approach a metal detector. I am definitely not used to this in the county schools. As I pass through and proceed down a long wide corridor, I begin to see the other students. Wow, a sea of blackness. Everyone is sharply dressed, with creases down the front of their starched jeans and hairstyles that are unique to African American culture. I really have never seen a student body of all black students, as I have been going to Bayless since the second grade.

Talk about culture shock, it is an entirely different experience to what I am used to. I do not know anyone, and everyone is staring at me like I am from another planet. I'm taking a writing course as my summer class, so this should be a breeze. I walk to my first class and find a sit. As the teacher begins to give us a quick lesson on writing 101, I look down and notice the textbook that has been distributed. The book is in poor condition, with gang writing throughout the pages. Some of the pages are missing, and when I look at the copyright date, I notice these books are over 10 years old. Matter of fact, this book I know is on the level of books I studied from in sixth and seventh grade. Why are these students so behind? No wonder why nobody makes it out of the hood, look at what we are learning from. This is another classic example of why I am going to try my best to pass these summer classes and get on to my senior year of high school. I am so disappointed in the teachings of my people, and I feel sorry for anyone who attends this school on a regular basis. The news surely doesn't tell you this side of the story.

CHECK YOUR LUGGAGE

It's graduation, and I am super excited, I finally decided to start classes for nursing school. I am enrolling in Forest Park Community College, and I start the prerequisites classes like English, communication, and college algebra. As an average teenager, I am so pressured to hang out, party, get into trouble, basically anything besides studying. But I really need to stay focused because I have about 3 classes this semester to take. I decide to go check on Tine and see what she is up to today. As I jump out of the car, rocking my long weave ponytail, yellow halter top, and black pants, I walk down the sidewalk headed for the porch. I suddenly hear a loud voice scream, Noooooooonnyyyyyy." I look in the street as a car pulls over to the side, as I look a little closer, I can see Tony, my ex-boyfriend hanging out of the window. The car pulls over at the corner, Tony jumps out and heads toward me. "What's up, Nony, where you been a girl? Now I have not seen Tony since my sister was chasing him down the street over four years ago. I say, what's up to Tony, why you out here calling my name like you crazy, what's up with you?" "Nothing, I am trying to see what's up with you, now you know you have to give me your number again, I'm sorry about what went down back in the day," He says. I roll my eyes, and said: "Sure you are, I wasn't even talking to the dude." "Well give me your number so I can call you." "Well I don't have a pen, so you better remember it. If it's meant to be, you will remember it. So, I gave him the number. As he mumbles and repeats the number to engrain it into his memory, I see a girl jumping out of the car yelling and approaching us. "Just what do you think you out here doing, got me pulling over for some girl. "Who is that," I ask. "Oh, that's my baby mama Renee." "Oh, you have a baby now, wow, well you better go then, she pissed," I smirked. She proceeds to march up to him and slap him on the side of the head and start to drag him by the shirt back to the car. "You better come on now, or you gonna be walking home, she screams. I just stand on the sidewalk shaking my head, then I yell, "Bye, Tony," as I turn and walk up the steps. "I'ma call you, Nony."

Tony holds his word, and we start to date again. Why am I even giving him a second chance, I have no clue but let's see how this goes? As I begin to go through community college, my mom gives me $1100.00 in tax money for me to get my first brand new car. I pick out a 1999 Chevy Cavalier with 11 miles on it. I am living life. Eighteen with my own car, can we say balling. Life is good, but I recently got word that Tony is talking to some other girl that I had ever heard of before. I learn of this through a co-worker that is dating Tony's brother.

Now I always give people the benefit of the doubt and try to listen to both sides, so I really didn't want to believe this girl. She has a whole boyfriend that is locked up currently, and really haven't got the entire story about what he is in for. So why should I listen to her? I am careful to her, and I pick her up every day for work as her car is down. She started dating my boyfriend's brother for a while, I am really trying to be careful with listening to who is bringing me information. But still, I am confronting him about this soon as I get off of work. As I head home to the southside, I try calling his phone, and he picks up after a few rings. "You need to come over after I get off of work because I have to talk to you." "Aight, I will be over there a little later."

So, I get home a little bit after 5:30 because I make a few stops before I head back. Tony pulls up around the same time but in an unfamiliar white Malibu. "Well, who car is that," I ask. "It's my baby's mama, she let me borrow it." He quietly says. "Well, why would she be letting you use her car, and by the way, I heard you have been talking to some girl anyway, what you got to say about that. As we go back and forth, with nothing but lie after lie coming out of his mouth, I finally yell, "Well you need to get your clothes and that car and get the hell out of here, go live with that girl," I screamed. "Well while you are talking, my brother said you been calling him, and he implied yawl did something." What, you need to get the hell out of here, your brother, please, you just trying to say anything to get out of this mess you in." I ain't never looked at your brother in any kind of way." Your brother called me and asked me if I wanted to plan a birthday trip for you to go out of town, and we met up to work out the details, at no time did I ever try to flirt with him or anything," I stated in such disbelief. At that moment before I could get another word out, Tony grabs me up by the shirt and pushes me into the wall. He attempts to choke me, but I am able to free myself loose. I see the same look in his eyes that he had the day he tried to fight me in the middle of the street. But this time, his eyes were a little darker and a little colder, and I can see a tear welling up in the corner of his eye. I guess the anger of thinking that I could betray him with his brother was just too much to bear and he is losing it. At this very moment, I see a little bit of hurt in his face. But why would you think I could do such a thing, and by the way, you are the one I heard is cheating, how did this get turned around on me.

As I struggle to get away from him, out of nowhere, I feel a sudden sharp pain and the warm feeling in my right eye. Did he just hit me, oh hell no, I'm thinking, did he just hit me, how can you do this I and I love you, I am a good person, I don't have it in my heart to cheat and especially with your brother? At this moment, I feel ashamed, like I did something wrong when I know I did not. Did I say or give off the wrong signal during my discussion with his brother? No, I did not, but now I am second guessing myself. How can a man that claims to love you possibly be the same person to harm you? All of this is pouring through my mind at this very moment. At this point, the words that are coming out of his mouth are muffled, and playing without sound, as I just see the anger, hurt, and aggression playing out in front of me. It's reminding me of a horror movie when the person is dreaming or running through the woods, trying to get away from the killer, trying to scream but no one can hear you. Then you wake up, but I'm still here.

I immediately grab my face and start to cry, over and over I yell out, "you just hit me, you just hit me, you just hit me, let me go. I'm out of here. I grab my purse and keys from the countertop and head for the door. "You ain't going nowhere, he yelled. He lunges and blocks the front door. "Look you better move, or I'm calling the police," I said calmly. As he moves slowly away from the door, I walked past him and headed for the car. I jump in and pull off as fast as I can. As I drive around town for over 4 hours, it begins to rain.

I circle the same streets over and over as I am lost in transition. Every thought is looping through my mind right now as I have never been hit purposely by a man. Tony may have grabbed me and pushed me, but he has never blatantly hit me before. The tears begin to stream down my face as I think about what I want to do next. I don't really want to call my sister because I know she will want to kill him. I don't want to invite my friends as they will want to do the same. I am a big girl I will handle this myself because I am healthy and very independent. But I still love him, I don't want to be alone, but I also don't want to be pounded on either. As I turn down a quiet side road, I pull over and park my car. I take a look in the mirror, and my reflection shows the soft tissue swelling that has formed around the base and side of my eye. Red, bluish color is starting to develop, and I know tomorrow all of my problems will show their selves. What am I going to do now? I have to work, and I don't want to call off, but I am not going to worry about that now. I am tired, exhausted and alone. As I lay my seat back as far as it can go, I turn over nestled in my plush seat and cover myself with a jacket. I stared at the window as the raindrops hit the window, connecting with existing sprinkles and slide down to the edge of the glass. The sound of the raindrops hitting the hood of the car is soothing, and it's my only comfort now as I close my eyes to escape from the nightmare I can't wake up from.

Over the next few years, I continue to work on a relationship with Tony. I've been dealing with a few other side women and a couple of his baby mama drama situations mixed with a few good times and vacations with fun. But I am growing tired of the back and forth and obvious jealousy that this man continues to show. My family and friends tell me I should leave him alone, but all I want to do is help him. His father was a cheat, and his mother is sensible, but growing up in a harsh and wild environment does not lead to a stable individual. Plus, I need to get through nursing school, and I do not have time to be dealing with this type of drama in my life. I am just ready to get started with my nursing career before I end up being a baby mama just like Tony's other 3 kid's mothers. I refuse to have that label, so I think I want to withdraw from community college and go into an LPN program, that is only 14 months. This is the quickest way to get my life back on track and give me more focus and stability.

Over the next 2 years, I study hard struggling even to find a way to get back and forth to class. My car was repossessed last month because I couldn't keep up with the car note payments and Tony is little help. He works odd jobs here and there but none that last more than a few months. To make it through school I have to work 40 hours a week from Friday through Sunday, all while I attend class Monday-Thursday. On most occasions I wake up at 4 am to catch the first bus because I have to be at work at 7am, then I transfer to the metro link light rail train, then to the small local bus to the nursing facility where I work. Rain, sleet or snow, I push through. I have to. Getting to class is no different. I bummed rides from friends, borrowed cars, caught buses to the commuter parking lots and walked to school. I am determined, and I am not going to give up.

Dang, it, I'm running late to work, I cannot miss this day of work because my rent is due, and I need this shift to add the last two hundred to the lease. What am I going to do, I can't catch the bus because it will take me over 3 hours to get there by bus. Tony is not going to make me because his tags are not right on his car. Oh, I can call Burton he works with me, and I can ride with him and his mother to work, I am sure they have not left out yet. So, I call Burton to see if I can bum a ride. He agrees and states he will be there in about 15 minutes. As I continue to get ready for work, I look out the window and see Tony pull up. He walks in and asks, "What you still doing here, you should be gone already." "I woke up late, and so I asked a coworker to ride with him and his mother," I said. "So, you are just going to call another dude to take you to work, you don't call no other dude to take you to work.". "Well you can't drive me, and I need to work this shift." As I say this, I look and see Burton pulling up, and he honks the horn. I turned and said, Look, I have to go, I'm going to be late." Before I could grab my bag, Tony runs out the door and starts to argue with Burton. I hear Tony cursing and going off, but Burton stays calm.

"This is my co-worker and his mother, what is the big deal?" As Tony begins to get louder and louder making a scene where people start to look out the window, I wave to Burton to just go. "Are you sure, you want me to go?" "Yeah man, just go, he is acting a fool" "Yeah you better go and get out of here before I whoop your ass," Tony yelled as he jumps in the driver side of his car and drives off. This is the last straw as I cannot take this behavior anymore, I am about to become a professional nurse, and I cannot be surrounded by people that don't have my best interest at heart. I guess it has taken me this long to be at my breaking point, but I am here now, and I need to focus on myself and not others for once. I need to succeed if I want to do better and be better.

Today I reflect back on the first day of school when our instructor told us, this will be the hardest next 14 months of your life. You will be tested, and most of the people sitting around you will not graduate with you. And these same instructors proved us true. We started our class with 38 and ended with 18 students graduating. Nonetheless, I am one of those students that have pushed through all the reading, quizzes, clinical rotations, and final exams. I forced myself harder then I knew I could be driven. And today I graduate with a high GPA, and I take my boards on Friday to become a licensed practical nurse. I am officially going to be a nurse now.

PRE-CHECK PLAN

This night shift started like any other shift. Getting in the car, putting the music on, pulling out of the driveway and beginning the familiar routine of left and right turns, until I reach my destination. Sometimes you never really realize how you got to where you are going, you just know that when you look up, somehow your internal navigation got you there. This drive is not any different.

At this time, I have been a nurse for about two years and had worked primarily in skilled nursing facilities. As a nurse, I always have had a passion for working with the geriatric population. In elementary school, there were memories of being a part of the school choir and taking a field trip to the community nursing home to sing Christmas carols to the grandmas and grandpas. Their friendly smiling faces were so warming, so how could you resist being around them and helping to care for them. Not to mention, I had a grandma that had older friends that always needed something from the corner store, so my outdoor play consisted of "Run around to that store and get us lunchmeat, here's the money and bring my change back." Often times I would be allowed to get a dollar worth of penny candy for completing the task. I was ecstatic about that and my friends that ran with me too.

    These memories lead me to start working at one of the largest skilled nursing facilities in town. I have always heard that working for Laclede Groves would be great. They care about the residents, and it doesn't smell of urine when you open the door. I sign up to work **PRN** at this time because there are no other available open spots. As I fill out my application, the human resources rep let me know they have plenty of shifts to pick up, so I should be fine. Well, this will work because it will allow me to have the flexibility to work in other areas of nursing as well, I thought. As I enter the building to start my shift this particular night, I thought to myself I really do need a full-time job, I have bills to pay. But for now, I just want to make it through this shift, as nights are not my preference.

    I approach the second floor of the building to clock in and check in with the shift supervisor to receive my assignment. The nurse supervisor is new to the position and always looks scattered brain and tonight is no different. "Well, girl, you are working 2 East tonight, with Erica." She stated as she looked down on her clipboard that held the schedule. The schedule always had a bunch of red lines and scratches on it from all the call off's and assignment changes. "2 East, great the Medicare floor, what a surprise, I always get this floor when I am dog tired and really just wanted to have an easy night, like when I work on a wing like 3 West. "Well, whatever!! I thought to myself, at least I was working with another good nurse.

    As I walk up the stairs to the second floor, I approach the huge heavy metal doors. I enter the security code on the keypad next to the door. All the floor levels have code systems as some residents tend to want to escape their living conditions and get back to the life they have always known. I open the door and take a right turn at the dining room area. I walk through the long dark hall as after 10 o'clock all the lights in the hallway are turned off. The walk always reminds me of my one of my favorite horror movies, Halloween, when Laurie Strode walks down the darkened hospital hallways wondering if Michael Myers was going to jump out at any time with a knife. I approach the nursing station and find the outgoing nurses flipping charts closed and preparing to give a report on their patients. I see my partner in crime for the night, and she smiles as I walk up to the desk. We count narcotics with the other two nurses that are leaving and say goodbye for the night. Continuing on to my assignment, I complete the typical nursing duties of making rounds on the patients, checking in the medications, preparing the treatments for the night, transcribing any leftover medication orders, and restocking supplies. I head to the nurses' station to finish my charting and chit chat with my coworker Erica, thinking to myself it's time to relax until the next unexpected patient who crawls of bed makes their approach to the nursing station.

As the night progresses, Erica and I exchanged stories. I mention to her that I am looking for a full-time job to have consistent and steady hours. Erica states "My other job is looking for some nurses to travel to prisons and see patients and they are paying big bonuses too." Puzzled I said, "Girl what the heck you do as a nurse in the jail." "Girl, it's easy money, we pass out medications, see them for sick call, and make sure they detox off of the drugs." Intrigued, I thought, this sounds interesting, maybe I will check it out. Erica writes down the website for me to check the company out, Correctional Medical Services. Huh, never ever heard of it before. Sounds like another agency to me, but maybe this is something that might be worthwhile. A few days later, I look up the website online, and it states, hiring full time, part time and PRN nurses to work at the Workhouse and the Criminal Justice Center. I definitely heard of the workhouse before as my ex had been there before and I had brought his son up there to see him. I haven't realized that they had nurses working there. This should be interesting, I thought. It takes me over 2 months to finally make the connection with the company. I am calling and leaving messages for the director of nursing and those that answer the phone tell me the same message. "She will give you a call when she can." I continue to wait patiently but continue to pick up extra shifts at the nursing home to make ends meet. I am very persistent as I learned back in my high school co-op class, keep calling, it shows how interested you are and how committed you are to the position. While sitting at home the following weekend, the phone rings. "Yes, this is Sharon from the workhouse, we would like to schedule you for an interview for an LPN position here. Are you available next week to come in?" "Sure, I am," as I smile on the other end of the receiver. Sharon gives me the address and contact information. I am excited, a new experience. I don't know what the next step will be, but I am sure it will be an adventure. I will just have to see.

BUCKLE YOUR SEATBELT

As I pull up to the jail, flashbacks to prison movies filled my head. The Green Mile, the Wire, what am I stepping into? As I approach the front door for my interview, I feel prepared, dressed in all black, trying to look unfazed by the environment around me. The sounds of keys are jingling, walkie-talkies making the staticky sound, and big metal doors slamming filled the air. As I sit in the blue metal chairs, I really don't know what to expect. How would this interview go? Would it be the typical standard interview questions? What are your strengths and what are your weaknesses? I run through the answers in my head. I prepared last night, so they are still fresh in my memory. As I get to what my weaknesses are, someone yells "who is here for medical"? I raise my hand and proceed to the officer's desk. "Through the medical detector ma'am," the officer barked. Here we go again, the metal detectors, it reflects back to the experience at summer school. It's hard not to notice the similarities to school and now prisons. Are they preparing you to what you will become accustomed to in the future? I sure as heck hope not, but you have to wonder sometimes. I step up to the metal arch and walk through. "Beeeeeeeep," the machine sounded. "Step back through ma'am, did you lock up everything in the lockers as we told you to," the officer replied. "Yes, I did, maybe it's my belt," I stated. "Walk through again." "Beeeeeeeep," the machine sounded again. "Come on through, face away from me and arms out to your side." The officer uses the wand to scans me down to make sure I did not have any contraband, like drugs, cigarettes, or money. "Turn toward me ma'am," she stated. As she wands me down near my stomach, the wand alarms. "Lift up your shirt." It was my belt. "Okay ma'am, you are good" the officer rolled her eyes and went back to her position behind the desk. The lady in the scrubs motions for me to step to the metal door and we walk through two sets of big doors, both slamming hard behind us.

We walk in silence down the long white hall, with the black jail bar gate near the end of the room. The scent in the hallway smells of an old basement, with a fresh coat of paint. I guess it is the way to hide all the many years of wear and tear to the building. We approach the black gate and wait as the barrier moves bumpily to the left to allow us through. We turn left at the crossroad of hallways down another corridor that had its own distinct smell of old dirty gym socks and sweat. As I search to figure out where the smell originates from, I find my answer. We are now passing the gym on the left side of the hall.

The eyes from the correctional officers and inmates who walk alone throughout the halls pierce my back like needles used in acupuncture.

Fresh meat, I assumed. It took me back to high school days when the new student walks the halls, and everyone would whisper to each other. "Who is that, what class they in, wonder where they came from?" We continue on to the medical unit where I complete my interview with the health service administrator. She is a black woman, tall, pretty and speaks very professionally. She wears a white lab jacket, and she seems nice, maybe nice enough to give me a call back I hope. A few weeks go by, I have not heard anything from the jail. Let me try to call again. I dial the number, and I am transferred to a gentleman this time. Hi, this is LJ, the lady you interviewed with is no longer here, but you are looking for an LPN, right? Okay then, I will pass your information onto the Director of Nursing at the workhouse, and she will be giving you a call", he replied. "Okay thank you so much, I will be waiting to hear from her," I said. A few days pass, and I receive a call from the DON, and she lets me know that I am selected for the job.

My first day on the job is going to be interesting I imagine. So, I return to the same building where I was interviewed, and during the first couple of days or so, I complete the standard new hire binders and watch a couple of ethics and sexual harassment videos. As I finish the videos, random nurses enter in and out of the room I am sitting in, which functions as a medication room slash break room. The nurses' filter in and out as I completed the paperwork to take their lunch breaks. I hear the nurses discussing who is dating who, which patient took their meds and which ones give the nurses a hard time, and what the nurses did last Saturday night. Often times, someone would ask, "are you new?" "What shift are you going to be working?" I answer yes, I'm an LPN and I am going to be working evening shifts. "Oh okay, well it's crazy on evenings, good luck." Not sure what "crazy" meant in this context but guess I will find out during my next few months here.

Evenings, I notice after a few weeks seem to be pretty well organized. We have about three different nurses that worked the evening shift and a couple of PRN staff. We have a beautiful middle-aged woman named Karrina, who is pretty as a button. She reminds me of Minnie Mouse with a cute button nose. She is charming and willing to help me out and show me the ropes. We also have an older lady who we called Mrs. Bennett. She smokes a lot but will run circles around any of us youngins. She will definitely correct you when you are wrong and tell you just how to do any task right, or what she believes is right. Then we have the lone male nurse, Mr. Kennedy. Kennedy as we called him as we always go by last names, is smart, organized and a good preceptor. He drives the other female nurses crazy by calling them "hens" and telling them what to do and what not to do. He laughs when he knows he has gotten under their skins, but I tell him all the time, you better quit playing with these girls before they beat you up. I describe our team as the "Dream Team," we work well together and operate as a family. We get the work done, and we leave together at night.... an epitome of a team.

Initially, just like any other job, I am being tested by the staff and inmates as I always come in the door with a huge smile. That's just my personality. I smile a lot, and I'm just naturally friendly. So today, I'm passing pills on the floor, and a female correctional officer approaches me and says "I just got one question for you, why do you smile all the time? Ain't nobody that happy all the time". I was a little thrown off by the statement, as no one has ever been bold enough to say something like that to me. I replied, "that's just me, I'm smiley, I'm bubbly, that's just the way I am." As she turns and walks away, she states, "Well you not gonna last a week around here, you will be gone just like the rest of them." At this point, I vow to myself that I will continue to maintain my personality and natural ability to be a good person.

After that encounter with the officer, I realize that this environment has begun to change the nature of the people that work here. It seems like to me, the more you are in this facility, the more you become accustomed to the behaviors of the inmate patients. Really a lot of these individuals grew up in the same neighborhood as I have. I even have seen a few inmates recently that actually grew up with me on St. Louis Ave or went to school with me. My passion seems to be growing for this population. When I think of nursing, the number one thing you want to do in your career is to help people. Who better to help then your own people that you recognize are having struggles, live in undesirable environments or lack a proper home structure. Shoot, some of these people didn't have mothers, fathers, or anyone to guide them the right way. My father is pretty absent in my life which leads me to make the wrong decision when dealing with men. I spent the last five years dealing with Tony that really didn't care enough about me because he always would get upset and fight me. I don't deserve that, but that guidance is missing from my life. From what I have learned your father is the man you should love first in life, and he should teach you how to enjoy not only a man but to love yourself. My life lessons, unfortunately, have come from those surrounding me, which does not always lend to the best advice or role models when it comes to relationships. In this environment, I guess that some of these inmates have the same experience with not having role models and people to help guide them on the straight path. I am seeing now that this is the population that I feel connected to because they need the help and as a nurse, your ultimate goal is to show compassion, understanding, and help improve health outcomes. I think I have found my nitch. I need to help my people to do better and be better like I have tried to do as I transcend from hood life to professional life.

    I remember learning in nursing school and from studying nursing theorists, that caring is central to nursing and promotes health better than curing, as stated by Dr. Jean Watson. If I really want to kick some more nursing knowledge to Ms. Correctional Officer, Hildegard Peplau's first nursing role reports patients should be treated with respect and courtesy, as anybody would expect to be addressed. So, I will treat everyone one with respect and smile while I'm doing it. I am determined not to let the environment in which I am providing care in to dictate my mood and demeanor. As I progress working in corrections, I am always going to try to stay true to that belief.

    So, it's my second year working in corrections, I was promoted to charge nurse after obtaining my RN license a few months ago, and I'm working my usual three to eleven shift today. As the hustle of patients and people moving swiftly throughout the medical unit, I am preparing for the start of my turn. After completing my daily routine of checking the 24-hour report board and making my diabetic supplies, I organize my desk and converse with other employees in the office at the time. In walks an unfamiliar face, and definitely someone who did not work at this particular facility. As the clean-cut gentleman wearing a grey suit approach's the medical unit, I see that he is stopping multiple times within the long corridor leading in the medical department, speaking to other nurses as they pass, shaking hands like a politician on the campaign trail. I wonder who this guy is, must be someone from the mayor's office or city hall, coming to check out the conditions of the facility. The DON walks up and meets him at the door as a few words are exchanged. As the DON introduces the man to everyone that is standing before me, finally they make their way to my desk. "And this our charge nurse, Nurse Hatter." "Hello, I'm Jackson, the boss around here." I briefly give him a shocked look as that statement was bold, but he begins to laugh so at this point I figure he is being facetious. The gentleman reached out this hand for a handshake and stated, Hello, I know who you are, I have heard all about you." I stated, "Well I am sure, it was all good things." He replied, "Well actually no, it was all bad." We share a laugh, and little do I know that this humorous guy will soon become my mentor and most prominent champion.

PREPARE FOR TAKE OFF

My personal life at this point is going well I guess. I living, making money and I am alive, so I can't complain much. I am living with my sister Kim and her two children still until I can save up some money to move in my own house. I have been through a physical domestic relationship and definitely not trying to go back down that road again. So, my focus is trying to find time alone to get my credit, housing situation, and overall financial goals in order. I really do not have a stable male partner in my life as the guys I am currently dating all tend to have some issue one way or another. One guy I am dating I describe as a socialite, always in the club, actually that's where I met him. But he does have a day job as a mailman, so I guess that is not too bad. He is into big trucks with big rims, no kids, but you can tell he is a playa. The other guy that I am seeing is an Indian guy, and he is in his residency at the hospital. He is studying neurology and plans to become a neurosurgeon who is pretty cool, but he has zero time to hang out, as school and work occupies his life at this point. The dating scene is becoming quite dull as most of these guys have major issues or just not really to commit to one person. I'm going to keep looking until I find my knight and shining armor.

As far as my work life, I am two years in and I felt like I am comfortable in my current role as evening shift charge nurse. I am learning a lot from the seasoned nurses with whom I work with, and I am getting more confident in my leadership role. There are times when hard decisions have to be made, or your leadership is tested by security staff, but I always push through and make the difficult calls. Today as I begin to start my shift, I overheard the nurses talking about the director of nursing at our sister facility just quit. As any noisy nurse would, I ask what happened to her, what did she do, and which nurse ran her off. There have always been stories about how bad the nurses are at the "other" facility and how nobody wants to work there. As the legend goes, the DON just sat around and did nothing while regional and corporate leadership was in the building cleaning and preparing for an audit. And to everyone's surprise, she is magically no longer employed with our company. That is the standard language used when someone has been fired or has voluntarily resigned from their position.

"I wonder who's going to take that position next," the nurses began to conversate. I said, "I don't know who will, but they are crazy as heck if they do." "Well you should do it, Leonora, you would be good at that job," one of the nurses yells out. "Puhuh, are you nuts, I can't deal with those nurses down there, they crazy. I worked a shift down there, and nobody would even tell me where the supplies were. I had to go on a hunt to muscle up what I needed to do my job. I will pass". The lone male nurse, who had also been a preceptor and mentor for me, just sat back in the chair and stated, "Don't you go down there, with all those hens." That was his answer for everything, every female was a mother hen to him. Until that very moment, the thought of becoming director of nursing never really crossed my mind. I have only been a nurse for five years, charge nurse for one year and I have no prior experience as a manager or charge nurse. I thought to myself, how could I possibly be successful in this role.

When I left the shift that night, I couldn't really get the idea out of my head. Could I actually be the DON? My mind starts to form all the possibilities and different scenarios that could occur if I choose to apply for this role and what if I am actually offered the position. Well, it would be more money, it would look good on my resume, but it would be one hell of a challenge, unchartered, and unfamiliar territory. I shook it off for the moment and continued my drive home.

Over the next few days, the conversation about me applying for the DON role just keeps coming up. Are you going to apply? Are you really going to do it? There are mixed reactions from the staff. Some people are saying, "are you crazy, why would you want to do that, nobody stays in that position more than a few months." Some others are encouraging, "girl you got this, you can do this." My family is very encouraging about the possibility of me applying. My sister, who is one of my biggest fans is excited about the possibility of me becoming the DON. Kim will remind you of the overly excited parent in the stands, yelling "that's my kid." She was a staple at all my high school basketball games at Bayless Senior High. So, this time wouldn't be any different. "Girl you need to do that, you would be the boss," she said. I said, "Well I know, but that would mean, I have to leave the medium security jail and go the maximum-security jail. I will need to pay for parking, it's further from the house, plus the nurses are mean." I'm coming up with just as many excuses that I could possibly think of at this moment. "Forget all that, you will be in charge, and you can make the rules." It's a win-win.

As I further weigh the pros and cons of taking the position, I ask my DON for the job description and internal application. As I review the application, I see that you need three years of management experience. Well, I didn't have that, so I don't think I have a chance. Also, I heard that another nurse that has been with the company for 10 years is applying. But I have made up my mind, I am just going to try it at least out and ask if I get it high, if I don't, I will only continue to work as a charge nurses until I decide to go back to school to get my BSN. So, I fill out the paper application and turn it in. That is, it, now we wait to see what happens next.

In a few days or so Mr. Jackson, the corporate manager paid us another visit in the medical department. As we conversate, he begins to ask a few questions like, "what do you think of the nurses at the other facility?" I said, well they were a little mean and stood offish when I picked up a shift there not too long ago. I believe they need someone to encourage teamwork, as it seems like everyone is really for their self, just trying to get their work done." "Well, what would you do to help them be better nurses," he said. "Well, first I would have a meeting with all them and talk about how we are a team and that everyone contributes to the overall nature of how the day will go. I would use my current situation as an example. On our evening shift, we all work together. If an emergency comes in, everyone jumps in to help, instead of saying, that's your patient. When we get done with medication pass, and we have finished our assignment, we help the other person that go back late. We all leave together on time, if someone is not done, we help them so we all can leave together, that's what they need to do." Mr. Jackson just looked and shook his head up and down revealing a small smirk on his face. At this point, I realize, am I being interviewed right now. I turned to him and said, "why are you asking me all these questions? "Oh, I just wanted to know what you would do if you were in that situation," he replied. "Yeah, okay Mr. Jackson," I laughed. "Well, I have been watching you and noticing how you interact with the staff. And I have heard good things about how you handle yourself here. "So, I heard you applied for the DON position, do you think you are ready for that role," he said. "Well, no quite honestly, I'm up in the air about what I should do or not. Those nurses need a lot of work, and most of those nurses have been nurses longer than I have been alive on this earth. How the heck is a twenty-seven-year-old going to come in and tell them what do. Not to mention I have no other management experience." I sharply stated. "Well I can teach you how to be a director of nursing, that's the easy part. But what I can't teach is your infectious personality". These types of roles require a certain personality. One that you have. You get along with your staff, they look up to you, you are friendly, and you listen." Those are the qualities that are needed in this type of role. If you have a bad attitude, fail to understand what the needs of your staff are, then you will not be successful. That is why I think you would do well in this position. Now, you will want to quit so many times in the first 6 months, because it will be hard. But if you make it through, then you know you got it." "Well that's nice of you to say, but I don't know. It will be a lot." "Just think about it, we will be calling you in for an interview with the regional director of nursing and the health service administrator in a couple of days, he stated. "Be ready."

Lawd, what have I just gotten myself into. Am I crazy, what does he see in me that I don't see in myself. All I want to do is come to work, look at my patients and make sure their needs were taken care of. Now I will have to ensure that nurses are behaving following standards, policies, and procedures, and be dedicated to treating the patients with respect and professionalism. That will be a huge task. All this time that Mr. Jackson has been coming to the facility really researching out those that he feels are qualified and ready for this role. I had no clue that others were always watching and observing and choosing my next steps without my knowledge. I really have never entertained the thought of becoming a manager so young in my nursing career as I am just focused on getting to the terminal degree of becoming a Doctor of Nursing Practice one day. But realizing that you are not in control of your life as much as you think you are, is something that I have better start getting used to and getting used to it fast.

TURBULENCE

"Good morning Leonora, this is the provider's offices, the dental suite, here is the break room, and this here is your office. Get settled and let me know if you need anything," stated my new boss who had the title of health services administrator. As I walk into the office, I am met with 4 bright white walls, and a dark brown L-shaped desk, with a black computer with a 15-inch monitor. There are two big grey metal cabinets with two doors on each side of the wall, with a grey 5 drawer cabinet that have been used for hanging file folders. As I look to the left of the desk, I can see a huge pile of paperwork stacked messily on the floor. It has to be about three feet of paperwork there, in which I have no clue what everything would be. I continue to look around, thinking, oh my God, I have an office. No windows, so if the world is coming to an end, I would have no clue, but it's an office nonetheless. I pull the black office chair with wheels from underneath the desk and sit down. Awwww, my own chair, my computer, my phone, as I pick up the receiver, listen for a dial tone and place it on the hook. All mine!!! I quietly laugh to myself, "Now what? What do I do now, I have been used to my charge nurse routine? Come in, look at the schedule and see who is working that day. Do the sharps count, check the emergency equipment, get ready for the diabetics. This is a new role, I don't have a checklist, what do I do now. Solve the world's problems. I presume my boss will get to that a little later. I circle back around to the mess on the side of my desk. I pick up a piece of white paper from the huge stack on the floor. Huh, a sharps count log, with missing signatures. As I start to scan through the next couple of sheets of paper, I notice a nurse standing in my doorway. "Hi, there, can I help you?" I said. "Yeah, we had a call in for the evening shift, and I can't stay, as she rolled her eyes and twisted her lips to the side." Well okay, where is the schedule? It's at the nursing station, as she turned and walked away. I don't know who that nurse was, as she did not introduce herself, but all I knew is, here we go." This is only the first call in, but certainly not the last.

  The next few weeks are full of action and full of tests. These days reminded me of when I was a child playing Super Mario Bros, and you had to make off the last level before you could proceed closer to beating King Koopa on the bridge. The bridge signified just being able to clock out to go home and make it through the last sliding sally port door and out the building before you get a call with another crisis. My tests in the beginning pretty much came from my staff. The thought that a young highly energized nurse is calling the shots was too much for some to handle. The nurse which whom I have beaten out for the position seems cold at times, but still is willing to provide help and guidance when I didn't know the answer. Others were more blatant with the disrespect as they refuse specific assignments, stated, "well, I'm not doing that" and rejects any request to stay over for mandatory overtime. I came in the door raising my hand and two fingers like Mini-Me from Austin Powers. "I come in peace." I held an initial introductory meeting, to discuss my expectations and to get to know each and every staff member. I even created a little sheet that told a little about myself and asked each staff member, what shift they worked, what off days did they prefer, what they liked to do in their spare time, what challenges they currently had, and what would they like to see changed. Guess that just wasn't enough. I was the enemy, and I was there to change up everything, and they did not have it.

As I struggle to find my identity in this new role, the hits just kept coming. Working in my office, I get a stern knock on my door. I peer through the small pane of glass in the left upper side of the blue metal door. It is the chief of security and the captain of the shift. "We need to talk with you, now." Okay, come in, I stated. "What's going on?", as I look on with a puzzled look. "Well, one of the nurses has been accused of bringing in cupcakes to one of the patients." Now you know that is not allowed and you need to do something about it. I only have two weeks on the job and did not know the staff well enough even to have an initial opinion on if this nurse would do something like that. "I'll take care of it," I stated. "Well, you better or that nurse is going to be out here next time we catch her doing something like that." As I escort the facility leaders from my office, I figure this will be my first corrective action I would have to give out. The thought of having to "write somebody up" just didn't sit right in my spirit. I'm a nice person and always want to give the person the benefit of the doubt. But I had to do it.

Not long after that, there is an EEOC complaint against me for race discrimination even though the complainant is black, and I am too, go figure. I have an employee layoff period where I have to decide which four nurses have to be let go. A nurse accuses me of hiring someone else for the job because of her age. A nurse calls in after his PTO was denied then called me a liar and slammed the door to the break room. And to put the icing on the cake, nurses are refusing direct orders to provide patient care. That is it, I have really reached my breaking point. Maybe this was not the job for me, I'm thinking. I am just too nice, and these people are going to keep doing things to try to run me away. I'm calling my mentor, Mr. Jackson. "I think it's time for me to go back to be a charge nurse." This job is too difficult, and I can't take all of this negatively, being accused of things that you know you did not do, and the constant fight to provide good care to patients. Mr. Jackson, just calmly stated, "What did I tell you, you were going to want to quit within the first 6 months because you are learning, people are challenging you, and you are figuring things out. By the date on this calendar, you have been here in this role about 5 and a half months. So, make it to 6 months, and you will see that it will get easier. Just stick in there from now and start managing out those bad apples."

CRUISING ALTITUDE

I have never been a quitter in my life, and I definitely didn't want to start now, so I'm going to take my mentor's advice and began managing these individuals that are negative, and really do not want to be part of the team. I am going to have meetings where I include the charge nurses and a few of the high performing staff who tried to make a change. We will talk through processes and decide what is best for the department and what doesn't make sense. I will work on improving the relationship with the correctional officer staff by opening communication and participating in their meetings and briefing sessions. Over time the culture will start to develop, and things will tbegin to change for the better.

In the middle of the culture shift, why is my health administrator resigning? We just got a chance to work together, and now he is leaving us. I can't complain as they are getting ready to hire a new familiar face, which will help to make the HSA-DON leadership relationship even stronger. The late HSA Keith has been a correctional officer before. This will bring an exciting dynamic to the team. Also, he has a mental health background that will help to get into the psyche of some of the staff members behaviors. He is also an advocate that assisted with me obtaining my current position as DON. He told the HSA at the time, "you need to run some interference between the nurses and her because those nurses are crazy." I appreciate the dedication from all of my own advocates to help me to get to where I needed to be. This change I hope will help to balance the department with a focus on client relationship and nurse relationship. Just two years earlier, I was working and listening to rules. Now, I was impacting change in patient and staff lives, and it feels so good.

Playing good cop bad cop, my new partner and I in crime are running our newly designed department. We are changing the culture and attitudes of those that work under us and bringing more of a professional environment to a chaotic world. We are touring and entertaining the best professionals in the company as we are the host jail in our corporate city. So we have to pretend we are Barrack and Michelle on the campaign trail, shaking hands and holding babies, making sure we say the right thing to impress our constituents. We also have a good group of other folks that bring balance to our world, because seeing four white walls with no windows all day can really take a toll on you. Our click, if you want to call it consists of Albert, our mental health professional, who is funny as heck, and passionate about the work he does. He is single and a respectable bachelor. We tease him all the time that he is afraid to settle down, but he is taking his time until he finds "Mrs." Right. Dr. Sade who is elegant, independent, dresses in all designer labels and knows her psych medicine. Let me tell you if you have ever been a fan of Sex in the city, Dr. Sade will remind you of Carrie Bradshaw as her fashion game is off the chain. Jimmy Choo, Prada, Gucci you name, I need a spin in her wardrobe honey, I would be in heaven. Together we are saving the world one day at a time, at least that is what we believe in our minds.

PREPARING FOR LANDING

Wow, I can't believe it, six years have passed. Nurses have come and went, policies have changed and are updated, more challenges have come down the pipeline, audits are still due, everyday healthcare life continues. The same day to day routine continues day after day. This year of 2012, I have made the decision to pursue my Doctor of Nursing Practice degree with a focus on adult-gerontology primary care. I met the man of my dreams two years ago and was set to get married in the year after I was accepted into grad school. Seems like everything in my life is on course now. I have become a director of nursing mentor and is traveling around the country training new DONs. It is exciting, and I got to do the one thing I love in this world, and that's travel to new places.

At times, I feel like okay, what is next? I am getting tired of the same old routine, and I think I have outgrown the site manager role, I wanted something better. My craving for learning and getting a sit at the table stays in my mind. I think I have to blame one of my earlier classes in the DNP program for infusing that in our brains, the DNP = Seat at the table. A seat where decisions can be made about what type of care that can be provided for the patient. What policies and procedures that could be set to ensure nurses are practicing at their full scope of practice. I am ready to do more and being in my current role is not going to cut it.

Right after my wedding to my handsome, charming husband, I find out I am pregnant with my first child. When my husband heard the news, he was smiling ear to ear just like the day I met him on that rainy day at the firehouse. I was leaving the jail after what seemed like a day that would never end. It was thunderstorms in the area, and it was raining cats and dogs. As I tried to ease through the medical department without being detected, I was cornered by one of my hard-working nurses. I always try to be incognito when I have had a long day because I know one small problem would equal another 45 minutes of your time.

Nonetheless, the nurse put on the puppy dog eyes and asked, Ms. Hatter can you please go pick us up some tacos from Jack in the Box, please, we love you." "Girl I am ready to go, it's raining, and I am tired." "Please Ms. Hatter, all those shifts I work extra, don't I deserve some tacos." "Dang, she knew she had me. Okay, I will call on my way back, so somebody needs to come down and get them from the front door. So, despite how tired I was, I caved in and drove in the pouring rain about 10 minutes down the road to pick up the nasty deep-fried tacos that you only eat if it's 3am and you just left the nightclub.

As I arrive back at the site, I pull up, hit the red button with the triangle picture on my dashboard, hopping out the car with umbrella and tacos in hand, ran up the building steps and handed the tacos to the officer sitting at the door. "These are for the nurses, they are going to come down to get them." I ran back to the car to avoid getting soaked as I had on white scrub pants on that day and didn't want to give the bystanders something to look at. As I pulled on the driver door level, the door will not open. "What in the heck?" I tried again. Still, it would not open. As I try to gain assistance from inside the building to help unlock my door, I realized that maintenance men were on their typical extended, I don't want to be found, lunch break. So next stop was the fire station that sat on the next corner of the street.

When I approach the fire station, a few of the firemen are sitting out in lawn chairs watching the rainfall. I approach and ask for help to unlock the door to my running vehicle outside the front of the jail. As more firemen circle round to see what pretty damsel in distress needed their help, my future husband appears from his slumber upstairs in the bunk hall. He is 5'5 chocolate brown in color, with a fresh, good grade of hair. No waves like I like it, but his lining is crisp and newly done. His cheekbones are high with small angled eyes similar to an Asian but not as much. His eyebrows are thick, and I can tell from the rest of the firefighters that he is the designated wingman, who attracts all the girls to their Spidey web. I think it's the muscles that contribute to the luring of girls to the cave as I can see the lumps peeking through the ends of the fire department shirt and the parallel lumps across the front of his chest as well. Looks like he lifts some weights which may be an automatic requirement to be on the fire department, but I am not sure. All I know is that every firefighter calendar I have seen, it looks like these guys live in the gym. As he walks toward me wiping the sleep out of his eyes, that same goofy smile surfaced that I had on the day he found out he would be a father again.

My husband Khalid is indeed a blessing from God. I remember crying and praying hard to God to send me someone that would love me the way I needed to be loved. Coming from a lot of failed relationships with men not treating me the way I deserve to be addressed, Khalid shows me the way. Khallid is a Muslim raised through the ranks of the Nation of Islam up until now he has found true Islam. He attributes his change in lifestyle to his former days in the United States Marine Corp working as an infantry officer during Operation Restore Hope. If you have seen the movie Black Hawk Down, yeah that's my man. I wonder if that is why his firefighter buddies call him the Hawk. Being a former Marine, he is stern and stubborn as it comes, but gentle and has an unbelievable heart. As I use to go home to an empty loft, with all the furniture and items in their place, the exact way I left them, I would remanence on having a family to come home to. The horrors of being in a relationship with a man who did not value my worth or respect it is the driving force behind my prayers for a better companion. God answered my prayers. He not only shows me undying love and compassion, but he has also opened up my eyes to a different way of thinking that I did not have. Well, I feel like some of the things I have been taught by him I really felt the same way when I was younger, but your environment and surroundings cause you to take on the same thinking like everyone else. So much of a waste, I believe I would have done things in life way more differently if I thought this way or had a stable father figure in my life.

Khalid shows me the way love is supposed to be. Supportive from the beginning, with material things at first, just to hook me, but now his true heart begins to show. From making sure that I make it work and make it in the house at night, he is there. In the beginning, it really annoyed me to have someone checking up on you all the time. I lived almost 30 years without having someone wonder about my whereabouts and moving from my independent lifestyle mirrored off of Beyonce to now I have someone that loves and cares about my wellbeing. He will always say, you wouldn't leave your wallet outside, so why would you leave your most prized possession (your woman) outside not knowing where she is. When you think about it, it makes a lot of sense. The selflessness of his spirit is the reason I love him, no matter who you are, he wants the best for you. The delivery may be harsh, but the intent of the message is undeniable.

About a year and a half passed after the delivery of our little princess Kimora, I am ready to leave the jail. So, the opportunity comes up to change roles, and I am jumping at the chance. I am now promoted to Regional Clinical Services Manager, in charge of thirteen different facilities nursing staff and Directors of Nursing. It proved to be an excellent experience as I still could not believe I have the chance to influence so many people on such a significant level. I am now able to attend leadership meetings, having meetings with the CEO and chief nursing officers. I am more visible at different facilities around the country, people were calling me for input on their practices at their sites, and I am included on the initial pilot and workgroups. Not to mention, I am able to travel to different cities and see new places, it is fantastic. I began to reflect on just how I got here.

None of this was in my deck of cards that I believed I was handed. I planned to work at the jail for a couple of years, go back to school until I got my doctorate and then go save the world. As I tried to get to my dream of being a Doctor of Nursing practice, I guess I never really thought about all the stuff in between, who would help me, lessons I would learn, what I would go through to get to the end goal. Who would be the haters, that would try to stop you at all costs because you are doing better than them and doing the things they would want to do. Most people are genuinely happy for you until you start doing better than them. And sometimes it's not because you are elevated above them, but sometimes it's because they are just not progressing in the time they think they should have, and they inadvertently take it out on you. Those are learning pains that I had come to understand over time and learn to dismiss when I came across it.

GROUNDED

It is indeed in my presence. As I unzip it and remove it from the long black jacket it is enclosed in, I get a whiff of that new clothes smell. It has a burgundy base with three long thick black strips on each arm. Down the center, it is laced with black velvet material with two square Brandman University logos on each side of the zipper. Along with the doctorate robe, there lays a deep orange neck hood and a black doctorate level hat with the tassel. It is now sinking in, I was a Dr. Ever since the phone rang, 15 minutes after I defended my DNP scholarly dissertation, I will now and forever be called Dr. Leonora Muhammad.

It is still surreal to this day that all the hard work, dedication, sacrifices, challenges, hard aches, long nights of studying and celebrations lead to this. Getting a terminal degree in nursing is what I had dreamed of when I wrote it in my senior newsletter in the year 1999, along with the fact that I wanted to make $ 85,000 a year. Funny how I thought that was a lot of money back then and I would be super rich. I have achieved that but knowing that I would encounter people on the way that would help me realize things about myself that I did not even know. I know I am good at a lot of different things but was often times I'm scared to speak up or pursue things that I feel are outside my reach. Other people around me often times saw what I was capable of, I just can't see it. From my mentor to my cheerleaders in my family, friends, coworkers, and fellow students, they all push me to be better. My initial destination was set, but the journey was unknown. Throughout all those trees I passed on the side of the road, many trees stuck out along the way.

Being a spontaneous and adventurous person helps me to make the decision to work in a specialty area that is not common to most nurses. I still remember when I was still working PRN at the nursing home and then working full time at the jail. The nursing supervisor asked as I received my assignment, "So you still working over at the jail, as she turned and laughed with another supervisor." I could tell how they laughed that this wasn't the first conversation that they had about my new career choice at the time. It is instances like that that has pushed me to do the best I can to prove the haters wrong and prove to myself that I can do anything that I want to do in life.

Obtaining the doctorate degree along with my NP certification is just the stepping stone to doing bigger and better things. I have become more involved in local and national nursing organizations participates in volunteer opportunities, and have been promoted again to a Senior Director position focusing on quality improvement and patient safety, publishing articles in magazines, presenting at national conferences, and still traveling the world. My mission now is to spread my knowledge that I have learned through all of my experiences and help the next generation of nurses fulfill their dreams.

    I often times reflect back to the day when I saw that young girl laying on the grass with the bullet wound and blood oozing from her leg and reconnect with that feeling I had that day. I felt at that moment that I wanted to be better and do better than what was happening in my neighborhood. If I could say what moment in my life defined me, I would say that was the best day of my life, as it pushed me to want to have better, do better, and be better, than be a product of my environment.

Dr. Leonora Muhammad is a highly qualified healthcare professional with extensive experience in leading healthcare organizations through change with a proven history of increasing productivity, promoting compliance and improving quality. She is a Doctor of Nursing Practice (DNP) with 15 years' experience in healthcare, managing clinical operations, instituting clinical policy and nursing programs and quality training courseware. Her most recent accomplishment involved the courseware development and company-wide implementation of the Nurse Preceptor and Core Process program that improved patient outcomes, reduced new employee ramp up time by 1 week and resulted in a 14% reduction in turnover 1 year after deployment. Under Leonora's leadership, she has helped correctional facilities nationwide successfully reduce avoidable emergency room visits and inpatient hospitalizations by improving utilization of in-house infirmary bed management. Currently, Dr. Muhammad is the Sr. Director of Quality Improvement and Patient Safety at Corizon Health. Leonora serves as a champion and advocate for the 3500+ Corizon Health nurses and clinical staff. She plays a key role in establishing and promoting best practices that consistently result in high quality care, improved health outcomes for our patients and better the communities we serve. She has also published articles in the Corrections Forum magazine which highlighted care for incarcerated Dementia patients. Leonora is an Advanced Practice Registered Nurse and Board Certified in Adult Geriatric Primary Care. She has obtained multiple certifications and achievements including becoming a Certified Correctional Healthcare Professional (CCHP) and serves on the CCHP Board of Trustees, awarded the Alumni Award by the University of Missouri St. Louis in 2017, she is an American Heart Association- Basic Life Support Instructor, recipient of the 2017 Under 40 Award during last year's NBNA National Conference, 2018 Administrative Nurse of the Year and finally a NBNA Lifetime Member.

CHAPTER 9

TRAUMADEFEATED!
by
Ramona Phillips

"Charlie just left for work 5 hours ago." I can't believe I am on my way to the hospital with my son, David, four years old with his daddy's dimples and beautiful chocolate complexion. I know he's afraid, he can tell something is wrong.

I need to get our coats, I will throw on my black suede boots. On this beautiful Thursday afternoon, sunny blue skies, I have to sit in a hospital waiting room."

Charlie hit his head, and he wants to see me, at least that's what the nurse said when she called. It does not sound serious, so I am going to take the bus instead of a taxi".

Stepping off the bus, I see a policeman. "Excuse me, officer, can you tell me which way is University Hospital, the ER entrance?" He said, "University Hospital is just around the corner, you will see the ER when you turn the corner."

Turning the corner, I see the blue and white sign going around the front of the building saying: Hospital of the University of Pennsylvania-Penn Medicine.

"I am here to see my husband," Charlie Phillips, what room is he in?" The nurse slid the window open wider, with her blue eyes, short blonde hair and tiny nose looking at me over her glasses as if I am disturbing her. Isn't this the ER?

"I was told that my husband hit his head, is it a concussion?" Watching the two nurses look at each other strangely, whispering, one told me to have a seat in the waiting room and wait for the Chaplain. "The Chaplain!" Is my husband dead or alive? " "I was told he hit his head!"

She pointed to the Chaplain's office. I walked over to the brown door that said "Chaplain." David and I entered the room, but it was empty. It was a lovely room, white walls, long brown leather sofa, inspirational pictures and a few white comfy chairs in the corner.

Sitting on the couch with my arms around David is comforting for me too. I am feeling anxious ... fighting a panic attack, my stomach nervous with anticipation. I am sorry that I bought David with me. I am feeling impatient because no one is telling me anything about my husband's condition.

Entering the room now is a light-brown-skinned woman with a long grey robe, the long white rosary around her neck with grey and white dreadlocks. This is actually the Chaplain? Reaching out to shake my hand, "Hello my name is Ramona."

"What is the odds of her name being the same as mine?" " Hello, My name is Ramona too." "Where is my husband?" Looking at me seriously, she said, "we first need to identify him." I'm thinking, "Please God don't let it be him."

"Does he wear his hair in short twisty dreads, I braced myself for what was coming next. "Does he have a Ram tattoo on his arm?" "Yes, tears start to flow down my face. David is crying now. "He is in surgery, and his condition is severe."

"What happened to him?" she said, "Something fell on his head." We sat down to wait, and after five minutes, I jumped up to grab Ramona's hands. "He is not going out like this, "Let's pray!" and she joined me.

Family members are on their way, including some co-workers. They are all roofers traumatized by what happened to Charlie. Now my fear has me feeling numb while waiting, my mind drifts back to the events before all of this happened. I rehearsed everything in my mind.

I got up at 5 a.m. I usually got up to give Charlie his lunch and see him off. He looks at me with a sad expression on his face as he walks out the door. I'm standing by the dining room window, on the 3rd floor, looking at him walking down the street. His keys are swinging from the pocket of his blue, khaki pants.

I guess he doesn't want to take the train today, because he will not run into Lilly, Olivia's daughter. A woman's intuition never fails her whether we listen to it or not. I don't know why Charlie's schedule has been changed.

They are getting acquainted on the train ... sitting together. Lilly is 5'9 brown skin with a big gap between her front teeth ... her hair is long and black. She has a 6-year-old son, just a few years older than our son David. We live in the same apartment building. Charlie passes their apartment before coming upstairs to apt F our apartment. Charlie is suddenly getting too friendly with them. I know something must be going on.

He's stopping to check in on Olivia, Lily's mother, so he says. As he's leaving for work, I'm looking at Charlie from the window in discuss, feeling hopeless and angry about this relationship. I don't believe I actually married this man. Chocolate brown, beautiful skin, handsome, 5'11 and sexy, but that's not the point. He's not trustworthy, has anger issues, and is too secretive.

So many times thinking about leaving this relationship has me exhausted. I am afraid to go and afraid to stay, I feel he could seriously hurt me someday but hoping that day never comes. I don't want to be with him anymore. I am tired of him cheating, drinking, smoking and his disrespectful mouth, thinking he can say anything to me.

I finally admit to myself that I am not happy with him. I'm lost in this crazy relationship. I don't want to pray for him anymore. All these years feels like a waste of precious time waiting for him to change. There is more to a relationship than chemistry.

I am jumping from the frying pan into the fire with Charlie, only six months after ending a seven-year relationship my ex-boyfriend Rob, tells me that marriage is too permanent. Two little girls born out of this relationship, feeling depressed, shameful and like a failure.

Memorial Day 1988, Charlie and I are at the same bus stop. I give Charlie a religious pamphlet to read. Standing with my girls, Inez is in the stroller, Monique is holding my hand. Why is he talking to me?" "This is not my plan." I really don't want to be bothered. Why is he sitting with me on the bus? Why am I talking to him and why is he getting off the bus with us?

Doesn't he have some place to go? He's helping me with the stroller, this is the beginning of our crazy relationship. Some months pass, and I hope that Charlie and I can make this relationship work. Yet one minute he is here and the next he disappears for a few weeks. I am pregnant, and he is accusing me of tricking him. I guess he forgot we purchased birth control together. Besides, that is not my character to fool anybody.

I can't believe I said yes that he could stay until Saturday so he could have helped to move out, now he's in the hospital fighting for his life.

WHY KEEP PRAYING FOR CHARLIE?

These two angels are on my shoulders. In one ear I hear "take him out of his misery" in the other ear, I hear "No. Pray for Him." I hear that still small voice inside of me saying, keep praying for him." I want to rebel but choose not to because of my faith.

Maybe this is why God told me to wait. A few months ago I finally found the strength, and courage to leave the relationship? I kept hearing "wait" not yet." Could this be why?

His co-workers are here before everyone else. "He is not out of surgery yet." They look so sad. I ask, "Do any of you know what happened?" Andrew, light skinned, 5'8 sitting down with me, begins to tell me a horrible story. He says that they were working on the roof of Compassion Hospital.

Charlie had gone to lunch. When he returned, an elevator with a hook attached to it fell on his head. His head split wide open brain exposed, losing most of his blood in his body, he died on the way to the hospital in the helicopter but was revived.

Devastated, trying to process all that Andrew is telling me. "So he died on the way to the hospital?" I thought. I don't believe that this is happening. I need to tell the girls what is going on.

Alicea is seven, Inez is nine and Monique is thirteen. My neighbor across the hall is taking care of them while I am at the hospital.

Waiting for Charlie to come out of surgery feels like forever. My mother-in-law arrived, tall, grey/black short hair, named Charity. We do not have a good relationship, I don't feel that I can trust her.

Charlie finally came out of surgery. Unconscious, the head was swollen and bandaged up. After hearing what happened, I am looking at a miracle, and I know it.

Returning to the room with my coffee, I see balloons and a card from some woman named Denise. I don't know about her. I know about Wanda, her little girl is about two years older than our daughter, this was before I met Charlie.

Wanda is here, outside of his room. I am glad that she is walking away as I am turning around. I don't want any drama at the hospital. I have enough to deal with.

I am at the hospital every day. I can't believe it's been three months. I am disappointed that my life has changed overnight. I feel like I am in a fog, I am waiting for it to clear. It seems to be getting heavier.

I am feeling remorseful, depressed and anxiety on a daily basis. I am trying to adjust but not sure how long I can go on like this. "God, why do you want me to be merciful to this man that causes me grief most of the time?"

I sit in a support group meeting feeling so disconnected. It is good to see familiar faces. I feel like my body is here, but my mind is someplace else. I can't focus. I still feel alone, even on a sunny day it feels dark. I am in a pit of despair. "Oh God help me get out of this mess."

Charlie's progress is moving along nicely but still slow. I meet with several people to decide if rehab is the next step for him. His brain injury is dangerous, and he needs a lot of treatment. Charlie is paralyzed on his left side and also has some brain damage. He remembers family and friends but has short term memory loss.

"What is life going to be like after rehab if he goes home?" I am happy that rehab is working for him and he is talking now. His left eye is damaged he has a big crooked scar on his forehead. His head is swollen, and he needs to use his wheelchair to move around.

He is quiet most of the time but sometimes sounds like his old self. He looks different and a bit scary when he looks at me. His lazy eye seems to get stuck in that position, focused on me. I have no idea what he is thinking.

Looking in the mirror at himself he says "I am ugly." I think this is the most vulnerable I have ever seen him. I actually feel compassion for him. I am hoping that maybe his heart is beginning to change. I go home to spend time with the children. They are real troopers on the days I bring them up after school. David helps by pushing him in the wheelchair.

I head back to the rehab only discovering a business card from Denise on the table. I went into protection mode, restricting his visitors to family members only, including putting his phone in the drawer. He later called the nurse to take it out of the drawer after I left. This left me feeling powerless.

The Social Worker called to inform me that my mother-in-law arranged for Denise to come with her. The staff is very kind to me, they all seem to look out for me. The Social Worker said they have seen wives drop their husbands off and never turn back. I just could not do that I am Mrs. Devoted. I feel that I must look out for him and make sure he gets the best of care.

Angry and disappointed that Charlie thinks its acceptable for his lover to visit him, I roll him into the bathroom and tell him how I feel. He looks at me and says, "Mona if I had not been in this accident, I would be doing the same things." I got my wake up call; his heart has not changed, not even after such a traumatic experience.

ACCEPTING REALITY AND THINKING BACK

Before the accident, I had almost 6 years of recovery from trauma, and today I feel like I am back at square one. I started my recovery journey by taking the girls to VA to spend some time with my aunt, Lassie. I am on my way to the airport, to spend 28 days in a Tampa Bay Florida Rehabilitation Facility.

My biggest mistake was not getting out of the relationship when I returned to Philadelphia. Charlie is not letting me go that easily using his anger to intimidate me. Attending meetings and making other changes like enrolling in school made me proud of myself. Charlie is not happy about the changes that I am making.

CHARLIE DON'T KILL ME!

I am sitting at the table and Charlie walks in. He is too quiet for me; my books are on the table. I was fearful as I see him in from of me. He plants himself in the chair in front of me and my stomach begins to churn. Charlie keeps staring at me. I maintain my pleasant attitude. "Do you want to eat something?"

He is looking at me and pointing at my book. He says, "So what does this mean?" I am trying to explain, but I feel that this is a trick question. "I am going to check on the children." Charlie is yelling "Don't go up those stairs!" I stop, I feel that I am in danger. If I run, he is going to catch me on the steps.

Maybe I can calm him down. "What's the matter, why are you so angry?" Charlie leaps on my neck like a cobra pushing me in the kitchen towards the cabinet. I am trying to catch my breath. Looking down I see David, "Charlie, "David is watching."

Charlie is yelling "I don't give an f__k!" Now things are turning white. "What is that noise?" Charlie is startled, he lets go. I am grabbing my throat, catching my breath, My oldest daughter Monique is hitting him with the broom. She is now running.

He runs after her, he knocks her down the curtains fall on top of her. He is distracted, I am calling the police. He looks at me with anger in his eyes and runs down the stairs.

I see him walking towards the train station. He is on the platform calling me from the pay phone. I answer the phone while signaling to the children to grab their coats. He says to me, "I don't have anything to lose!"

I am terrified. I am being triggered by what he just said. I can barely breathe from the anxiety. Taking short breaths, I can hear the glass door crashing. It's in my mind, memories from my childhood. In reality, I am calling my brother. "Tommy, please come get the children and me, Charlie is acting crazy."

I am feeling safe now that Tommy and his wife, Julia are here. I am hoping that Charlie is not on his way back as we climb into the SUV. Walking into their house, I am thinking, we can't stay here.

A few hours pass, Charlie calls, he is apologizing, we are going back home. I don't want to be a burden to my brother and his wife, I have four children. What am I doing? This reminds me of exactly what my mother did when we were kids. I hated it.

WILL CHARLIE BE HIMSELF?

Nine months later, the Dr's say it is time for Charlie to be transferred to another facility. This time Charlie will get vocational training and support with taking care of himself. He will be taught with other clients. This is good for him.

I just want to get away from it all. I feel trapped, I need time to take care of myself, but I feel like I have to be at the rehab every day to support him.

Charlie is now in the new rehab in Wayne PA. I am meeting with the staff, and they are telling me that I can only visit two days a week. This program actually set some boundaries for me. He needs to learn how to use his one hand and push the chair on his own, that included cognitive training.

Staff asks me if I want to take Charlie home after he completes this program. I feel I have to do so, so I begin looking for a home that is wheelchair accessible. I have a hard time finding something.

TRAUMADEFEATED!

This is all new to me. I feel like things are hopeless, I feel like my back is against a wall. Deep inside I know I want out of this relationship, regardless of his condition. He is not a good husband. I need to get away and think.

I am exhausted, depressed and numb. It is a beautiful mid-Summer day. I sit on the bench at Rittenhouse Square in Philadelphia. A tall black middle-aged woman comes over and asks if she can sit next to me. I want to be alone, but I say yes.

Now she is talking about her son. "Why is she talking to me about something so personal concerning her son?" I feel safe enough to tell her what I am going through with my husband before the accident and up until now. I guess I need to talk to someone.

I believe she is an angel. She looks at me strangely and says "Honey do you need this man?" No one has ever asked me that question. I have never asked myself that question. I pondered the question in my mind. I came up with the answer. No.

I don't need him. Reality has smacked me in my face. She says, "God has already removed him from your life." Then I realized how things were already shifting, such as his program would only allow me to visit a few days a week. This is God helping me.

I enjoy speaking with her. I feel better with negative energy is leaving me. I feel the warmth of the sun. We are walking to the bus stop. I thank her as we exchange numbers. As they say, some people come into our lives for a time, to teach us something and then move on.

While Charlie is doing so well in this vocational rehab, I file for divorce. He moves into a condo with his Mom's supervision. He reconnects with old friends and even travels to Las Vegas. I think...Wow!

I feel better that he is living somewhat of a normal life again. It helps me to move on without feeling guilty. I still have suppressed anger and needed to heal.

Laying in my bed watching TV, the children storm into the room and say, "daddy's dead!" Charlie is dead 5 years after his accident before the divorce is finalized. Blood clots travel from his heart and lungs. I feel so anxious by the shock.

Experiencing the damage from the trauma of it all. I am taking a flight to New Orleans to attend a conference, I need time to feel. While on the plane, my mind goes back to a movie I saw.

It was called: Diary of A Mad Black Woman. By Tyler Perry. In some ways, I think it helped me feel some feelings I needed to explore. I could Identify with the wife. "I know I shouldn't laugh, but laughter is good for the soul."

Her husband's name is Charles. He treats her like crap, cheats on her, puts her out of the house and leaves her for another woman. He's shot and is paralyzed. His wife chose to take care of him because she wanted him back. Parts of this movie reminded me of my life with Charlie, although I don't want him back and not happy that he is dead.

He's in the wheelchair talking to his wife being disrespectful and no remorse whatsoever. She turns on him, and her anger turns to rage. She starts treating him like crap too.

She rolls him into the jacuzzi and leaves him there in his wheelchair. She watches him as he blows bubbles to keep from swallowing water. She sits on the edge smoking a cigarette angrily reminding him of how bad he treats her.

I must admit this movie is helping me in some strange way. I feel a stream of emotions. It has a happy ending, she met the guy of her dreams, the one God chose for her. I thought she got him back for me. I don't believe in getting revenge, but it was sure fun to think about it. She had a change of heart and decided to forgive him. I did the same for myself and Charlie.

MY MOTHER'S EX PLOTS TO MURDER ME!

I am in the back seat of this strange man's car, vomiting up blood. I thought..."am I dying?" "Is this what it feels like?" "I'm only fifteen." "I am not in pain." The warm blood is coming up from my stomach. "I am not choking, but I want it to stop."

Why would God allow me to go through this? I will never ever forget, it is October 14th, 1976. It's a beautiful Fall night, the Moon is full and the street lights shining brightly. I walk up on the porch. I open the front door, I hear a strange sound at the top of the stairs. It's coming from my bedroom, it sounds like someone heard me come in and closed something, but what?

My siblings are outside playing at least I think all six of them are. My mother is not home from work yet, I slowly walk up the stairs, walking down the hallway quietly so I can catch this person. As I am opening the door standing in front of me is Michael. He is my mother's ex-boyfriend.

They had a fight and broke up because he wants to move in with us, but my mother said no. Michael is 5'11", dark brown complexion, brown eyes. He isn't a very handsome guy neither stylish. He likes wearing jeans, weird tee shirts with a fake tuxedo picture in front, sneakers and a short tight black leather jacket.

Looking at him suspiciously I say, "Michael what are you doing snooping around in my room?" He looks at me with his snake eyes, and creepy smile, as if he is up to something.

He smirks, then asks me about the broken pieces of glass on the walls. My brother had this room first. He decorates the walls with broken pieces of glass, then adds some sexy neon colored velvet posters.

"Michael doesn't change the subject!" He fiendishly grins and walks past me. I watch him as he walks down the hall, down the stairs, and out the front door. I cannot shake the feeling that he is up to something, we don't have anything to steal, I thought. Looking around the room, it does not look like anything is missing. The window is down. "I wonder what was the noise I heard?"

My siblings are asleep, my mother is in bed. I start to boil water to dye my trench coat. Mission accomplished, it turns out a beautiful sky blue, it is no longer beige, which was too casual for me. I want to look stylish, now in high school.

I am having trouble washing the dye from my hands. I'm tired and going to bed, I roll on my stomach to fall asleep. I feel my body jump high, I'm awake. Startled, I sit up on the edge of the bed. I look around, my sister is sleeping next to me everything looks normal, except the window is wide open.

I hear a strange sound, a spitting sound like when you puncture a hole in a pipe. My neck feels wet, there is blood on my hand. Strangely, I feel peaceful as I sit on the edge of the bed, shaking my sister to show her the blood on my hands. Lifting her head, she falls back asleep.

Putting on my slippers, I hear a still small voice say, "go wake up your mother now!" Getting up and unlocking the latch on the door, I am walking down the hall to wake my mother.

Banging on the door, she opens it, I show her the blood on my hands. I cannot speak. She is yelling, "what happened?" Looking at her, I nod my head, I don't know.

She grabs me, we are running down the stairs almost falling. Opening the front door, not letting my hand go as we run across the street. "Club 1990" is still open a few people come out. Mom yells to a light-skinned man with a light blue suit, and an afro, "please help me!" "Somebody did something to my daughter!"

He and his girlfriend grab me and put me in the backseat of his car. He's driving so fast, I hope we don't have an accident, his girlfriend looks terrified as she looks at me in the back seat. I'm throwing up blood in this man's car.

I can't believe I still feel this strange peace. I think, as the car is shaking and swerving as he turns the corner, driving over the old cobblestone trolley tracks, weird, I feel no fear.

I see a big red sign that says ER and a large white sign that says Presbyterian Hospital as he steps on the breaks to stop for the paramedics. The lights are flashing, and it all feels like a dream.

I can see the first responders coming towards the car; they are talking as the nurses are walking fast to assist. I am quickly lifted onto the cold stretcher, still throwing up blood.

I am being wheeled through automatic doors, rushing down the hall, pushed through double doors and stripped from my beautiful flowered dress. Strangely, this night, I slept in my favorite dress for the first time, was too thin to wear in the Fall anyway.

Someone is saying, "who is with her?" I am being attached to some monitors and medics are talking to each other trying to figure out why my nails are blue. I can't speak, so I can't tell them that I dyed my coat before going to bed.

I hear someone shout, "we have ten minutes to get her upstairs!" I feel crashing through double doors, speeding, I feel bumps, as I roll down the hall. Oh, "here is my Mom!" We stop, in front of the elevator she looks at me. "Are you alright?" Signaling to her "are you alright?" I know this is tearing her apart she is so protective of her children and now feeling powerless.

The elevator doors open then closes, then opens. I see entries that say O.R. is rolling swiftly through the doors, they are grabbing at my arms, there is so much going on. I am beginning to feel weak. I see someone coming towards my face with what looks like a mask. I am going under, "but am I going to wake up?" If I die tonight at least I am not in pain, I am sure Heaven is beautiful.

I wake up in a hospital room, I can not move or speak. My wrists are tied to the bed and my neck, stiff from the bandages. I can barely move my head. The door is open, and I see bright lights in the hall.

I see two men standing outside my door. "Who are they?" I feel tears slowly coming down the side of my eyes. "What happened to me?" "Who would try to kill me and why?" "I don't go around hurting people." "What if the person comes here to finish me off once the word gets out that I am still alive?"

A red-haired nurse comes into my room peeks at one of the machines and leaves. I want her to untie my wrists, but she is gone. A tall black man maybe 6'2" dark blue suit clean cut comes into my room and stands by my bed. A chubby white guy follows him in.

They tell me that they are detectives. The big guy says, "do you know what happened to you?" I nodded no. The tall guy says, "Do you know who would try to hurt you?" I slowly and sadly, nodded my head no. "Did you see anyone when you woke up?"

Again, I nodded my head no.

"We will look for your mother, don't worry we will look more into this." They leave the room, I hear my mother talking to someone outside the room. She comes in and stands by my bed. She looks at me in shock, I can tell she is angry but not at me.

She says to the nurse, "why are her wrists tied to the bed?" The nurse says she has been in surgery for eight hours under anesthesia, it is a precaution. She walks out and comes back, then cutting my wrists loose with the scissors.

The detectives call my mother and are questioning her. She is angry and waving her hands, she is not one to cry right away, she is in fight mode.

I am in bed looking at the glass window wondering what is being said. I see a sign that says ICU. The door is closed so I can't hear. Tears are rolling down the side of my face, my hands are untied, I can wipe my tears now.

Mother comes back into the room after the detectives leave. She tells me, after she put me in the man's car, running home to get the children she runs into Michael. She tells him what happened to me and that she needs someone to watch the children and take her to the hospital.

My mother tells the kids that something terrible has happened to me. Michael helps organize the kids. They are taken a few houses away to Michael's room. They are terrified and confused.

Arriving at the hospital, they are directed to the waiting room while I am still in surgery. My mother talks to him while trying to make sense out of what happened. She watches him as he looks nervous and smoking cigarettes one after the other.

She says, all of a sudden something clicked "he did this!" She accuses him, and he says he did not do it, she looks at him and angrily says, "she better not die!" Michael starts walking fast down the hall.

My siblings tell my mother when Michael is back in his room, they see him nervously wiping off his boots, they have mud on them. My siblings suspect him. They are afraid. My mother calls a taxi to drive her back to get the children out of Michael's room, just in case he is the one who plotted to murder me. She calls my oldest brother and some of his friends.

During surgery the Dr's give me a tracheostomy, putting an incision in my windpipe with a tube assuring that I can breathe. There are stitches around half of my neck including some areas where there are puncture wounds. I also have some vocal cord damage. The Dr.'s say, "we are not sure if she will ever speak again."

My Mom receives sympathy cards in the mail the next day, the person thought I would have been dead and wanted to cause more pain for her. My mother meets with police to share this information.

Mom is looking for another place to live. She finds a house but not too far away in a car. I am glad that I do not have to go back to that house.

A candy striper named Laura 16 years old, very compassionate, she is white with beautiful long blonde/brownish hair. She comes to my room to suction me when there is too much mucus in my chest from the blood in my stomach.

I hate this experience. Sometimes I call the nurse to do it because I can barely breathe, tears run down my face as I try hard not to panic. My voice sounds funny when I put my finger over the hole to speak. Thank God I do not have to go home with this thing in my throat. Three weeks in the hospital it is time to go back. "I wonder what the new house looks like." We now live only 15 mins from the Philadelphia Zoo.

Michael is arrested, but they don't hold him while under investigation. After moving to our new home, one night, my sister and my brother's girlfriend and I are going to the store. We see that we are being followed.

We turn the corner and see a dark red Chevy slowly pulling up on us. Michael is following us! Running home, my mother calls the police, the following day she files for a restraining order. Michael follows my little brother home to find out where we live. He stays away, we wait for our day in court.

We're on our way to City Hall the building with its creepy beige corridors and dull lighting. I see Michael standing in the hall a few feet away with a lawyer. I feel sad, disappointed, confused, angry. He does not come over to me and say anything to plead his innocence. I guess this means he is guilty.

I look forward to the justice system putting him in jail. I enter the courtroom, and I am called to the witness stand.

Raising my hand as the court clerk tells me to, saying some words and I sit down. I believe this is going to go in my favor. Before I can take a deep breath, his lawyer is asking about my personal life, my smoking weed, drinking, if I had a boyfriend, things that have nothing to do with what happened to me. I am now confused and angry.

I do not feel valued by a judicial system that I thought would defend me, a fifteen-year-old girl that had not hurt anyone but herself, trying to deal with the feelings of trauma from her childhood.

His lawyer got him off on circumstantial evidence. How could this be? A sizeable bloody nail found in the trunk of his car, muddy boots in his room. The handwriting has never been checked on the sympathy cards.

Just because he's a Veteran my life isn't meaningful? This psychopath did not do a day in jail. The good part is I am still alive. I am eighteen years old now, riding on a bus and I see Michael walking down the street.

Looking out of the window, feelings of anger come up immediately, I want to get off of this bus grab a bottle and hit him in the head with it. Some months later, I hear that he stabs his girlfriend. I never heard anything else about it or about him. I hope he is in jail.

TWO PSYCHOPATHS TRY TO KILL US ALL!

My mother is screaming for help, I wake up, go to her room, and she is lying on the bed bleeding. She has been stabbed three times, just missing her heart. I call the police. Her psycho ex-boyfriend, Walt, followed her home and tried to murder her.

Mr. Walt, short, stocky, light-skinned, mole on his face, healthy, kind of cute but crazy. I am 11 years old watching him become obsessed with my mother. He questions every move she makes and is very jealous. My mother is short 5'2 built, stylish, Indian hair and beautiful, sometimes wearing wigs of different styles.

She is angry at times, stubborn, feisty, prideful and a little bit crazy herself. She's a fighter, she suffers in silence always trying to be strong for us. She loves to cook, loves her family, outspoken, an artist, poet, serving others and loves to sing old-time gospel.

A few weeks later, in bed sleeping. I hear windows breaking, I smell smoke, I jump up, run to the stairs. It's Mr. Walt he starts a fire on the stairway, trapping us all upstairs. My cousin leaps over the railing and runs out the door to get help. Mr. Walt disappears, we never see him again.

Mom meets Kenny sometime later... Kenny, a light-skinned, 5'11, with two personalities. Kenny was jealous and creepier than Walt. I would peek in the bathroom and watch him in the mirror talking to himself. He would say "I am a pretty Motherfuc--."

I hear Mr. Kenny and my mother arguing while we are watching Soul Train on TV. I come out of the room, and he has a large knife, threatening her at the top of the stairs. I duck under them and run down the stairs, almost hitting the front door, he shouts to me, "get back up here!" "I will kill your mother and your sisters and brothers! I turn to go back up the steps hoping he does not stab me in my back.

My mother talks him off the ledge, he leaves, thank God. He later returns. I am in bed and smell smoke, Kenny starts a fire in the kitchen. Thank God again for divine intervention. We move to another home. Mom has a hard time breaking up with Kenny, and He keeps coming back. I come home from school, I am thirteen, My uncle Jim now lives with us, tall in stature, thick like a lumberjack.

Mr. Kenny has my mother at the top of the stairs again holding her at knifepoint. Terrified, we call uncle Jim for help. His runs down the stairs with a hammer and starts hitting Mr. Kenny in his head. We are horrified and run into the backyard to hide.

My mother calls the police, he is taken to the hospital. Later, we're in bed and hear someone walking up the stairs towards our bedroom. We jump up. It's Mr. Kenny, head bandaged up, he says, "where is your mother?" in his threatening voice. We run to the other side of the bed, "I don't know where she is." He leaves.

A few weeks later, my sister and I coming out of a store, see Kenny walking down 52nd street with the same brown work boots, dark brown khaki pants and brown jacket. He looks like a zombie in a trance, focused and just walking. He is walking in the direction of our home.

Running to the pay phone, I call my mother. She is on the roof waiting for the police. Kenny is pushing the door trying to break in. He has just stabbed his new girlfriend 30 times.

Sadly, the lady he murdered has seven children and her oldest son found her dead. I feel so sorry for the children whose mother was killed by Kenny. That could have been me discovering my mother's body. Kenny was arrested in front of my home, just before being put in the police van, he looks up at my mother and says, "thank you." We never saw him again.

MY HUSBAND HAS BORDERLINE PERSONALITY DISORDER!

In the middle of the night, in a threatening voice, I hear Allen say in my ear, "you don't know who you are sleeping with." My heart races, I go into the bathroom and pray.

While living in the US, in my beautiful home in Voorhees NJ, large bedroom, jacuzzi tub. I feel as if something is missing from my life. I say to God, "I have a purpose for being here, so what is it?" "I will go wherever you want me to go." I have no idea what is about to transpire in my life as the month's pass.

Going on vacation, I am on a flight to St Lucia, a little island in the West Indies, 45 mins from Barbados. I plan to attend the Jazz Festival. I can't wait to see these two talented women from England called "Floetry."

I am on this beautiful island enjoying the magnificent view from my villa. I meet people making a difference, one of them say to me, "there are so many people hurting here, but tourists only see what is inside of the resorts.

"I hear a still small voice inside me say they need you here?" "You can teach recovery." "Leave my country?" I think. "God this can't be you. I later broke the news to my family. "I am relocating to St Lucia in 2 years." I was still fighting the reality of it, somewhat in denial, knowing that God is calling me NOW. God's still small voice says, "Do you know how many people you can help in 2 years?" Obedient, I started making plans to sell my house. My two youngest children and I left the US Dec 2004.

I met Allen redbone, gentle eyes 5'11 handsome. We are now friends and getting closer. We decide to get married a few years later. I notice times when Allen's personality would shift, suppressing his anger, too needy and very controlling. If he is angry with his son's mother or a job-related incident, he would eventually explode. I try to console him, he slaps me, or throws his plate of food across the room., or has an affair. "I'm devastated, I cannot believe I am in another crazy relationship."

His shifting in behavior continues, he becomes manipulative, angry. Not knowing what is going on with my husband I pray. Feeling led to go to the bookstore in Rodney Bay. Walking in the bookstore, I see a book that jumps out at me. "Stop Walking On Egg Shells, Borderline Personality Disorder. It helps me take back my power.

Allen's trauma started with his dad, a retired police officer who abused and neglected him when he was a young boy. Allen has been acting strange all day. He grabs a can of insect repellant and lands it on my shoulder blade... OMG it's so painful, cut and bruised. I call the police. We separate, he goes to anger management counseling, but the relationship is not meant to be. I divorce him.

SUMMONED BACK TO THE U.S.

My mother is sick with cancer, I take her back and forth to the hospital for 6 years. The cancer returns, this time in her brain. The Dr's say, there is nothing they can do for her this time.

Fortunately, family and friends are able to spend some time with her before she passes on September 19, 2016. She lives for 5 weeks.

SAINT LUCIA

Living in the Caribbean for six years, I am grateful for God's favor, My Bishop, and his family. The local gospel artists from my church who helped me. Watching my son grow from a young boy to a teenager. I am grateful for the years on International radio.

I think of all I have been through, I think to myself...TraumaDefeated!!

I took some years to learn my lessons still teachable I asked God to heal my heart. When I returned home to the U.S., I did not know what would transpire once I returned...

Ramona Phillips, a mother of four adult children, a grandmother of seven. Speaker, Trainer, I am the Vice President of Speranza Human Compassion Project, responsible for Communications and Mindful Care. Founder of TraumaDefeated.LLC, Radio Host of "Radio Show: "Loving Me, Loving You" with FMhdmsradio.net, and former

TRAUMADEFEATED!

International Radio Host, of New Awareness and New Perceptions, Transforming Teens shows. Former Teen Mentor, A Peer Supporter, Prison Ministry facilitator, Published Author, Leader with World Changer Sister Tribe.
Founder of: Traumadefeated.LLC
Website: Traumadefeated.com
Blog: Traumadefeated.blogspot.com

CHAPTER 10

GIRL OF PRAYER
by
Zizo Mda

Nomthi is a short name for Nomthandazo, which has two meanings the first being a girl of prayer in Xhosa, one of the eleven official languages in South Africa. She was always a smart, bright young girl with dreams that no one else could comprehend but herself. She grew up playing with her brothers and sisters by the well down her mother's sweet shop in Willowvale a small rural village in Eastern Cape. She would always sneak out of the crowd to play dress up with her mother's clothes while everyone else went out to play on the well. One day her mother caught her playing with her new earrings and gave her hiding, but that would not stop Nomthi from sneaking in to make herself up with her mother's accessories. Her lips were blood-shot red with pink cheeks, and she had God-given talent in everything she did. She was a middle child and had all the problems that come with being a middle child like insecurities and continuously wondered what her part in this world is.

One day Nomthi woke up late and everyone else had gone to the well, they had left her in the village house alone. Nomthi panicked and quickly grabbed her yellow ....dress and ran down to the well but her brothers and sisters were not there instead she found an extraordinary looking woman who looked at her straight in the eye and asked her to follow her to the hut which was located just a few kilometers from the well. Naively so Nomthi followed the lady, they went through a small forest that had a defined pathway with many footsteps from stray dogs and cats. Funny bird sounds and hisses were coming from in between the trees that made Nomthi doubtful, but her bravery would overcome her fears until they got to the hut.

Before they stepped inside Nomthi noticed the structure of the hut. It was round, built with what seemed to be cow dung and clay. It was painted light green with a black belt at the bottom. Everything seemed reasonable at that point until Nomthi noticed this strange woman's outfit. What was shocking about it was that it was not just an everyday outfit, it was nothing like Nothi's yellow dress. It was more complicated than that. It was a combination of red cloth with white beads, and before Nomthi could notice the more delicate details of the outfit, the woman whispered in her ear that "I'm going to turn you into a Sangoma."

Now a Sangoma is what we call a traditional healer in the Xhosa culture. The word "ngoma" means "song" and the prefix "sa" is "send." Now a Sangoma is believed to be sent by the ancestors to convey a spiritual song to the chosen ones, it's Godly, perhaps not the type that a 10-year-old would have expected let alone understood, so she ran away even before she entered the hut. She got back to her home, and she never told anyone about it. She just took off her dress, put it back in the drawer and curled herself back in the position she was before realizing that everyone had left her alone to play in the well.

The second meaning of the name Nomthandazo is a girl with prayer. It was not by chance that she would go by her name and follow an unstructured routine of worship. It was unstructured because she didn't know what she was praying for, but because Nomthandazo needed comfort and protection from the world, she would kneel and connect with God regardless until one day when a tragedy happened five years later when she was sent to boarding school to better prepare for University.

It was a Wednesday evening at around 7 pm after she had written her second exam in Literature, her phone rang, and she saw it on the screen that it was her sister. Always delighted to speak to her, she picked up the phone.

"Hello Nomthandazo" her sister always greeted her with a warm voice.

"Hello Penny" she responded although she could tell that this time her sister's voice was a bit shaky.

"My mother is going to book you a bus ticket to come back home tomorrow night ." Said her sister.

"Alright!" She uttered. That was the end of their conversation on that day.

As promised the following day her sister arranged her tickets, and she got on the bus which took about 9 hours to get to Willowvale bus station where she was picked up by her sister in a 1994 silver grey Nissan Skyline. Immediately when she got off the bus, she ran to her sister forgetting her luggage behind. She was overwhelmed by the excitement of seeing her sister she had not seen in 3 months on the other side of the road. The bus drivers were yelling at Nomthi to get her suitcases, but she couldn't care less about the luggage at that point. What was more important was the sight of her sister and how warm they embraced each other with hugs and kisses while the bus driver went after her with her suitcases still yelling and ranting that "this child is disrespectful." Both she and her sister looked at the driver and started laughing followed by an apology and excuse that they were carried away.

All that excitement lasted for a couple of minutes until they both got in the car and Nomthi couldn't help but notice a sad look in her sister's eyes. She could tell it was bad news she was anticipating. She was trying to hold back on the question but curiously and anxiety got the better of her and pushed her into asking her sister "what's wrong?"

"Nothing" answered her sister, with so much hesitation that Nomthi could tell that her sister was trying to protect her by postponing the truth for as long as she could. Nomthi fell into a trance of prayer. This week time is structured because she knew exactly what she was praying for and that was not to hear bad news.

They drove 30 minutes from the bus station to their farmhouse, when they finally arrived Nomthi jumped out of the car to open the gate for her sister to drive in. Immediately she noticed strange noise of prayer and mourning hymns from where the vehicle was parked, and she knew that her father had passed away.

Still, in disbelief, she ran back to the front seat of the car to ask her "so what are we going to do now?" Her sister Penny was just as confused, and they burst into tears. Their father had passed away from HIV related illnesses.

The following day they went to visit the corpse of their father in the mortuary, and both sisters had a little idea of what HIV was and its effects on the human body. Penny had a better knowledge as she was older but not enough to spare her the shock when she saw her father's corpse lying in the casket with its head as tiny as a fist, eyes closed deep in their socket and lips as thin two lines. It was an unbearable sight for both sisters and not even the support from their family could comfort them. It was a sad moment to have lost someone they love to a disease they both had little knowledge of.

Later on that night Nomthi woke up in the middle of her sleep and put on her sandals and a gown and started walking to the well that was down the road from her mother's sweet shop. This time it was dark and seemed to be no stars in the sky to light up the road for her, she felt afraid as though she was alone in the dark with no idea where she was headed, but she kept walking regardless.

About 10 feet from the well the same strange looking woman she saw from her childhood appeared. She had the same red piece of cloth wrapped around her waist, a white strap top and beads on both her arms and her forehead. She looked at Nomthi strangely again and yelled "Camago!".

Camago is a way of greeting and celebrating the gift given to someone by their ancestors. It was difficult for Nomthandazo to embrace this calling. She was young and as with HIV had little knowledge on this calling as well, in fact, she felt as though it was too much of a responsibility that was put on her shoulders, but that did not stop her from following the Sangoma to a place that seemed like a hill with green pastures and lonely trees. The Sangoma started chanting and chanting, at that point Nomthi thought it would stop it did not, it carried on for about five minutes until Nomthi involuntarily joined in.

The two chanted under the trees on the pastures, singing songs of praise until it was time for Nomthi to head back home. Before she went down the hill, Nomthi noticed something strange in the Sangoma's eyes and before she could ask what was wrong, the Sangoma whispered to her that "you need to go on a journey."

It was not clear at that point as to what this journey entailed, but it would manifest itself a couple of years later when Nomthi moved to a bigger city in Johannesburg together with her three-year old son. It was their first time abroad, and everything was different from the life they were used to at home. The people all spoke a foreign language she could not understand. The food tasted different from what she was used to. It was always grey when she looked up in the sky. There were many people in the streets of Johannesburg, some good some bad.

Nomthi worked as a clerk at a junior school in the center of Johannesburg. As one would expect, life as a vulnerable woman in a big city like Johannesburg would be anything but ordinary – at least not by her standards and experiences. It was difficult for her to fit in. Even in a cosmopolitan city like Johannesburg, the air of hardship could not be ignored – it was different from the kind that she was used to. This seemed tainted with a type of despair she could not quite put her finger on. Not wanting to focus on such, Nomthi put her energy into her work and her son. It did not escape her that she had taken him away from his family and culture. It did not escape her that she had ripped him apart from his roots. It did not escape her that Willowvale is not just a place, a mass of land, but the spiritual center of their ancestors for as long as she had existed. So she had taken him away.

She told herself that she would not let him forget. She promised herself that she would continue to teach him about his culture, that she would never allow him not to have pride in his heritage. She promises herself, she promises herself.

She's always been a bit of an adventurous spirit, still trying to follow the urge to try different things. When the opportunity came for the move to Johannesburg, naturally she jumped at it. Of course, she would try. Any objections were dealt with swiftly and logically. Nothing was going to hold her back from her destiny. Not her family. Not her job. Not her friends. Not her son. And not some strange feeling. Though it wasn't new, she had just learned to push it aside. Figured it was best to give it no credence and to mention it to no-one. What would she even say? For lack of a better word, she had been 'haunted' by the Sangoma since the day she first laid eyes on her. For a long time, she told herself that these are just the feelings that people have after encounters with Sangomas. Spiritual people are a little weird. Right? Nomthi would likely never be able to tell you how many times she had this conversation with herself — convincing herself.

Moreover, she would succeed too – until she fell asleep. She would dream of her. Every night, she would dream of their encounter. So much so, that she didn't even notice that she hadn't done so, since her move.

Life in Johannesburg could have been a bit overwhelming, had she not had her little boy to focus on. Her little boy and jumping all the cultural hurdles that come with moving clean across to a big city and diving into another existence. However, she had a handle on it and was focused. Even created little routines for herself and her son. While she found the market on Saturdays a little claustrophobic, her little man loved the adventure. So many people, so many vegetables and goodies to try; so many people. She would often find herself just standing and looking out into the hustle and bustle of it all. Watch the old ladies screaming out the price of their products, watch customers walk past, walk up, stop, haggle (shouting – it always seemed like shouting to her), arguing – and right when she thought for sure the customer was angry and walking away, a sale is made. Every single time. It was always so different. It was still the same. She would find herself standing in some 'corner,' or merely stationary in the crowd, observing this intoxicating exchange with a slight smile on her face. This day would be no different. After placating her son with a banana, she found herself paused and watching two old ladies going at it. This was a particularly energetic exchange, and Nomthi thought to herself "Oh my word, it's going to happen. She isn't making this sale.

There is no way this one is buying from her".

"Ma. Ma-aaa", her son tugs at her hand.

"Wait. One second Love."

"Maaaaa," he tugs, almost in desperation. She tears her eyes away from her drama, looks at him with slight irritation and says "What?"

"I've finished my banana."

She sighs and says "Okay, give me the peel," and looks up to quickly scan for a bin in the sea of market goers. In the exact moment, she locates one, her body freezes, and she stares motionless into the distance until she is pulled out of it by her son's screams. "Ow Ma, owww, you're hurting me."

Disoriented, she apologizes to him, while looking around wondering if she is going a bit crazy. "It can't be. I'm in Johannesburg, for crying out loud. There's no way", she says to herself as struggles to gather her composure.

Little did she know that the calling was starting to haunt her. There were lots of episodes such as these that were taking place on a regular basis. A distinct one was when she and her son together with a colleague were on their way to drop her son off at a local primary school. It was crowded on the bus as usual and all of a sudden Nomthi noticed a strange red cloth on the floor and immediately fell into a trance, and in a blink of an eye, everyone had disappeared except for herself and her son. She felt scared, not sure if she was hallucinating or haunted by the reality of her calling. Before she could process that thought, the Sangoma reappeared in front of her. Dressed in the same red cloth, she had spotted on the floor and covered in white beads. They both started chanting on the train in Shanghai; then the Sangoma whispered in her ear that "I would like to borrow your son."

Immediately the chanting stopped, Nomthi fell out of the trance and held on tight to her son's hand. The train stopped at the next station, and she was pushed back and forth by other passengers, they were pushed back and forth by other passengers, and before she knew it, she and her son's hands had parted, and her son was pulled and swallowed by the crowd that was departing the train.

"Lonwabo!" She cried "Lonwabo!" she cried again. Her eyes started tearing up, her throat was as though a lump had stuck on it, her voice could not come out clearly, but she kept screaming out loud for her son. She pushed through the crowd to try to get off on the next stop. She was a bit tiny, almost the same size as the locals with dark chocolate skin. That made her stand out from the rest of the crowd and even because of her screaming. She screamed uncontrollably while people were trying to pull her away from almost breaking the window from the frustration of parting with her son. He had disappeared in the crowd that departed the train on Xixaway station in Shanghai China, and it was starting to sink in that there was nothing she could have done to prevent it. It was the Sangoma that had her son.

She did not sleep that night; instead, she went to the nearest police station to open a case, but no one understood her in Chinese. She phoned her school principal who came to give her support but could also not speak Chinese. Nomthi found the school principal easy to talk to so she poured her heart out to her. The two sat down at a local coffee shop outside the police station, and Nomthi told the principal everything from her childhood to her experiences with the Sangoma. The principal was a very supportive listener and advised Nomthi to search for the calling first.

Nomthi was not sure what searching for the calling entailed, but as always she relied on her bravery to guide her. She would pray every day for her son to return but no answer. She decided to go back home, so she took a bus from Grahamstown to Willowvale where she was picked up again by her sister in the same 1999… silver grey Nissan Skyline. They looked at each other in the eye and again burst into tears. They had lost Lonwabo. They drove again for 30 minutes from the bus station to their home where Nomthi quickly changed into a red cloth wrapped around her waist, a white strap top and wore beads around her wrist and forehead. She felt uncomfortable in the outfit as it was her first time in it, but she continued on her journey to search for her son. She ran down the veld to the well hoping to find the Sangoma, but the Sangoma was not there.

A spirit let her to the same hut the Sangoma has taken her as a little girl, and it had the same green painting with a black belt at the bottom. Nomthandazo opened the door, and the Sangoma was sitting there, on the floor wearing the same outfit and told Nomthandazo to sit down across from her. She did as she was told, then the Sangoma said to her that waters were calling her. That waters of her ancestors.

The Sangoma explained to her that she had gone through the first three stages of the calling and the last one would have to be her going in or coming out of the water. Desperate to get this over with and put it behind her Nomthi went down to the river bank where she took off her dress and shoes and sunk inside the water. She immediately fell unconscious and woke up in the hut with the Sangoma besides her, She could not remember what had happened after soaking in the water, but she felt a huge relief, and she felt as if she had achieved her goal. The Sangoma started chanting songs of praise congratulating Nomthi. There was a knock on the door, Nomthi still in confusion got up from the floor, walked towards the door, pulled it open and there was his son standing right in front of her. Both the mother and son were overwhelmed with joy that they were both reunited. The Sangoma smiled at Nomthi and welcomed her to her calling.

For the next couple of months, Nomthi underwent an initiation process, where she was trained by the Sangoma of all the stages of becoming a traditional healer. It was difficult for her at first but soon embraced the calling, and after the initiation process, she started accepting the calling.

A couple of weeks after finishing the initiation she found a new job as an administrator at a local university. She would wake up every morning, walk a few kilometers to drop her son off at a preschool nearby then hop on a minibus taxi to jump off at work.

One day when she was in a minibus taxi from work on her way to pick up her son from preschool, Nomthi met a charming young man who started chatting her up and to walk her to fetch her son at school. This was uncomfortable for Nomthandazo so she asked the man nicely if she could have his phone number. Instead, they gladly exchanged numbers and started a full-blown communication from then on. They would visit each other every other day and soon began a relationship.

Nomthi's life seemed to be going well; she had her son, good job, a career and a good relationship. They were engaged to be married when Nomthi found out that she is pregnant with her second child so she went to a nearby doctor to get a medical checkup. That day was a fun day for Nomthi, she woke up, did her daily routine of praying, made breakfast for her son and her husband and sent her son to school. She made sure to be on time for her 9 am doctor's appointment, and she was in the doctor's room at 9 am sharp. The doctor greeted her with a smile and asked to sit on the chair opposite his. They made some small talk before the doctor asked her a couple of personal questions followed as if she has tested for HIV in the last year. Nomthi had never gone for an HIV test before so this whole topic made her uncomfortable and nervous. "No" she replied to the doctor. The doctor followed with a series of other questions and asked Nomthi if she would like to do an HIV test. Nomthi responded with a yes, and the doctor got up from his chair, opened a small drawer to take out an HIV test kit. All the while Nomthandazo was feeling a few nerves, but she kept comforting herself that she had nothing to worry about. She was loyal to her husband after all.

The doctor did a bit of counseling and finally conducted the test. They were both in anticipation while waiting for the test results to come out. After about 5 minutes the doctor looked down to check the results, then showed it to Nomthandazo who immediately noticed two red lines through the glass thin glass of a chase buffer. She was HIV positive, and it was clear that she had contracted it from her husband.

Since that day, she and her husband had difficulty reconnecting. They eventually went their separate ways, and Nomthi went back to the Sangoma where she practiced traditional healing. She now lives in Willowvale with her son and has her same hut like the one the Sangoma had. She has since disclosed it to her family that she has a calling and finds joy in healing people for a living, she is managing her HIV status well and tried to help those around her find purpose in life and remain healthy.

I'm Zizo Mda, I was born and bread in a small town called Umtata in South Africa. I completed my grade 12 in Umtata High School and went on to study a BA with English

Literature and Political Science at the University of the Witwatersrand which was voted the best University in Africa in 2017. I've lived and worked in 4 countries including my home country South Africa, Thailand, China and Saudi Arabia. I've learnt how to interact with people from different backgrounds and I know how to speak four languages like conversational English, Xhosa, conversational Thai, Zulu, conversational Tshwana and I play around with most. One thing that distinguishes me from the rest is my personality and people's skills. I'm a certified Speaking Examiner and I teach Reading and Writing but most of all I'm a storyteller.

ABOUT FUMI HANCOCK

Dr. Princess Fumi Stephanie Hancock, DNP., M.A., BSN, B.A.

Bestselling Author, NAFCA African Oscar & Indiefest Film Award Winner, TEDx Talk Int'l. Speaker, African Heritage Leadership Recipient, TV Personality, DR. FUMI: The Doctor of Nurse Practice™ Show &Transformation Interventionist, Philanthropist

Dr. Hancock with her love for the literary arts and behavioral health sciences, she has managed to strike a balance between the two, through her TV /Radio shows, documentaries, feature films, books, and her mental health-wellness presentations. To date, she has written over 21 books, 11 of which have become bestsellers and on the heels of releasing other books in the success development, health & wealth arena. Her book series, Your Vision Torch™ has been received by organizations, ministries, and colleges, in Africa, USA, Pakistan and other countries as a success strategy tool. Quit Your Job in 90 Days as equally allowed her to speak in front of Moslem women from all over the world, who converged in London, United Kingdom. In 2018, she got an incredible opportunity to be the first black woman to grace the stage of TEDx Talk-Al Anjal National Schools in Saudi Arabia.

When she is not writing or making movies, she is a sought after International Public Speaker, (a member National Speakers' Bureau & Women's Speakers Bureau-USA), with interesting topics ranging from spirituality, mental health, & wellness, self-help development, personal & success growth. She has been invited to train traditional and political leaders in Africa on Innovative Leadership as well as be a keynote speaker in some African Universities during their convocation ceremonies. Her doctoral dissertation, *using mobile application as an adjunct in treating patients with anorexia nervosa (AN) in communities that regard AN as taboo* earned her invitation to speak at the Sigma Theta Tau International Convention in United States of America.

Some say she is a Social Changer; others say a Transformation Catalyst seeking to extend the hand & heart of social justice, and many, call her a Story weaver who strives to bridge the gap between Africa and America.

Dr. Fumi Stephanie Hancock, DNP, M.A., BSN, an African Princess living in Diaspora is an Advanced Nurse Practitioner turned Screenwriter, President of The Princess of Suburbia® LLC (Cambium Break Pictures), and the host of a nominated NAFCA African Oscar Lifestyle & Health Talk Show, The Doctor of Nurse Practice Show with Dr. FUMI broadcasted by The Princess in Suburbia®. She was a columnist for over two years at The New American Times, Tennessee where she wrote on "Mental Health & the Media" and has been featured in several newspapers such as the Princeton Packet, The Advertisers' News, Tennessean Tribune. Recently, she launched International Diaspora Network and an Online Virtual Incubator for Professionals in Transition & Emerging Creative Entrepreneur.

Her accolades span from Africa to the US, as the most recent NAFCA African Oscar Peoples' Choice Award Winner~ as Favorite Screenwriter, Indiefest & Accolade Global Films Merit Award Winner, and Depth of Field International Film Festival, Woman of Excellence in Films Award Winner. On the heels of her recently released award-winning movie, Of Sentimental Value, she launched a woman-centric radio show, The Southern Warrior Sister-Tribe which is gaining grounds globally from her homestead, Nashville Tennessee.

Her greatest achievement besides her husband, Dr. David Hancock & their 4 grown children is her philanthropic work in Africa (The Princess of Suburbia Foundation). Dr. Hancock's ultimate mission is to inspire, motivate, empower, and equip others; helping them to value themselves, connect/reconnect with their true calling, and live a well-balanced life. Her desire is to create platforms for others who have not had the opportunity to be heard by telling their stories, one woman at a time. September 2015 alongside a Nobel Prize winner, Dr. Wole Soyinka is being honored by the NAFCA Africa Oscar Film Critic Association in Hollywood, California for their contribution to Literary Arts Globally.

AWARDS OF DISTINCTION:

NAFCA (Nollywood Films Critics Association, Hollywood, CA) NAFCA *African Oscar* Peoples' Choice Favorite Screenwriter

Indiefest Films Merit Awards for *Women in Films*

Accolade Global Films Merit Award: *Women in Films*

African Heritage Award: Contributions in Films, Writing, & philanthropic work in Africa (African Heritage Festival Nashville, TN).

Depth of Field International Film Festival: Merit Award, Screenwriter

Doctor of Nurse Practice (DNP) in Mental Health with Areas of interest: Self-Image, Eating Disorders in silent cultures, Mood Disorders.

2015 Prestigious Honorary Award by NAFCA *African Oscar* Organization, Hollywood, California.

www.drfumihancock.com
www.princessinsuburbia.com
www.storytellerbistro.com

MORE RESOURCES

Other Books
www.drfumihancock.com
http://www.theprincessofsuburbia.com/

For information on booking Dr. Princess Fumi S. Hancock BSN, MA, DNP to your next event, please log in to:
www.worldoffumihancock.com / www.theprincessofsuburbia.com

My Blog
www.yourinneryou.com

My Podcast: Storyteller Bistro
https://www.spreaker.com/show/storyteller-bistro-podcast

My Film Production Company
Cambium Break Pictures/ The Princess of Suburbia Films
For details on her upcoming movies, please log on to:
www.cambiumbreakpictures.com
http://ofsentimentalvaluemovies.com

E-Learning Masterclasses
www.storytellerbistro.com

DR. PRINCESS FUMI STEPHANIE HANCOCK, DNP, MA, BSN.

The Princess of Suburbia® Brand
www.theprincessofsuburbia.com
www.drfumihancock.com
*LITERARY ARTS *FILM/TV/RADIO PRODUCTION
*SPEAKER/COACH
(Psychiatric Mental Health-Wellness Expert for the Entertainment Industry)

&

Find out about
The Princess of Suburbia® Foundation, Inc.
The Adassa Adumori Project

DR. FUMI STEPHANIE HANCOCK, DNP, M.A., BSN, B.A.

Manufactured in Africa....
Assembled in United States of America....
Dispatched to the World.

This is just the Beginning....
One Event Can Change Your Life Forever!
Be the CHAMPION in your own Story.

©Copyright 2018~ THE PRINCESS OF SUBURBIA®

MORE PRAISES FOR PRINCESS FUMI'S BOOKS

Dr. Fumi Hancock is an incredible woman with an incredible passion to see people, women and men alike fulfill their purpose on this earth. She has witnessed first-hand in her own life, and in the lives of friends and family, huge circumstances and challenges that have come to distract and derail them from the plan and purpose that Creator has created them for.

As you read, I believe you will be freed to dream once again. You will gain a heart-felt determination to become all YOU are intended to be and be moved to action to finish your race despite all odds."

~Snr. Pastor Janet Conley – Cottonwood Christian Center, Los Alamitos, California.

Your Vision Torch is just that, like a light down a dimly lit path, a bright, beautiful, and bold wisdom packed life manual for successful and very soon to be successful individuals.

I challenge anyone to read Your Vision Torch from cover to cover and not be inspired! Truly this has impacted me, and I know many others, to achieve your dreams and goals not just for the sake of oneself, but for us all! Thank You Dr. Princess Fumi Hancock, for all the good you pour into others!

~Interior Designer/Stager

"With hopes of healing herself and helping others, Fumi writes these words of inspiration to others"

~Lynn Miller, West Windsor & Plainsboro Newspaper

"Fumi shares the message of hope in the midst of tragedy."
~ **Star Ledger**

"Dr. Fumi is a breath of fresh air to those who cannot see their way out and have lost hope. She is a modern-day Esther understanding her past, recognizing her season and Creator's timing, while embracing her future. She reigns supreme as a communicator, a visionary, a spiritual giant that the world is about to discover, only we knew it all along."
~ **Dr. Phyllis Carter Pole, Author: Temperament – Your Spiritual DNA.**

Spring Hill resident Princess Fumi Hancock has been riding a wave of success since her new book, The Adventures of Jewel Cardwell: Hydra's Nest hit the shelves in September 2012
~**The Advertisers' News- Spring Hill**

PRAISES FOR DR. PRINCESS FUMI HANCOCK'S U.S.-BASED TV SHOW
THE PRINCESS IN SUBURBIA® TV
(AN INNOVATIVE & INSPIRATIONAL MENTAL HEALTH & LIFESTYLE TALK SHOW)
WWW.PRINCESSINSUBURBIA.COM
CHECK OUT WHERE IT IS BEING AIRED

Despite our bad international image, some Nigerians, like Dr. Princess Fumi Hancock, still believe in promoting our image and African culture through her online TV Show. Bravo! ~ **Prince AF**

OMG just realized you have lots of videos, before and after this. I am off to watch them all ~**CY**

I really enjoyed one of your videos some minutes ago online. Keep the fire of good work you are doing burning, you are a source of inspiration to me and my family, Creator will increase your knowledge ~ **SO**

I am a new fan of the Princess in Suburbia Show! ~ **FL**

Didn't realize you had other episodes. Just got back you're your channel. I am a new fan! ~**LS**

I don't know how to thank you for your activities and your online TV programming. Creator will continue to strengthen your ability, provide more grease to your elbow ~ **OB**

You are so funny princess. You make me laugh so much ~ **RV**

I love your laughter and the way you approach life, Princess ~ **EB**

More grease to your elbow, Princess in Suburbia. I will keep watching ~ **GL**

Just found your video and I loved it. I am off to watch others on your channel ~**JL**

I came across your channel, Princess in Suburbia USA and found the content to be quite engaging and empowering. Thank you for making us laugh ~**YS**

Your show and the Let's Go Innovate Africa group online is quite inspiring. I am happy to be a part of this movement ~ **KC**

www.ingramcontent.com/pod-product-compliance
Lightning Source LLC
Chambersburg PA
CBHW020225170426
43201CB00007B/328